Napoleon's Light Infantry and Artillery

To Pierre Juhel
Thank you for your friendship and support of my endeavours.

Napoleon's Light Infantry and Artillery

Uniforms and Equipment

Paul L. Dawson

FRONTLINE BOOKS

First published in Great Britain in 2025 by
Frontline Books
An imprint of Pen & Sword Books Limited
Yorkshire – Philadelphia

Copyright © Paul L. Dawson 2025

ISBN 978 1 03615 057 0

The right of Paul L. Dawson to be identified as
Author of this Work has been asserted by him in accordance
with the Copyright, Designs and Patents Act 1988.

A CIP catalogue record for this book is
available from the British Library.

All rights reserved. No part of this book may be reproduced, transmitted, downloaded, decompiled or reverse engineered in any form or by any means, electronic or mechanical including photocopying, recording or by any information storage and retrieval system, without permission from the Publisher in writing. NO AI TRAINING: Without in any way limiting the Author's and Publisher's exclusive rights under copyright, any use of this publication to "train" generative artificial intelligence (AI) technologies to generate text is expressly prohibited. The Author and Publisher reserve all rights to license uses of this work for generative AI training and development of machine learning language models.

Typeset by Mac Style

The Publisher's authorised representative in the EU for product
safety is Authorised Rep Compliance Ltd., Ground Floor,
71 Lower Baggot Street, Dublin D02 P593, Ireland.
www.arccompliance.com

For a complete list of Pen & Sword titles please contact

PEN & SWORD BOOKS LIMITED
47 Church Street, Barnsley, South Yorkshire, S70 2AS, England
E-mail: enquiries@pen-and-sword.co.uk
Website: www.pen-and-sword.co.uk
or
PEN AND SWORD BOOKS
1950 Lawrence Road, Havertown, PA 19083, USA
E-mail: uspen-and-sword@casematepublishers.com
Website: www.penandswordbooks.com

Contents

Acknowledgements   vi
Introduction   vii

Chapter 1	The Light Infantry	1
Chapter 2	Dress Regulations	12
Chapter 3	Bardin	28
Chapter 4	Getting Bardin into Service	36
Chapter 5	Regulations in Practice	54
Chapter 6	Other Regiments	146
Chapter 7	The National Guard	166
Chapter 8	Foot Artillery	195
Chapter 9	Horse Artillery	211
Chapter 10	Artillery Train	237
Chapter 11	Guides and Other Troops	246

Notes   260
Bibliography   272

Acknowledgements

More than twenty ago I made my first visit to the Chateau de Vincennes, the home of the French Army Archives. It is a place I have come to know intimately in that time, and the 'holy grail' it keeps within its walls of millions of documents from the 1^e Empire. My two or three annual pilgrimages to 'worship at the shrine of archive research' came to a juddering halt in March 2020. My writing stopped, and this book hit 'the buffers'. At the height of Covid, Yves Martin sent me copies of records for most of the legere regiments that he had already made: without his unfailing support and friendship, this book would not exist. I owe Yves a huge debt.

I am also indebted to Ian Smith and Jean Charles Lair for their assistance with, and photographing of, archival material at the Archives Nationales and Service Historique de la Défense Armée de Térre, in Paris. Sally needs special mention, as she has accompanied me willingly on my pilgrimage to Paris more than twenty times, and spent hours and hours photographing archives and developing 'Vincennes Back' from standing for hours at a time photographing records. Without her help, friendship and dedication, this book would have taken years longer to write.

Martin Lancaster, Ben Townsend, Terry Crowdy and Robert Cooper must be heartily thanked for their encouragement of this book and my research: their support and critical input to my thinking have kept this projecting progressing for the last seven years. I hope, Gentlemen, that the finished thesis lives up to your expectations and the thousands spent on air flights, hotels and dedicated patronage of Le Drapeau at Vincennes has been worth it.

Bertrand Malvaux is to be heartily thanked for allowing me to use images of his extensive collection. Bravo Sir! Without your help this book would have far fewer illustrations!

The long-suffering staff at Service Historique de la Défense Armée de Térre need to be thanked for answering questions and locating items of research that have made this book possible.

Paris, 15 August 2024

Introduction

This book set out to describe what light infantry – Infanterie *légère* – wore during the course of the 1ᵉ Empire. Our goal was to chart the dress of every regiment across the course of the Empire from previously unused archive sources. Our goal was, however, thwarted by the virtual absence of material from the Grande Armée leaving the camp of Boulogne to the fall of the Empire in 1815. Therefore, the project's boundaries naturally changed to study the dress and equipment of Napoléon's army in its twilight years. This refocusing allowed us to answer a perennial question: did the famous Bardin regulation exist? This book lays the facts bare warts and all.

This book explores those who came behind the glittering columns of cavalry and grenadiers in towering bearskins: 'those who also served'. The support troops, spies and women. We describe as well as we can based on the limited archive sources the dress of the horse and foot artillery, artillery and equipment trains, as well as a plethora of almost forgotten units that made up the Grande Armée.

The archive material presented in the following chapters are transcripts of the original material used by the author. The narrative for each regiment's clothing and equipment has been constructed from the sources available to the author. The starting point is the official War Ministry decrees for what was to be worn, the War Ministry decree detailing the specification of items, and lastly regimental purchase accounts and inspection returns.

Official inspection returns and regimental standing orders are key primary documents. They document in minute detail what was being worn on the day of inspection, what the regimental *dépôt* contained, what was purchased and in the case of the standing orders says exactly what was worn, when and how. This data gives us a snapshot of the Grande Armée as it was at the very close of its existence. This incredible source of information, along with regimental account books for expenditure on clothing and equipment, has been used to present the Grande Armée's appearance 'warts and all' for the first time. The data allows us to reconcile the realities behind the Bardin regulation and shows the army as it really was.

I have endeavoured to let the primary sources speak for themselves without having to fit what they say into a superficial construct, created by other authors. This approach has allowed a fresh and revisionary narrative to be produced on the uniform of the Line and Light Infantry.

It is our task as historians to acknowledge that it may never be possible to fully align iconographic and written sources. We should start from quantifiable data – the regimental records – and work from there. Dress regulations, original items and iconography help us visualise what these items look like and how they were worn. Yet in many cases the iconography shows uniforms that simply cannot be reconstructed from official documents. Yet which is correct? Where more than one independent eyewitness iconographic source presents similar information, we can be sure that the iconography is reliable, or whereby the iconographic source is backed up by eyewitness written testimony.

Many readers will be disappointed that we can say nothing about how most trumpeters and drummers were dressed, or if their favourite regiment had epaulettes and what colour they were. The archive sources do not answer these questions: the documents where the colonel wrote down in facsimilia exactly what was worn and when simply no longer exist. Less than a dozen sets of regimental standing orders from the Line and Guard from 1791–1815 have come down to us. We have to admit that we will never know exactly what a regiment wore in the overwhelming majority of cases. Hence we have to compare what records we have with contemporary iconography and come to a conclusion based on facts rather than speculation.

Chapter 1

The Light Infantry

Originating in the eighteenth century on an essentially experimental basis, in 1788 the Minister for War recreated twelve ostensibly light infantry battalions, designated *chasseurs a pied*. Each battalion was to have a staff, and each of the four companies was to have six officers and 102 men. The men were to be robust, need not be particularly tall, and *sous-officiers* were eligible for promotion to officer status. Each company was to raise a squad of 12 men designated as *carabiniers* who were to act as marksmen. Under the reforms of 1 April 1791 the *carabiniers* were done away with, but the number of battalions was increased to 14. Each of these battalions became the nucleus of the thirty-two new *demi-brigades* from 12 August 1793. These were reorganised on *18 Nivôse An IV* (8 January 1796) to 30. The decree of 1 Vendemiaire An XII (24 September 1803) restored the title of regiment, and the *demi-brigades* were consolidated into 27 regiments, each of three battalions, the third being the *dépôt* or training battalion.

From 1786 the light infantry had worn green *habits*, *vestes* and *pantalons* with a felt *chapeau* for a headdress, replaced from 1791 with a helmet. From 7 September 1793 the light infantry were dressed in blue short-tailed *habits*, with blue lapels (*revers*) that were piped white and ended in a point, a red collar piped white, red cuff flaps with blue flaps with four buttons, piped white, a blue waistcoat (*veste*) a pair of blue ankle-length trousers (*pantalons*) and black gaiters: the *légère* had its own distinctive look. The turnbacks and pockets on the tails of the *habit* were figured in white piping, while the tails were lined in blue serge. The buttons were to be copper, and the headdress a helmet. One innovation was the adoption of short tails. The infantryman wore at his neck a black stock (*col noir*) with two spare lengths of white piping (*rabats*) and on parade a white stock (*col blanc*). He also had three shirts (*chemise*) and a pair of underwear (*caleçon*) as well as a long pair of woollen stockings and two pairs of linen ankle socks, and last but not least three pairs of shoes as well as a cleaning kit. He was also issued three pairs of gaiters – one pair in white linen, a pair in black twill, a pair in grey linen. He would also have alongside his *havresac*, an ammunition box (*giberne*) and if a member of the elite company his sword (*sabre briquet*) and belt (*baudrier*). Every man had a firearm, even drummers, as well as a bayonet. The bayonet was carried on the *giberne* belt (*porte-giberne*) or for grenadiers and *sous-officiers* (the *sous-officier* ranked as a corporal and above) from the *baudrier*, with sabre and sword knot (*dragonne*).

The *chapeau* and *helmet* began to be unofficially replaced from 1798 with a felt cylindrical *schako*, which had a detachable peak. From *4 Brumaire An X* (26 October 1801) the *légère* was to adopt a cylindrical *schako* with a fixed peak.

Chasseur of an unknown *légère* regiment c.1804. This side view captures very well the appearance of the first model *schako*.

Clothing Fund

All of these items were provided to the soldier by the state out of the man's pay, called the 1st Issue (*1ᵉ Messe*) along with sundry items like stocks, shirts, cleaning kit etc. The men of the Grande Armée were paid professionals. They were paid, in theory, weekly, according to rank and status. In all cases, the pay was subject to a number of deductions for communal funds (*masses*), which left very little actual pay. The purpose of the pay was

The Light Infantry 3

Chasseur of an unknown regiment drawn in Germany sometime in 1806.

Chasseur of an unknown regiment drawn in Germany sometime in 1806.

The Light Infantry

Carabinier and *chasseur* of an unknown regiment in Germany, sometime in 1806.

actually not to give the soldier pocket money to spend on wine, women and gambling but so he could pay for fines, pay repair bills for his clothing and equipment, purchase soap and cleaning equipment and if needed buy new items of clothing.[1]

Prior to 1806 there had been the *masse générale* or general fund, from which the soldier's uniform was paid for. The decree of 25 April 1806 established the *masse d'habillement*, literally clothing fund, and set this at 48fr 29 centimes per man per year in the line infantry, and some 49fr 53 centimes for a soldier in a light infantry regiment. From this fund, the regimental Council of Administration drew its necessary funds to buy raw materials, equipment, headdress as well as to pay the regimental workmen. It also covered sundry items such as the epaulettes of the *adjutant-sous-officier*, lace for rank stripes, service chevrons, musicians' and drummers' lace, plumes and pompoms. The fund was to provide a soldier with his full issue of uniform and equipment.[2]

Linen and Shoe Fund

A soldier, in addition to his basic issue, needed more than a single shirt, stock and pair of shoes. This was paid for with more stoppages from his pay being sent to the Linen and Shoe Fund. The fund was paid for at the rate of 12 centimes a day for a *sous-officier* and 7 centimes for other ranks. Prior to 25 April 1806 this had allowed for a pair of white parade gaiters. With the removal of the white parade gaiters, the money saved from their purchase was carried over to issue every man a pair of linen canvas overalls for use in camp and on the march. The fund also covered the cost of providing a soldier with three shirts, two white stocks, two pairs of cotton or linen socks, one pair of woollen stockings, two pairs of shoes, and a set of four buckles: stock, knee buckles, breeches back buckle, and shoe buckles.[3]

The Ordinary

Once the conscript had given over most of his pay to buy his uniform, most of what money the soldier had left was retained by his unit to pay for his daily ration, the 'ordinary' (*Masse Ordinaire*). At the start of the epoch, 14 to 16 men in the same company were grouped into an ordinary, which was not necessarily the same group as the squad. The company captain would appoint a *chef d'ordinaire*, literally a 'chief', who was often a corporal, who was required to be literate, and understand the new metric system of weights and measures. Each ordinary possessed a register (the French army adored paperwork. Lots of little men running around with lots of bits of paper even on campaign, made the army either a bureaucratic nightmare or dream depending on one's viewpoint!). In the register the 'chief' was to record all expenses from the purchase of groceries to laundry expenses. Each man was to contribute the value of one shirt per week to the fund. The chief would write the expenses in the registers and sign it, recording the names of the men in the ordinary, and the name of those who accompanied him on his chores. The numerous 'chiefs' were paid by the *caporal-fourrier* (the sergeant major's clerk in essence). Every fifteen days the captain inspected the books to ensure fair play, that the men were not being defrauded out of food and the *chef* was not spending the money on drink. To ensure food was being purchased, the company sergeant major visited the butchers, grocers and bakers recorded in the register to double check the accuracy of the records, to ensure the records were accurate and to satisfy himself the ordinary was not in debt.

The regulation amount of food was established on 12 March 1806 and stated that each day, a soldier was to receive three ounces of bread for thickening the soup; half a pound of meat and vegetables. The fund was set at 17.5 centimes a day for each member of the ordinary.[4]

The Light Infantry 7

Chasseur walking out in female company. Of interest, he has a black sabre belt – regulation up to September 1804 – and the early-pattern *schako*.

Two *chasseurs* witnessed sometime in 1804 to 1805. They have black cross belts. An order dated 18 April 1793 stated that blackened cow hide was to be used due to the scarcity of buff leather. This was not rescinded until 23 September 1804, but thousands of black cross belts were in use throughout the 1805 campaign.

Repairs and Losses

All repairs were carried out under the auspices of the *caporal-fourrier*. Minor repairs were to be carried out to clothing and equipment by the soldier, while for more major repairs, the *caporal-fourrier* took the soldier and his damaged items to the captain clothing officer, who authorised the regimental workmen to undertake the repair. If the repair was judged to be the fault of negligence by the soldier he had to pay for the work or a replacement item from his pay.[5]

The definition of negligence and clothing simply falling to bits because it was badly made was a fine line.

Making it All

Clothing was issued on a regulated basis. Each item of clothing had a specified duration period. A *habit* had to last two years, for example. Every year a regiment would be inspected on 1 October, and the condition of the clothing assessed. A return of all the clothing to be struck off/disposed of was made, and the appropriate number of new items ordered. Clothing and equipment needing repairs was also logged, as was how many items had been repaired since the last inspection. From this data, the clothing officer was able to report the total number of items needing to be replaced or repaired. Every year a third of the regiment's cloth work was replaced, so every 36 months a soldier received a new *habit*. It was very much make do and men by the time the cloth items of equipment were coming to the end of their service life.[6]

The regiment's clothing and equipment was overseen by the regiment's clothing officer, who had to oversee the purchase of all items of equipment and clothing for the sub-officers and troopers. Officers provided their own uniforms and equipment. The clothing officer also had to ensure that all regimental property held in the regimental magazines at the *dépôt* was in good condition and all accounted for. The clothing and equipment of men in hospital was also the responsibility of the clothing officer, who had to ensure it was stored in good condition while the member of the regiment was hospitalised. Each company commander had to keep a report of the items of clothing and equipment issued to their company, and note what items needed repairing, what was beyond use, and what items were new. These reports were submitted to the clothing officer, who then collated the information. The magazines and regiment were to be inspected every year by a Commissioner for War to ensure that the paperwork of the regiment matched reality, and to agree to the disposal of worn-out clothing, and equipment.[7]

Clothing was made in two ways: regimental workshops or direct purchase. Each regiment had up to six master workmen. Their workshops were located in the regimental *dépôt*. Each workman would take on at least two of the regiment's children as apprentices. The workmen included:[8]

> Master tailor. He ranked as a sergeant and was responsible for manufacturing uniforms for his regiment, as well as making repairs to the uniforms.

> Master cordwainer. The master shoemaker ranked as a corporal and was responsible for the manufacture and repair of shoes and boots.

The Light Infantry 9

Officer of *légère* wearing the 1802 regulation uniform.

Chasseur wearing the 1802 regulation uniform.

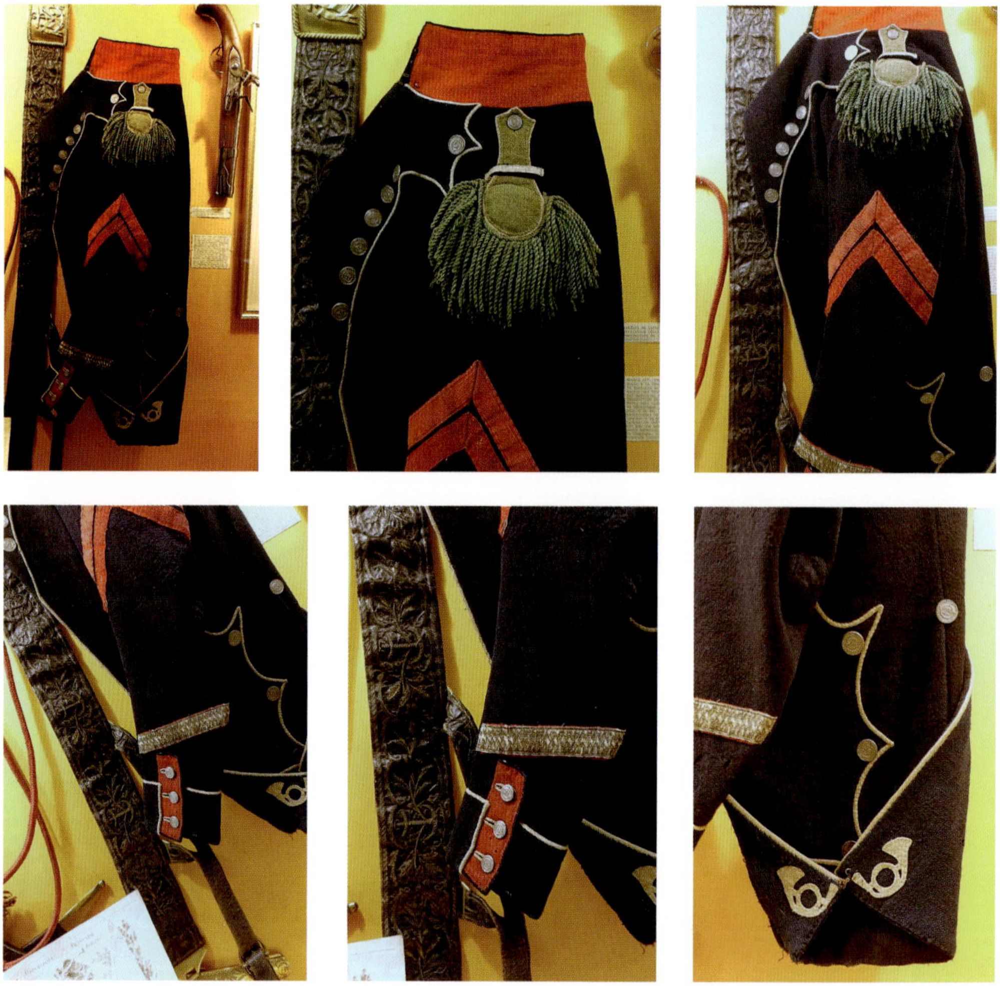

Sergeant's *habit* of light infantry of the type worn in the first half of the empire. No evidence from the epoch supports the use of silver and red epaulettes or other distinctions by *sous-officiers*. (*Musée de l'Empéri, Collections du Musée de l'armée, Anciennes collections Jean et Raoul Brunon*)

Master gaiter-maker. The gaiters of a regiment had prior to 9 September 1799 been made by the master tailor; after that date the duties were passed to the gaiter-maker.

The master workmen ran their own workshops: by and large from 1812. The contracts for work were 'put out' as 'piece work' to the seamstresses, cobblers, leather cutters and other artisans around the *dépôt*, and their work overseen directly by the master craftsmen because the workshop staff simply lacked capacity to reclothe the army. Workshop staff tended to come from the lame, the old and crippled of the *'compagnies des hors rang'*. Uniforms came in three standard sizes. This standardisation in size made production far easier logistically. The regiment bought materials locally as cheaply as possible, seldom with recourse to army standards out of necessity. In most cases the master tailor would cut out material for the required number of *habits*, *gilets*, *pantalons* etc and then would engage a number of people who came into the *dépôt* to collect 'kits' to sew into garments at home. They then handed the finished items back to the master craftsmen, and only when the contract was completed and items approved as being of acceptable quality were they were paid, roughly three months later. These 'kits' appear very frequently in regimental records. We know external tailors, seamstresses and cobblers were used out of necessity on campaign, particularly in Spain, Germany between Essling and Wagram, and in 1813 for the men who were billeted in Prussia and survived the Russian campaign. These survivors were issued funds from their regiments, in real terms promissory notes of credit that were never paid, to get their new kit made up where they were living, using whatever kit they had with them that had survived the campaign as examples to copy.

French light infantry *schako* of the first issue, in use from 1800. Offering greater protection to the head than the *chapeau*, it was the model on which the 1806 *schako* was based. Some models of the light infantry *schako* as late as 1803 had detachable peaks. (*Musee de l'Armée*)

Due to demand, it was often the case that the regiment would employ a subcontractor to make *gibernes*, *schakos*, shoes as well as uniform items from specialist firms whose trade was to supply the armed forces. These companies operated out of large factories in urban centres such as Metz, Strasbourg and Paris. The worker force stitched up 'kits' in the warehouses on a set wage per week or again as piece work. In all cases, to standardise clothing and equipment, rather than relying on the written word, one of the innovations of the 1812 regulations was that the War Ministry issued sealed patterns or *effets de modèle* for each item of equipment, which was the established model to be copied.[9] Disputes over cost of materials and clothing could run and run for years, with it seems most military suppliers being somewhat corrupt or they at least chased a healthy profit.

Chapter 2

Dress Regulations

The decree of 22 February 1802 laid out the dress of the Line and Light Infantry as follows:

Line and Light Infantry.
objects	duration
Cloth *habit*:	2 years.
Cloth jacket:	2.
Tricot breeches:	1.
Hat:	2.
White buffalo waistbelts or shoulder belts:	20.
Giberne:	20.
White Buffalo *giberne* belt:	20.
Musket sling:	20.
Drum and drum carriage:	20.
Sapeur's apron:	20.

IV. Non-commissioned officers and soldiers will be required to provide *bonnets de police* at their expense.

V. *Sous-officiers* and soldiers will not be able to dispose of the breeches from the previous issue until after the end of the year, so that each soldier always has two pairs.

VI. The clothes and *habits* that will be replaced in year X, will belong to the regiment; the best will be kept for the clothing of the new soldiers, for the guard house, the prison and the discipline room.

VII. *Sous-officiers* and soldiers will be allowed to provide white linen *pantalons* for the summer, while complying with the provisions of the instruction which will be written and addressed to each regiment by the Minister of War.[1]

Nothing was formally written down for four years. In theory a French 'squaddie' under the terms of a decree of 12 March 1806 was issued a *schako*, an undress cap (*bonnet de police*), a coat (*habit*), a short jacket with sleeves (*veste manches*), a pair of breeches (*culottes*), a pair of linen overalls (*pantalons de toile*, also known as *pantalons de route*) and two pairs of gaiters, one pair made from black twill with leather or horn buttons, and a pair made from linen, with horn buttons. In wet weather and on the march, he was issued a top coat (*capote*) and his coat was to be carried in his backpack (*havresac* or *sac de peau*: both terms are used in the period for the same object). From 1802 in summer a squaddie could buy at his own expense a white linen waistcoat (*gilet sans manches*) to be worn in lieu of his broadcloth *veste*, which also provided an extra layer for warmth in the winter.

Dress Regulations 13

Drawn by Berka, these *carabiniers* – red plumes – and *chasseurs* of an unknown *légère* regiment were drawn c.1806. The *voltigeur* officer with a colpack – the only period source to show this – is clearly a mounted officer – which *voltigeur* companies never had – and both he and the *chasseur* officer have scarlet cuffs to their *habit*s, again distinctly non-regulation.

Carabinier carrying a battalion fanion *c.*1806. Of note, he accompanies a *chasseur* company.

Capotes

The *capote* was an item of clothing that was not in general issue during the late eighteenth century and first years of the Empire. It was issued to men on sentry duty in bad weather or at night. Thus, the *capote* was part of the equipment of the guard house.

During the eighteenth century, the *veste* was the everyday jacket of the soldier. The *habit* formed the soldier's top coat, being cut so that the tails, which were normally hooked together, could be opened out, and the *revers* (lapels) could be buttoned over, giving the soldier a bad weather garment. In general, the *revers* were normally folded back to show the facing colour, as were the skirts of the *habit*. As fashion changed, the *habit* became ever more tight fitting and it transitioned into an everyday jacket. Thus, the need arose for a top coat. *Capotes* had existed in the army before 1806. They were part of the guard house equipment and were for sentries on duty in the cold or wet weather. *Capotes* for everyday use had been introduced for service on 25 April 1767 for troops stationed in colder regions during the winter. All regiments at the Camp of Boulogne or on service in north Italy were issued *capotes*: the order of 25 *Prairial An XI* (14 June 1803) resulted in 80,000 *capotes* being made and distributed by September. This regiments still lacking *capotes* were ordered on 29 June 1804 to purchase materials to make these items in the regimental workshops.[2]

Carabiniers

Authorised 12 August 1793, each demi-brigade had eight companies of fusiliers and one of *carabiniers*. The law of *10 Messidor An VII* (28 June 1799) clarified that each battalion was to have eight companies of fusiliers, one of *carabiniers* and one of *chasseurs*. From *14 Pluvoise An VIII* (3 February 1800) the *chasseur* or marksman company – the forerunner of the *voltigeurs* – were removed, and the *carabiniers* were to be armed with rifles, the fusiliers being designated *chasseurs*. Enshrined as part of the 1801 regulations, grenadiers were allowed to wear bearskin caps and red-fringed epaulettes. These items appear in inspection reports and regimental accounts. We stress, however, that they seldom do appear, which makes us wonder how many regiments actually put the decree into action.

Colloquially known as the beehive, the most characteristic feature of the uniform of the grenadiers were their tall *bonnets a poil* (literally fur hats) and scarlet epaulettes, authorised in April 1791.

The 1801 dress regulations stated that the *bonnet* had a leather carcass that was to be 352mm tall and 231mm wide. The carcass was covered in bear pelt. A leather sweat band adorned the bottom. At the top rear of the bearskin was the back patch, some 162mm in diameter. It was quartered blue and red and decorated with a white lace cross. In full dress the bearskin was adored with scarlet worsted cords. The knotted portion of the cords was to be 921mm long, the tassels to be 88mm long, and the *raquettes* to measure 115mm deep by 74mm wide. At the front of the bearskins was a copper plate, to be embossed with the flaming grenade. The plate measured 137mm tall, 205mm wide at the base and 135mm wide in the middle.[3] Iconography suggests *légère* regiments did not use plates.

At the end of the Friedland campaign, with the army on a peace footing, the decree of 18 February 1808 authorised that the line and light infantry regiments were to be reorganised into five battalions. *Carabiniers* were no longer the best soldiers in a regiment, but now had to be the tallest – the criteria laid out for the men nominated as *carabiniers* based on valour, proven courage, good conduct, that they had served for

Carabinier and *sapeur*, potentially of the 3ᵉ *Légère*, drawn by Suhr sometime in 1808.

Dress Regulations 17

Rear view of a *voltigeur cornet*. Archive documents support the accuracy of the image of these men being armed with light cavalry *mousqueton* and being issued *gibernes*.

Drummer, of a *voltigeur* company, potentially of the 3e *Légère*, drawn by Suhr sometime in 1808. We know from a drawing executed in August 1813 showing the 13e *Légère* found in Rousselot's papers in the Musee de l'Armée that this type of uniform remained in use for some time across several regiments rather than Imperial Livery. The *sapeur* is perfectly plausible.

two years and were 1m 73 tall, set in 1788, were done away with. *Carabiniers* henceforth had to be the tallest men in a regiment, and have served for four years or taken part in two campaigns. The decree of 18 February 1808 also formalised *sapeurs* in a regiment, four per battalion drawn from the *carabinier* company.[4] The regulations of 26 October 1801 refer to equipment for *sapeurs*, notably the apron, axe case and belt. The *Journal Militaire* for 1804 notes that the company *sapeurs* were to be drawn from the senior mess of the grenadier companies in the infantry and dragoons and that they were to be given instruction in the use of engineering tools and issued with axes, aprons and ordered to grow beards: 'When the troops are on campaign, 8 grenadiers (sic) chosen on a rotating basis will be given axes and aprons and will perform the duties of a sapeur.' A War Ministry circular of 29 August 1804 refers to *sapeurs* being authorised to carry a *mousqueton* and bayonet.[5]

Voltigeurs

The major change to the uniform of the infantry had been the introduction of *voltigeur* companies with the decrees of 13 March 1804 and 24 September 1804 in regiments of light infantry only:

> On the report of our Minister of War,
> The Council of State heard, decrees:
> **Title I. Organisation of Voltigeur Companies**
> Art. 1. There will be, in each battalion of the light infantry regiments, a company which will bear the name of *Voltigeurs*.
> This company will always be the third of the battalion, counting that of grenadiers; but as the number of companies in the battalion must not be increased, it will replace the second fusilier company, which will be dissolved and distributed among all the others in the battalion.
>
> 2. The company of *voltigeurs* will be composed of well-formed, vigorous and nimble men, but of the smallest size. The non-commissioned officers and soldiers admitted to it may not stand more than one metre five hundred and ninety-eight millimetres (4ft 11in); officers over one metre six hundred and twenty-five millimetres (5ft).
>
> 3. It will be constantly maintained on a war footing, and composed as follows:
>
> 1 Captain,
> 1 Lieutenant,
> 1 Second Lieutenant,
> 1 Sergeant Major,
> 4 Sergeants,
> 1 Fourrier,
> 8 Corporals,
> 104 *Voltigeurs*,

20   Napoleon's Light Infantry and Artillery

Group of *légère* soldiers witnessed in Hamburg sometime in 1808. The variety of plume shapes is notable. The artist correctly shows the *carabinier* being much taller in height than the *voltigeurs* and his *chasseur* colleagues. If the artist is to be believed, the *carabinier* has copper fish scales to the his epaulette boards to offer a degree of shoulder protection we suppose, as well as to be decorative. Again we see some *voltigeur* have white schako cords.

2 instrumentalists
Total: 123.

Instead of drums, this company will have as military instruments, small hunting horns.

4. The officers, non-commissioned officers and soldiers of these companies will be drawn from the regiment, and appointed to their rank, by the colonel, from amongst

those of the height indicated and who will show the most aptitude for the kind of service that the *voltigeurs* must make.

5. The strength of this company will not increase that of the battalion, which will remain composed, in number of men, as fixed by the organisational decree for the year 12; but to keep the battalion in full complement, each company of line infantry, that of grenadiers excepted, will be reduced by fifteen men.

Title II. Armament, Clothing and Instruction of *Voltigeurs*
6. The *voltigeurs* will be armed with an infantry sabre and a very light musket, the dragoon model
Officers and *sous-officiers* will have a rifle instead of a musket.

7. The *voltigeurs* will be dressed like the light infantry, and they will bear the distinctive marks of their respective bodies; but the collar of their coat and veste will be in chamois.

8. The *voltigeurs* being especially intended to be transported quickly by the troops on horse in the places where their presence will be necessary, they will be exerted to go up quickly, and jump on the rump of a horse behind the rider; to descend with lightness, to move quickly and to follow on foot a rider either walking or trotting.
   They will also be particularly trained to shoot with promptness and great accuracy.
   In Paris, Imperial Printing.
   22 Ventose XII[6]

Not a word was mentioned about epaulettes, plumes or special patterns of *schakos*! *Voltigeurs* were allowed to wear epaulettes from 19 September 1805, which were to be yellow.[7] However, contemporary iconography shows a preponderance of green epaulettes with yellow crescents. The practice, although not officially abolished, was frowned upon by the War Ministry.

The War Ministry issued a circular of 10 February 1806, reminding colonels that it authorised only epaulettes for *adjutant-sous-officiers* and *grenadiers* or *carabiniers*. Epaulettes and sword knots were strictly forbidden for *chasseurs* and *voltigeurs*, but those in use could remain in use until life expired.[8] A second circular was issued on 27 December 1807. In it, the War Ministry stated yellow epaulettes and *schakos* cords for *voltigeurs* were to be suppressed.[9] This implies that standard *chasseur* epaulettes remained in use. *Voltigeurs* had lost their symbol of being elite soldiers, the *sabre briquet* used by grenadiers, with the decree of 7 October 1807.[10] A War Ministry circular of 11 January 1809 forbade the use of government money, i.e., the clothing fund and stoppages from the men's pay, to pay for sword knots and epaulettes for *voltigeurs*, ergo if colonels wanted these items, the officer's corps had to foot the bill.[11] We suppose therefore that colonels made sure they got value for money for items in use, and in most cases epaulettes and sword knots were discontinued. The lack of inspection reports prohibits any conclusive study on the widespread use of epaulettes etc for *voltigeurs* and *chasseurs* in 1809 to 1814.

Rear view of a *légère* officer by Weiland *c.*1812. (*Collection KM*)

Porte-Aigle

In new year 1808, with the army on a peace footing, the line and light infantry regiments were reorganised into five battalions. Grenadiers were no longer the best soldiers in a regiment, but now had to be the tallest – the criteria laid out for the men nominated as grenadiers based on valour, proven courage, good conduct, that they had served for two years and were 1m 73 tall, set in 1788, were done away with. Grenadiers henceforth had to be the tallest men in a regiment, and have served for four years or taken part in two campaigns. The decree of 18 February 1808 also formalised *sapeurs* in a regiment, four per battalion drawn from the grenadier company.[12] The decree also introduced the 2ᵉ and 3ᵉ *Porte-Aigle* or eagle guards:

> Article 17
> Each regiment shall have an eagle which shall be carried by an eagle-bearer having the rank of lieutenant or second lieutenant and having at least ten years' service, or having made the four campaigns of Ulm, Austerlitz, Jena, and from Friedland. He will enjoy the pay of a first-class lieutenant.
>
> Two brave men taken from among the former uneducated soldiers, who, for this reason, could not obtain advancement, having at least ten years of service, with the title, one of second eagle-bearer and the other of third eagle-bearer, will always be placed next to the eagle. They will rank as sergeant and will receive the pay of a sergeant major. They will carry four chevrons on both arms.
>
> The eagle will always remain where there will be the most battalions together. The eagle-bearers are part of the regimental headquarters. They are all three appointed by us and can only be removed by us.[13]

The circular of 18 September 1809 provided the eagle guards with bearskins, spontoons and pistols:

> The Emperor has decreed that the 2ᵉ and 3ᵉ *porte-aigle* of each regiment will in future be armed with a spontoon in the form of a lance, attached to it will be a banner, red for the 2ᵉ *porte-aigle* and white for the 3ᵉ. On one side of the banner will be inscribed in gold letters the name of the emperor, the other the number and indication of the arm of the regiment.
>
> The spontoon will be 6 pied 6 pouce; 5 pied to the bottom of the banner, which will be 8 pouce tall and 28 pouces long and end in a point. The first part of the lance, after it has passed through the banner, is 10 pouces, the horizontal arm will terminate in a rounded blade at one side and a point at the other. To carry the spontoon, the shaft will be from blackened wood, like a bayonet, the red and white banners will serve to mark where the eagle is.
>
> The 2ᵉ and 3ᵉ *porte-aigle* in addition to the spontoon, will carry a pair of pistols which will be in a case, on the left side of the chest, in the manner of the Orientals.

Martinet presents this *voltigeur* c.1810. Oddly his *habit* has pointed cuffs rather than with cuff flaps as per regulation and was presumably a now lost regimental variation.

The case, so it can rest against the body will be flat on the inside and round on the outside; it will be made of strong black patent leather like the *giberne*, the top and bottom will be trimmed with a two-inch serrated trim.

The lower end will be passed and contained in a loop, which is attached to a belt worn on the coat, and will be closed by means of a loop, covered by a square plate, decorated with a N. in relief: this plate and the end intended to receive the rounded end of the belt will be polished copper, and the belt black patent leather. The headdress of the 2^e and 3^e *porte-aigle* will be a grenadier's bearskin with a white braid.[14]

The Suhr brothers show this uniform in use in 1813. Did any of this equipment exist prior to 1812? We know that some items were made as the War Ministry issued a reprimand to colonels on 31 October 1809 stating 'there is a great irregularity in the appearance and dimensions' of the spontoons, pistol holsters, banners and bearskins. All production was to cease at regimental level until a new *item de modèle* had been prepared at the War Ministry and copies sent to regiments.[15]

Musicians

Military bands first appeared during the Seven Years' War. The Royal Ordinance of 17 March 1788 allowed each regiment to employ eight musicians and a band master. Light infantry battalions were allowed to hire four musicians, who had to play the cornet or other brass instruments. The establishment remained the same until 8 December 1802, when all regiments of line and light infantry were allowed eight musicians, to wear the dress of the regiment's drummers and to have the uniform ornamented with a single row of lace 27mm wide at the cuff. From 29 August 1804 musicians were allowed to carry a dragoon musket and bayonet. It was common for colonels to expand the regimental band with hired men, *gagistes* who were professional musicians, who would be offered a contract to last no more than two years. To meet this unofficial expense, a private fund could be established, with money docked from the officers' pay from November 1807. Musicians were officially allowed to wear the same dress as the drummers of a regiment, but the *arête* of 8 December 1802 allowed a single gold braid 27mm wide at collar and cuff. This was confirmed 5 May 1811.

The War Ministry circular of 20 November, 1807 informs us that:

There exist in several infantry corps a large number of musicians which the regulation does not allow. As there should only be eight in number, those in excess of this number may be admitted as soldiers, but in those cases where they have been admitted as 'gagistes' (musicians not on the strength), they should undertake a military engagement, and if they refuse and if the regiment wishes to retain them they will have no right to any allowance or supplies and will be entirely the charge of the officers, provided that the expense the band needs does not exceed one day's allowance of the officers per month.[16]

Martinet gives us this *carabinier* c.1810. Most regiments by 1808 lacked bearskins for the elite company, and what Martinet shows was the typical appearance of these companies.

Inspection returns add some information about the dress of the bands. Musicians seldom appear in archive sources, given their clothing was private purchase.

In July 1811 a commission was assembled by the Minister of War in order to determine the new uniforms for all branches of the army but their propositions were sent to a second commission. The commission was headed by General Bourcier, while General Sorbier represented the artillery; Colonel Dautaurt the cavalry, Major Bardin, who also acted as secretary, the infantry, and Intendant General Dufour represented the administration and staff.[17] The commission worked with great speed, and any attempt to hinder or obstruct the work largely failed once the initial idea to also reclothe the Imperial Guard had been dropped. Imperial Livery was actually not part of Bardin and had been introduced to the army on 15 May 1811, when the War Ministry authorised a trumpeter's *habit* to have wool lace 24mm wide, and required 15m 30 of lace, of a model yet to be determined.[18] Something more formal about the dress of the trumpeters was enacted with the decree of 30 December 1811:

This portrait shows the elaborate and unofficial level of excess that many *légère* officers adopted. (*Musée de l'Empéri, Collections du Musée de l'armée, Anciennes collections Jean et Raoul Brunon*)

1. The *habits* of drummers and trumpeters were to be laced with 2m 70 of lace 27mm wide, to be sewn on to the *habit* conforming to the decree of 1 October 1786.

2. The *habits* of drum majors, trumpet majors and master musicians are to be no longer laced in gold or silver; the drum majors and trumpet majors will not be distinguished, but the master musicians will be by a double row of silver lace 22mm wide at the cuff, and the musicians by a single row in the same place.

The body of the *habit* will be green. The lining of the *habit*, the cuffs, the *revers*, the collar, *veste* or *gilet*, the *culotte* or *pantalons* will retain the colours of their corps and are not to be affected by these changes. No further changes to the remainder of the uniform, such as pompoms, *retroussis* etc are to be made.

However, upon consideration the uniform of the light infantry will change concerning the lining of the *habit-veste*, *gilet* and *pantalons*, which are blue. This colour has a disagreeable effect with green, it is therefore decided that the lining of the *habit-veste*, the *gilet* and *pantalons* are to be green, and also the *habit*, for the drummers and musicians of this arm.[19]

Major Bardin notes that the 1811 decree was not enforced rigorously and that the lace amount and *habit* form was changed with the decree of 19 January 1812.[20]

Chapter 3

Bardin

The Bardin regulation of 1812 brought sweeping changes to the dress of the *légère*. As before the *habit* was entirely blue with white piping to the *revers*, cuffs, collar and pockets. What marked it out was that the *revers* closed to the waist, and the cuffs became blue and pointed like the light cavalry. About the cut and fit of a soldier's clothing, the Bardin regulations commented that:

> Article 1. Dress of men.
> 1. The dress of the *sous-officier* and soldiers of our corps of infantry, artillery, sappers and veterans, shall be composed of a *habit-veste*, a *gilet manches* with sleeves, *pantalons de tricot*, linen *caleçon*, linen *pantalons* and a greatcoat, and a *schako*.
> 2. The clothing will be made according to the proportion details as follows, except the items specific for each arm. The pieces made from broadcloth, which meet the proportions once made.
> 3. The *habit-veste* and *gilets manches* shall be cut following the height and build of the men, so that the cut shall allow the men to perform with ease the movements ordered, without danger of ripping the seams. To this effect, the body shall be cut very large, the rear of the *habit* and *gilets manches*, and the sleeves, and arm holes shall equally be cut large. The measure shall be taken of each man on the body, the shoulders held well up and back, to take the measure of the back the arms are held forward. The *revers* are made so that a hand can be passed between the *habit* and the *gilets manches*; the collar when closed shall be able to take two fingers behind it. The *pantalons* shall be cut large enough to easily contain the *caleçon*, and for the man to be able to place his knee on the ground with ease. When the measure cannot be made on the man, the *habits, gilets manches*, and *caleçons* shall be cut for three sizes for the infantry and two sizes for the artillery.[1]

As well as his *habit-veste* and legwear a soldier needed other items of clothing, which the army also provided. About small clothes, Bardin regulations comment:

> 183. Composition of the Linen and Shoes.
> A soldier shall have 3 shirts, 1 black stocks [*col noir*] with 3 rabats, two to be carried in the *trousse*, 2 pairs of socks, 1 pair of black half gaiters, 1 pair grey half gaiters, 1 pair of *pantalons* in linen canvas, 2 pairs of shoes, 2 handkerchiefs, 2 night caps.[2]

The Bardin document went through various edits and redactions. Rather than producing a new document each time the regulation changed, Bardin simply edited the original: crossing out words, adding in new sentences as superscript words above the line, or even gluing in new pages covering the original wording in April 1813 when the 'definitive' version was finally agreed to. We have copied Bardin's text as far as practicable, complete with his edits. Where words are struck out in the text we have done so, ~~comment~~; where words are added in later, we have used superscript, ^{comment}; where Bardin has added in notes, we have italicised these words, *comment*.

The soldier's shirt came in three sizes – like all items of kit – and Bardin's description merely confirms that of 1786: the shirt had cuffs fastened with links, the collar fastened by a 'Dorset button', a low collar made from superfine white linen and shoulders reinforced with 'epaulettes' made from a heavy-grade linen. A soldier was also issued '*petit equipment*', and this was paid for with a 40fr gratuity to the conscript by the state. The *petit equipment* comprised:

> **168.** Details of the first issue
> Under the name of first issue we will include the *petit equipment*. Linen and shoes the uniform, petit monture and items for maintenance.
> **169.** ^{Distributed under the name of 1st Issue, it will comprise the petit equipment, and will comprise the items of dress, of petit monture} [illegible] the petit equipment will comprise the *havresac*, the linen *sac à distribution*, the *aigrettes* Viz. no. 42 et 43, pompoms for fusiliers viz No. 41, the cockade, the ~~stock buckle~~, sword knots for grenadiers and *sous-officiers*, small canteens. These objects will be renewed at the expense of the ^{clothing fund} ~~the linen and shoe fund~~ ^{with the exception of the havresac as well as the sac a toile, the major part of which will be still funded from the linen and shoe fund. The small canteen will be supplied from the campaign fund} and then renewed at the expense of the men of the battalion.³

As well as items of *petit equipment*, the soldier received items of *petit monture*. The *trousse* contained these items, which included according to regulations:

> Art 8. Objects of clothing and *Petite Monture*
> 189. The objects of *petit monture* will comprise items for cleaning and carrying out necessary repairs, and will comprise a *trousse*, a brush for cleaning copper, a *vergette* for the *habit* and a shoe brush, needles and a box of grease.
> 190. The *trousse* and items of clothing.
> The *trousse* will contain linen thread for sewing, material for mending uniforms, a pair of scissors in a case, needles, an awl, two sets of gaiter foot straps, spare buttons for the gaiters, *habits* and breeches, a spare needle file for the *épinglette*, a piece of leather to protect the leg, two rabats for the stock, a button stick, a comb, a razor.
> 191. *Petit Monture*
> A pay book ^{contained in a white metal case}, *giberne* cover in waxed linen, a cover for the *schakos* made from oil cloth [funded by the clothing fund at the same time as the *schakos*], a musket worm [provided by the magazines of the empire], a screwdriver, a piece of

grease, lead to hold the flint, a wooden flint, a bottle of oil for the musket, every corporal will have these objects as well as a spring clamp for his squad.'4

The case for the paybook appears to have been cylindrical, and carried from a cord. For personal hygiene, the soldier would have some soap, and a linen towel, a comb (*peigne*). He would be shaved by the company barber twice a week.[5]

Carabiniers

For *carabiniers* they lost their bearskin, and instead wore a grenadier-model *schako*:

> Art 3. Grenadier *Schako*.
> 37. The *schako* of the grenadiers will replace the bearskin; it is the same form as that of the infantry, except that it will be 200mm tall and the top will be 250mm in diameter; it will be garnished with scarlet lace and be surmounted by an *aigrette* as detailed at No. 42.
> 38. The top of the *schako* with be garnished by scarlet lace of the pattern Cul de De. It will be 40mm wide. On each side there will be a double chevron in the form of a V, made from red worsted lace 20mm wide. The width of the V measured at the top where it joins the horizontal lace is 90mm. The distance of the two pieces of lace at the origin is 5mm. The bottom of the point is at the bottom edge of the *schako*. The second row of lace follows the same shape as the first and is placed 10mm apart. It will conform to the engraved design No. 38.
> 39. At the back of the *schako* there is an escutcheon which is adorned in the *schako* of the infantry with a buckle to adjust the size of the *schako*. The escutcheon will be surmounted by a grenade. There will not be a copper buckle on the back of the *schako*.[6]

Carabiniers were marked out by scarlet-fringed epaulettes worn on the *habit*:

> 7. The *sous-officier* of grenadiers and carabiniers, and the grenadiers and carabiniers will wear a scarlet epaulette with fringes, lined in broadcloth the same colour as the body of the *habit*; it will be made from scarlet worsted braid Cul de De. The board of the epaulette will be 60mm wide, and be 45mm long where it passes through the bride, the length of the remaining portion will be 60mm. It will be held in place with bride 10mm wide cut from scarlet broadcloth.[7]

The tails for the *habit* were decorated with cut out flaming grenades, their *schakos* adorned with a horse hair *aigrette* in parade dress and a red pompom on campaign. The *gilets manches* worn under the *habit* was decorated on the sleeves with red cut out flaming grenade devices:

66 *Gilets manches de Grenadiers*. The grenadiers and *carabiniers* of Light Infantry will wear on the upper sleeve of the *gilets manches* a grenade cut from red broadcloth, the same as on the turnbacks.[8]

In prior years, under the 1796 regulations, the collars and cuffs of *carabiniers veste manches* or *gilets manches* had been scarlet. Under Bardin they swapped to blue. The plates accompanying the regulation show the use of the fringed epaulettes on the *gilets manches* and confirms the presence of the grenade badges on the arms.[9] Bardin is clear that *carabiniers* and *voltigeurs* did not carry sabres:

Section 4. Armament and Equipment
Art 1 Composition
90. The armament of the infantry will comprise a musket with bayonet. The dragoon musket will be used by *voltigeurs*. The sapeurs will use a *mousqueton* with bayonet. The *sabre-briquet* will be used by the drum major, the sergeant majors, Vaugmestre, chief workmen, sergeants, drum master, *fourrier*, corporals, *sapeurs*, musicians, drummers and *cornets*. There will also be issued to the *sapeurs* and *porte-aigle* a pair of pistols, a pole arm to the *porte-aigle* and also an axe to the *sapeur*.[10]

Yet the Vernet plates accompanying the text contradict this, as does the detailed description of sword knots for grenadiers and *carabiniers* as part of the regulation: we are left with an enigma of what was, or was not allowed.

Voltigeurs

Voltigeurs were marked out by the chamois collar to the *habit*, and hunting horn devices to the tails of the *habit*:

70 *Distinctions des Voltigeurs*. The uniform of the *voltigeur* will be no different to the infantry of the Line except that that their collar and their epaulettes will be in chamois broadcloth. The turnbacks are garnished with a hunting horn cut from chamois broadcloth. Their *schako* is to be the same as the fusiliers except that it is ornamented with a ~~citron yellow~~ chamois *aigrette* conforming to model No. 42.[11]

What does epaulette mean? The regulation reads that the *voltigeurs* used the same shoulder straps as the fusiliers, but cut from chamois, piped in scarlet, or as the plate accompanying the regulation shows, fringed epaulettes.[12] The vagueness of the regulation presumably gave colonels a marked decree of latitude in adopting fringed epaulettes or not. The regulation is very clear that the *voltigeurs* wore fusilier *schakos*.

Sapeurs

For *sapeurs*, Bardin stated that the man was to be dressed in the standard uniform of the grenadier or *carabinier* company in which they served but with the following amendments:

> **68 *Distinctions des Sapeurs*.** The *sapeurs* will wear a distinctive mark on the upper arm, above the fold of the elbow, namely two crossed axes cut from yellow broadcloth exactly as drawn in engraving No. 68. The arms of the axe will be 10mm wide and 130mm long; the axe head is 25mm tall from extremity to extremity and 55mm wide. There will be furnished to *sapeurs* a pair of gauntlets.
>
> **69. Headdress.** Their headdress will be a bearskin, a grenadier *schako* and a *bonnet de police*. The ~~hat of the sapeur~~ bearskin will be of the form indicated in the engraving No. 60, it will be 320mm tall and 180mmm in diameter when measured at the base. There are to be placed in the centre of each side a chinstrap made from scales, set 10mm from the bottom edge. They will be fastened to a copper hook placed on the back of the bearskin 10mm in diameter. The hook is sewn to the body of the bearskin [illegible] on the front of the bearskin, placed 70mm from the summit is placed a red tassel 70mm long. The head of the tassel measures 25mm. The bearskin will not be ornamented with a plate, nor a plume, nor pompom.13

So, a *sapeur* had a bearskin and a *schako*! The *sapeur* was also issued an apron made from sheep hide, and axe with case that also doubled up as a *giberne*. No waistbelts were listed as part of the regulation. The belt that carried the axe case was totally devoid of any ornamentation. At the rear, it had a buff leather loop, through which the handle of the axe was passed when the axe was carried in the axe case.[14] Artists and re-enactors are fond of showing *sapeurs*' cross belts festooned with brass badges, and large buckles – this is simply not true. Nor were *sapeurs* issued any special kind of sabre – they wore the *sabre briquet*.

Cornets

Under Bardin, *voltigeur cornets* had their own distinctive uniform:

> **Art 4. *Distinctions des Cornets***
> **88.** The clothing of the *cornets* of the *voltigeurs* of the Line infantry and light infantry will be the same as the drummers, Viz. No. 82 however the collar of the habit will be cut from chamois broadcloth and their headdress will be the same as the men, Viz. No. 32 except the bonnet de police, which will be the same as the drummers. Their distinction to their headdress will be a yellow *aigrette* as for their company Viz. No. 71. ~~They will carry the *sabre briquet* as well as the *baudrier*,~~ Their linen and foot wear will be the same as their company. They will carry the sabre briquet and baudrier.15

The basic uniform was the same as the drummers of the *Légère*, about which Bardin states:

Distinctive marks: *Habits*

33. The habit of the drummers is made in green wool-cloth, the top of the collar, the cuffs, the pockets, and the edges of the turnbacks are decorated with a dark-green lace, which carries an eagle and a crowned N in green, on a yellow escutcheon conforming to the model. The parts laced horizontally carry Type 1 lace, those vertically Type 2. The habit has no *revers*; it closes across the chest by means of 9 large buttons, placed upon 4 double ranks of the lace of Type 1. These double ranks form the buttonholes and terminate with a point; their length measured from the edge of the *habit* to the point shall be 130mm (4 inches 9 *lignes*). The ranks are equally spaced; those at the top join the seam of the collar and that of the bottom lies along the bottom edge of the front of the *habit*.

34. The sleeves are covered with 7 bars of lace stitched in the form of rounded chevrons at equal distances, the top chevron of the sleeve follows the curve of the armhole, it shall be 60mm (2 inches 3 *lignes*) from the seam; the lowest lace comes to 20mm (9 *lignes*) from the edge of the cuff, measured from the stitch lines.

35. The buttons are stitched on to the lace; each button of the pockets is on a buttonhole formed by a double lace which ends in a point 70mm (2.5 inches) long. The buttons of the tail are surrounded by an escutcheon, square in form, round the button in a double square; the inferior part of the lace enters into the seams; each of the three sides is 80mm (3 inches) long; the base of the seam in the middle of the tail is decorated with the point of the lace conforming to the type, with a height of 50mm (22 *lignes*). The three points which form the escutcheon of the buttons and those of the middle of the tail rest on the seams of the tail, that of the middle comes up 5mm (2 *lignes*) more than those of the sides.[16]

When we consult the printed decree, the *habit* body was made from green broadcloth, so too the cuff flaps and turnback ornaments. The tails were also lined in green broadcloth. The collar was scarlet piped with green. The shoulder straps were green piped scarlet, as were the cuff flaps, the cuffs being scarlet piped white. The tail facings (*retroussis*) were cut from white broadcloth, and the front of the *habit* from the collar to the start of the tail facings was also to be piped white. The upper body lining, sleeves, internal pockets and button stands were made in linen. Furthermore, a *habit* required 12m of No. 1 Lace, which is listed as horizontal, and 3m of Lace No. 2, the vertical pattern. A *habit* needed 17 large buttons, 8 small and the collar was closed by 3 hooks and eyes.[17] However, when we consult another version of the printed decree, we find the tails are lined in white serge along with the collar.[18] We suppose the reference to white tail lining was a typing error. Light infantry drummers and *cornets* had green *retroussis* and tail lining.[19]

Bardin notes that new lace design was finally introduced on 17 September 1812 with the introduction of Imperial Livery.[20]

Bands

Musicians from 1811 had a single row of silver lace to the cuff of the *habit*. In theory the band were to be dressed in green.[21] Bardin makes the following specific recommendations on the dress of musicians in April 1813:

> *Art. 5 Dress of the Musicians*
> 89. The clothing of the musicians will comprise that same as the soldiers. Their headdress and footwear will be the same as the soldiers Viz No. 30 and 187. Their pompom will be the same as for the état major, and their *bonnet de police* will be cut from green broadcloth in the same model as the men. The *habit* will conform to that described No. 790. The collar and cuffs will be ornamented with a lace the same as used by the drummers. The musicians will wear *veste* and *pantalons* cut from green broadcloth in the same form as the men. Their *vestes* and *pantalons* will be cut from white broadcloth for the regiments that have *pantalons* the same colour. The *vestes* and *pantalons* will be green for those regiments whose *pantalons* are of the darker colour. They will be armed with the *sabre briquet* and *baudrier*.
>
> The Chef de Musique will be marked out by the same rank stripes as the sergeant major of their arm, and will be in gold or silver lace. The collar with be decorated with rows of gold or silver lace, the same as appears on the cuffs.[22]

Presumably line infantry had white *veste* and *pantalons* in light infantry green. The reference to drawing No. 790 is clearly a mistake as when we check the drawing register, item 790 is part of a saddle! Quite why Bardin himself wrote this is not known; unless of course a new drawing of regiments was generated in April 1813 that is now lost, or misplaced in an archive awaiting discovery by an intrepid researcher. A tantalising prospect indeed. However, it is undeniable that we are left with an enigma about the form the *habit* actually took. Bardin himself adds a footnote that seems to answer that question:

> The *habits* of the drummers, musicians, drummers and *cornets* will conform to the general model viz 83 to 88, their *bonnets de police* will be in green broadcloth. The ornaments of the turnbacks of the musicians will be a crowned N in green broadcloth the same as ~~the drummers of the grenadiers~~ the drummers of the fusiliers, ~~the same colour as their arm and their company. Their *vestes* and *pantalons* will be made from green tricot and the lining to the *vestes* will be white. The drummers of the line infantry will have white *pantalons* and *veste*.~~

Therefore, we must imagine that the musicians, drummers and *cornets*, as well as the trumpeters of the mounted units, all wore the same *habit*!

Thanks to Bardin editing his original text rather than starting again, it means sadly that the original January 1812 text is lost. The text was redacted by Bardin gluing over the original text a new piece of paper to present the amended regulation. The original decree is very likely represented by the Vernet prints accompanying the original text. Vernet shows musicians with a single row of imperial livery to the collar and dressed in a green *habits veste* with white piping and scarlet collar, and green tricot *pantalons* with gaiters, sabre carried off a *baudrier*, and fusilier *schako* with white *houpette* for light infantry, and for line infantry he shows a green *habit-veste* with white tail lining, scarlet cuffs, cuff flaps, collar and *revers* piped green, and the collar decorated with a row of Imperial Livery. Again, they have white tricot *pantalons* worn with black gaiters. The *Chef de Musique* has an épée worn from a waistbelt, officer's boots and sergeant major's stripes at the cuff but no lace to the collar. The scarlet facings are most striking. We are therefore left with an enigma about what was worn.

Eagle Guards

Under Bardin the 2e and 3e *Porte-Aigle* were issued:

> 57. Distinctions of the *Porte-Aigle*.
> The second and third *porte-aigle* will be distinguished ~~by the colour of the pennant on the spontoon~~ by their headdress, which will be a carabinier helmet, a helmet of particular form and by the colour of the *criniere* on the helmet and pennant; that of the second *porte-aigle* will be red; that of the 3^e *porte-aigle* will be white; they will wear this and other distinctive marks, those of the sergeant major; there will also be placed four chevrons in gold or silver corresponding to the colour of the buttons, as for the service chevrons on each arm. Their will remain in usage the epaulettes of grenadiers garnished with scales. The remainder of the uniform is the same as the men.[23]

By *criniere* we assume *chenille* is meant, we are unclear as to the chosen form of the helmet: many of these 'particular' helmets exist in museums, while Vernet does show the *carabinier* helmet in use: this suggests some degree of latitude in what was allowed. Bardin makes no design comment on the 'particular helmet'. In addition, they carried a pair of pistols in a shoulder-mounted holster, which Bardin describes in great detail. Their sabre was carried off a black leather waistbelt that held in place the bottom of the pistol holster. In lieu of a musket they carried a spontoon.[24] At the time of writing, no archive documentation can be found that tells us these provisions were enacted in the *légère*, and certainly based on the documentation reviewed by the author, the *légère* never seem to have had *porte-aigle* with halberds and helmets, or pistols.

Chapter 4

Getting Bardin into Service

Despite the decree being signed off on 19 January 1812, nothing yet had been said about authorising production. On 2 April, the Comte de Cessac wrote from the War Ministry warning colonels that he would be issuing instructions concerning changes to the uniform of the army. He requested that inspections be carried out for the number of new items needed for replacements for the year 1813, and no items were to be made until he issued instructions.[1]

As the army readied itself to march on Moscow, the first stage in implementing the new regulation came on 12 April 1812 when the War Ministry decreed that the replacement clothing for the year 1812 was to be the old model, i.e., more of what was already in use, and the replacement clothing for 1813 was to be of the new pattern.[2]

Months past until finally from his desk in the War Administration, the Comte de Cessac wrote to regimental colonels of the *ligne* and *légère* regiments on 21 July 1812 warning them that he would shortly pass an order requiring them to begin the production of a 'clothing reserve' as outlined in the decree of 3 October 1811, anticipating the needs for 1813. All items were to be made according to the decree of 19 January and 7 February 1812.[3] *Habits-vestes* were go!

The War Ministry ordered three days later, on the 24th, that as huge quantities of leather equipment existed in regimental stores, government stores and arsenals of the Empire, an immediate audit was to be carried out to assess just exactly how much kit existed, and that this stockpile was to be issued before any new equipment was to be made.[4]

Two days later, in a War Ministry circular of 26 July 1812, *légère* colonels were ordered to being the production of 200 *habits-vestes*, 200 *gilets manches*, 200 pairs of *pantalons de tricot*, 200 *capotes*, and 200 *bonnets de police*. The colonels were also ordered to provide the same number of *gibernes, sacs de peau dit havresacs*, etc for issue in 1813. To do so, the regimental workshops of the *légère* regiments were to obtain 47m of blue broadcloth, 4m white broadcloth and 2,000m of blue tricot, for which the sum of 575fr 29 was advanced from the state treasury. Regimental funds were to be allocated to purchase 0m 40 red broadcloth, 98m of blue serge as well as small and large buttons for the production of *habits*.[5] Bardin regulation, a full six months after the decree had been past, was at long last going into production, but in limited numbers.

Several months would pass before any more official utterances were made about clothing. On 12 September 1812, the War Ministry stated that no changes were to take place to items of *petit equipment* and the regulation of 1801 was to remain in force for these items. After complaints had been received about the poor design of the new *havresac*, the order

Martinet's excellent study of battalion commander *c.*1813 wearing the new Bardin uniform.

Martinet gives this *carabinier* wearing an approximation of the Bardin-regulation uniform during the 1st Restoration.

Voltigeur officer wearing the Bardin regulation *habits-vestes*. (Musée de l'Empéri, Collections du Musée de l'armée, Anciennes collections Jean et Raoul Brunon)

to make the new *sac de peau* was in essence rescinded; again the new-pattern canteen and sundry other items were all cancelled.[6] Included in the *petit equipment* were epaulettes: here was tacit approval for the continued use of epaulettes by not only *carabiniers* but also *voltigeurs* and *chasseurs*, which had been paid for by the regiment's officers since 1809.[7]

Days later, a second decree was issued on 17 September 1812 that authorised the production of new Imperial Livery for drummers, and the purchase of silver lace for drum majors and musicians. The same decree brought into use the new-pattern *schakos* in two types: grenadier with red lace and red *aigrette* and the fusilier model for *chasseurs* and *voltigeurs*, along with the two new patterns of *schako* plate – grenadier and fusilier/*voltigeur* – Schako covers and yellow *aigrettes* for *voltigeurs*. *Sous-officiers* were allowed *gibernes* of a special, smaller pattern, and their *giberne* belts officially had no bayonet frog. Because of the smaller size of their *gibernes*, officially they lacked *giberne* plates. The decree also witnessed the introduction of the new crowned 'N' *giberne* plate for *chasseurs* in white metal. *Carabiniers* retained a flaming grenade and *voltigeurs* had a hunting horn, again in both instances in white metal. The decree notes *carabiniers*, *voltigeurs* and *chasseurs* all used the same pattern *giberne* belt with the bayonet frog. *Sous-officiers*, drummers and *sapeurs* were allowed *baudriers* and sabres. *Sapeurs* under the terms of the decree were no longer allowed to wear bearskins, but were allocated axes with cases and belts and aprons. The decree again mentioned short black gaiters with copper buttons and short grey linen gaiters with bone buttons, and linen *pantalons* for campaign use.[8]

A week would pass until the War Ministry ordered that from 25 September 1812 all new clothing would be of the new pattern. From 1 October 1812 each regiment was to receive from the War Ministry an example of each item of uniform for the master tailors of the regiment to copy, along with a written copy of the regulation.[9] Rather than hoping that the master workmen would interpret the text correctly, between February and September 1812 the War Ministry produced hundreds of 'sealed pattern examples' of every item of uniform and equipment, which were then distributed to every regiment of the army. In this way there could be no mistakes in how an item looked. This was a pragmatic and common-sense approach to regulating the dress of the army.

On 14 October 1812, the war administration advised the Emperor that clothing to the new regulation would be firstly issued to regiments in Germany, and all old-pattern clothing sent to the troops in Spain.[10] Even issuing the stockpiled clothing, the army needed more, so much so that by the end of 1812 or the beginning of 1813, the order is not clearly dated, Napoléon authorised regiments in great need of uniforms to issue the stockpile of 200 items authorised in July 1812 to be issued and ordered that the reserves were to be replenished.[11]

As 1813 progressed, colonels reported backed to the War Ministry that they were struggling to clothe their men. The Comte de Cessac wrote to line and light infantry colonels on 21 April 1813, to press into service old articles:

> Within many military stores, there are leather accoutrements that while not new, are still considered to be in good condition. It is my intention to allow those infantry dépôts that, by their geographic location or their distance from supply lines, are experiencing difficulties in providing new equipment to the conscripts of the last six levies, to make use of them …[12]

About three weeks later, on 10 May 1813, the War Administration wrote to the commissary inspectors, sub-inspectors and the regiments of all branches of service informing that:

This portrait of an *adjutant-sous-officer* shows the non-regulation application of three rank stripes – allowed only for Vaugmestre, the regimental post master – and silver and red-fringed epaulettes. He also carries his cane of office. (*Musée de l'Empéri, Collections du Musée de l'armée, Anciennes collections Jean et Raoul Brunon*)

You are aware that I am only responsible for supplying fabrics and that I have not been able to provide, nor am I responsible for providing, articles that the units are supposed to acquire for themselves. In any event, I have used all means at my disposal to aid those units most in need. I have therefore agreed to purchase a certain quantity of leather accoutrements, as well as knapsacks, to be delivered to the stores in Paris in May and June […] Those units in need of such articles may send requests, validated by a Commissioner for War, to my attention … Regiments are to leave only the minimum number of articles in their stores to carry out their duties and replace them as and when it is possible to do so. I expect the strictest and promptest execution of these measures but, at the same time, I will also hold those responsible that by negligence compromise or disrupt military duties.[13]

Thus, regiments were authorised to empty out their store rooms of whatever clothing remained, so men would be clothed in brand-new Bardin clothing and a mix of old-pattern items. Even with the measure of making sure that whatever buff and leather equipment that could be pressed into service, even if it had been in a *dépôt* for years, was used the army still demanded more than supply could meet. By spring 1813, the French state, like in the 1790s, was never going to be able to provide enough buff leather to meet the needs of the army. Thus, on 22 June 1813, the Comte de Cessac wrote to the commissary inspectors, sub-inspectors and regimental colonels:

> The Regiments' Administrative Councils are to let me know on a daily basis the difficulties that they are experiencing to get hold of leather accoutrements destined to equip their conscripts. These difficulties are notably problematic in southern France and Italy. After taking into account the different reports detailing why such difficulties were persevering, I have come to the conclusion that they are due only to the scarcity of buff leather, that was already being felt last year, as a consequence of the high demand of this product over the last two years. Since buff leather can be replaced by black cowhide to manufacture cartridge boxes, musket slings, cartridge box belts and drum belts, I have sanctioned, with the agreement of the Minister of War, the following:
>
> 1° The light infantry regiments, *chasseurs à cheval*, hussars, artillery train battalions, engineer and equipment train, irregular troops, veteran battalions, coast-guards and national guards that, as a result of my decision, are to buy leather accoutrements are permitted to use black cowhide in lieu of buff leather;
>
> 2° Line infantry regiments, *carabiniers*, *cuirassiers*, dragoons, *chevaux-légers*, foot and horse artillery are exempted from the above decision and will continue to use buff leather;
>
> 3° The prices allocated to these objects are as follows:
>
> | | |
> |---|---|
> | Cartridge box belt in black cowhide | 3fr 25 cents |
> | Musket sling in black cowhide | 0fr 70 cents |
> | Leather belt in black cowhide | 3fr 50 cents |
> | Drum belt in black cowhide | 3fr 50 cents |
>
> 4° The ten per cent increase, granted on the general tariffs for leather goods, is not applicable to articles in black cowhide;
>
> 5° The lifespan of black cowhide articles is set for six years;
>
> 6° Those units permitted to use cowhide in lieu of buff leather will, as much as possible, not distribute these articles to the men in the *dépôts* and the battalions serving inside imperial borders;

Getting Bardin into Service   43

Chasseurs wearing the new Bardin regulation by Vernet.

His Excellency the Minister of War and I believe that these arrangements will allow greater latitude for the different units to acquire, in a timely manner, all the leather equipment they are lacking. On the one hand, the permission given to light infantry regiments, irregular troops and other units designated by article 1, to use black cowhide will increase the buff leather available for the line infantry and other troops described in article 2 and, on the other hand, it will allow the units designated in article 1 to have access to more abundant material sources. Should the units authorised to use black cowhide in lieu of buff leather find themselves unable to get hold of articles in black cowhide, they are to acquire the necessary materials and direct their regimental workmen to make cartridge boxes and belts.[14]

The cost of the new black leather work was fixed with a ministerial decision of 12 August 1813, and was now extended to cover to the line infantry.[15]

We note that the War Ministry had decreed that no old-pattern clothing was to be issued after 8 June 1813.[16] Presumably by this date, none existed in regimental stores

Carabinier wearing his regulation uniform. Very few, if any, grenadier-model *schako*s were issued to the *légère*.

anyhow! Because of the ongoing shortages of buff leather, from 17 November 1813, black leather work was to be used universally by the conscripts of the class of 1814 called up under the 15 and 20 November Levy.[17]

Due to the cost of buying indigo to dye cloth Imperial Blue, with the decree of 8 January 1814, the *légère* was henceforth dressed in green *habits*. Rather than using expensive indigo, logwood and woad, which were cheaper and more readily available, was to be used to dye cloth green after serin or similar dye had been used to dye the cloth yellow. The new *habits* were to be made from green broadcloth, with white piping – the decree states ecru i.e., natural unbleached wool – and lined with green serge. The collar remained red – in essence all the blue elements of the uniform were replaced with green. The *gilets manches* and *pantalons* were to be green tricot. Due to an acute shortage of beige broadcloth, henceforth the War Ministry allowed that *capotes* were to be made from green, chestnut brown, white and *brun-beige* broadcloth and tricot. Furthermore, realising that regiments lacked the capacity to mass produce uniforms rapidly, the War Ministry authorised the production of 18,000 sets of green uniform by state workshops.[18] State production of the green uniforms began on 10 January and was suspended on 26 February.[19] We wonder how many of the 18,000 uniforms were made? As we shall see, some regiments did indeed adopt green and also black cowhide cross belts! A radical departure from how we imagine French light infantry!

By 1814, after three campaigns, the army was exhausted. Bardin regulation had evolved, many aspects not being implemented due to lack of time and lack of funds. The most visible impact of the changes to Bardin were the black cross belts, nut brown *capotes* rather than grey, and tricot *gilets manches*! Time and lack of funds, as well as the hugely displaced deployment of the army meant Bardin was not in universal use, nor was every regulation fully implemented, by the time the Emperor rode away from Fontainebleau.

The War Ministry *circulaire* of 22 April 1814 stated that the decree of 19 January and 7 February 1812 for the dress of the army was to be enforced. Any clothing not made to these regulations was to be removed from use. To assess the clothing needs for the army, every regiment was given a shake-down inspection that summer. The War Ministry, as part of the 'rebranding' exercise, made the following amendments to the Bardin regulations, the fifth such major change:

On the retroussis of the *habits* the crowned N will be removed and replaced by a *fleur-de-lys*, 70mm tall (2 pouces ½ or thereabouts) and of proportionate width.

The crowned N will be removed from the *schako* plates
The crowned N will be removed from the *gibernes*
The crowned N will be removed from sabretaches
The crowned N will be removed from the buttons of the gendarme
The drummers, trumpeters and musicians will abandon the colour green and will use *bleu de roi* in its place for *habits* and will use the Livery of the Royal Household.
All other aspects will be in strict conformity to the two decrees.[20]

Voltigeur wearing his regulation Bardin uniform.

At the same time, a second circular from the War Ministry ordered that all the codicils that made up the Bardin collation of orders generated from January 1812 through to June 1813 were to be deleted:

1. Black leather work was to be replaced
2. *Pokalems* were undress headgear
3. All *gilets* were to be made from broadcloth
4. Grenadiers had scarlet epaulettes, *aigrettes* and elite company *schakos*. Bearskins were abolished for all but *sapeurs*
5. *Voltigeurs* were allowed yellow *aigrettes* and yellow epaulettes were tolerated
6. All *capotes* were to be beige
7. All pre-Bardin clothing to be taken out of service

In campaign dress Ligne and Legere (left) were almost indistinguishable as this image by Vernet shows. By 1813 most legere units were nothing more than badly trained conscripts incapable of carrying out true light infantry functions. The earlier model of greatcoat was single breasted, and was either mid grey or brown in colour.

In essence, all non-standard clothing and equipment was to be replaced. This was the first time that the War Ministry had the chance to impose on the armed forces the Bardin regulation, and vast sums of money were allocated to the task of remaking the Imperial Army in the Royalist mould.

In order to ensure uniformity across the army, the War Ministry, rather than relying on *circulaires*, drew up a detailed set of new regulations for the army. Thus, the 1814 collation of orders was codified into the dress regulations of 8 February 1815, or Bardin Mark 6.

The regulations were framed in the Bardin regulation of 1812. It was the first time that the army had had a chance to be totally re-equipped with new-pattern clothing and equipment, although some regiments clung on to the old-style *habits*, and other idiosyncrasies. A huge reclothing programme began in spring 1815. The dress regulations of 8 February decreed that the clothing and equipment was to be:[21]

Linen for lining 104cm wide	1fr 40
Linen for *pantalons* and *caleçon*, 89cm wide	1fr 65
Large buttons	40 centimes a dozen
Small buttons	24 centimes a dozen

Labour costs

Habit	2fr 45
Drummers' *habit*	8fr 52
Gilet manches	1fr 15
Pantalons	1fr
Capote	1fr 50
Bonnet de police	60 centimes
Caleçon	40 centimes

Lace

Silver for *sous-officier*	8fr 50
In white wool for corporal	55 centimes
In red wool for chevrons	55 centimes
Silver for drum major and musicians	5fr 60
Livery for drummers No. 1	90 centimes
Livery for drummers No. 2	90 centimes

Epaulettes

Scarlet wool for *carabinier*	3fr 40
For adjutants	25fr

Aigrettes

Scarlet for *carabinier*	3fr 50
Yellow for *voltigeur*	2fr 50

Houpettes for *chasseur*	60 centimes
Hooks and eyes	10 centimes
Braces for *pantalons*	60 centimes

Schako with no neck cover for *carabinier*, cavalry model, garnished with scarlet wool lace of Cul de De type 22mm wide and 40mm wide, plate bearing Arms of France and regimental number and chinscales — 10fr 40

Schakos without neck covers for fusiliers and *voltigeurs* with plate and chinscales	8fr 60
Schako plate of the new model	55 centimes
Chinscales	75 centimes
Chinscales bosses	25 centimes

For equipment the regulations stated that:[22]
Giberne for *sous-officier* with no plate
Giberne for soldier
Entwined LL cypher with crown for *giberne* of *chasseurs*
Grenade plate for *carabiniers*
Hunting horn plate for *voltigeurs*
Porte-giberne with no bayonet frog for *sous-officier*
Porte-giberne with bayonet frog for *carabiniers, voltigeurs* and *chasseurs*
Musket sling
Baudrier, 62mm wide for *sous-officier*
Drum, drum sling, drummers' apron in sheep hide or lacquered buff
Sapeurs' axe, axe case, gauntlets, apron
Horn for *voltigeurs*

Petty equipment was to comprise:[23]

Pair of shoes	5fr
Shirt	4fr 75
Half gaiters in black twill with flat copper buttons	3fr 15 a pair
Half gaiters in grey linen	1franc 85
Pair of ankle socks in wool or cotton	90 centimes
Black stock	40 centimes
Pantalons du toile after the regulation of 19 January 1812	3fr 16
Sac à distribution	3fr 70
Havresac	8fr 30
Cockade	15 centimes
Musket worm	30 centimes
Épinglette	10 centimes

Chasseur officer wearing the new Bardin-regulation uniform by Vernet.

Drummer of *carabinier* company wearing the Bardin-regulation full dress and undress uniforms by Rousselot. (*Collection KM*)

This document is very informative. It is clear that only *carabiniers* 1815 had the taller cavalry-style *schakos* with red lace. *Voltigeurs* wore the same *schakos* as *chasseurs*, but were allowed a yellow horse hair *aigrette*. Only *carabiniers* were allowed fringed epaulettes, while *voltigeurs* had shoulder straps like the *chasseurs*.

In new year 1815 Napoléon returned to Paris. The army had been mobilised over the Saxon Crisis of new year 1815. As Napoléon took back the reins of power, men were flooding back to the army from leave, which they had been on since the previous summer. Realising he had to face a war on several fronts, Napoléon began preparations to massively expand the small peacetime army of the Bourbons.

The Army Napoléon inherited was decked out in new Royalist uniforms and symbols. The army was to be re-styled in the Imperial Image. At the start of the 100 days, yet

Excellent Bardin-regulation *schako* of the 1e Légère. The plate is distinctly non-regulation. (Photograph and collection of Betrand Malvaux)

another collation of dress regulations appeared. According to the decree of 28 March 1815, the two decrees of 19 January and 7 February 1812 were to be re-instated: drummers and trumpeters were to wear green with Imperial Livery, the Royal Cypher and *fleur-de-lys* were abolished in favour of the crowned 'N'.[24] Under the Bourbon regime, 6,550,224fr worth of clothing had been made and issued but largely not paid for. Of this massive 6.5million French debt, Marshal Davout agreed to pay 4.7 million fr to manufacturers and suppliers.[25] As in 1813, the army by April 1815 had run out of supplies of buff leather for equipment. A supplementary regulation was issued on 1 April 1815. The tariff removed from the *voltigeurs* and grenadiers the sabre and belt, and allowed for the *porte-giberne* and musket sling to be made from blackened cowhide. Whitened cowhide could be used for the manufacture of *havresacs*. Remarkably, rather than regimental buttons, all buttons were to be the model of the Imperial Guard made in white metal.[26] Standardising all buttons to a single model made a lot of sense logistically! This left regimental allocation purely down to the *schako* plate.

A second decree was issued on 17 June – largely repeating that of April – to speed up the process of supplying the army and to make the process cheaper. The infantry, *légère* and foot artillery were allowed a *capote*, *habit-veste*, *pantalons de route*, *schako*, *giberne* with belt made from blackened cowhide, and blackened cowhide musket sling. A major change with the decree was that the *gilet manches* was officially done away with, and the artillery were authorised beige *capotes* to save blue broadcloth for uniform *habits*. As in April, no chamois broadcloth was allowed for *voltigeurs* and no epaulettes for *carabiniers*: every man in the *légère* wore the same *habit-veste*! *Carabiniers* were forbidden to carry sabres, and the *sous-officiers* were allowed blackened cowhide *baudriers* costing 3fr 50 each. All buttons were to be '*modèle de la Garde Imperiale*'. Drummers were allocated 248m of Imperial Livery, costing 216fr, and tellingly not an inch of green broadcloth.[27] As in April, here is official sanction of drummers wearing standard *légère habits* adorned with Imperial Livery, as no special allowance was made for a different drummers' habit. How far the decree was implemented we cannot say as it was issued ten days or so before the Empire fell.

What this chapter has shown is the Bardin was not a static decree, The decree as written down in January and February 1812 never made it off the drawing board. The Bardin regulation so beloved of re-enactors and wargamers was not a single document, it comprised four different collations and went through eight major changes and revisions. The development of the Bardin regulation has, to my knowledge, never appeared in print or been acknowledged. Therefore, this 'revelation' about Bardin, added to my ground-breaking research that has taken over a decade to untangle, fundamentally alters our understanding of how the French Army was dressed from 1811 to 1815.

Far from simplifying how the army was dressed, the eight different regulations in three collations made things worse: a grand idea was 'derailed' by the chaotic situation France found itself in from summer 1812.

Chapter 5

Regulations in Practice

So much for the theory, what of the practice? What follows is a discussion of the clothing and equipment of the 36 *légère* regiments. Due to the vagaries of history, the documentation that can be located dates primarily to the end of the Empire, and thus our study centres on the Bardin regulation.

1ᵉ *Légère*

We only have a limited amount of information about the regiment's clothing. That which can be easily located is from the years 1814 to 1815. When the *Régiment du Roi* was formed in August 1814, all paperwork generated prior to this time appears to have been lost as it cannot be located at the French Army Archives. The only document we can find is an inspection report dated 20 August 1814 and this presents the following information about clothing and equipment:[1]

220m beige broadcloth for *capotes*
1,120m 78 blue broadcloth
54m 35 white broadcloth
350m blue serge
2,861m 80 tricot
1,034m linen
797m 72 linen for *caleçons*
252 *habits*
224 *gilets manches*
400 *schakos*

With only limited archive sources for the dress of the line infantry in 1815, thankfully, however, a report produced on 18 to 20 June 1815 gives us some information about what the army was actually dressed like. The review reads as follows:

1st Light Infantry
In the next 20 days, the regiment will receive the broadcloth and tricot to complete the clothing of 1,000 men and for the replacement items for the year 1815. The corps is to receive in the next 20 days 600 *schakos*, *gibernes* and *porte* gibernes, 500 musket slings and 150 *baudriers*.

The corps has received only 504 men from the 1,000 assigned by the minister, of which some 496 have yet to arrive with the regiment. This is sufficient to complete

Officers' *schako* of a *chasseur* company of the 1e Légère. The wide silver lace band may denote the rank of captain. (*Private collection UK*)

the 4th Battalion. The 4th Battalion which is in the *dépôt* has 18 officers, 205 *sous-officiers* and men. The three first battalions are with the army at the present time and muster 67 officers and 1,880 *sous-officiers* and men.[2]

We know nothing about the dress of the regiment until 21 September 1815, when it was disbanded. At this date, the 711 men present under arms had the following equipment, which they carried away with them:[3]

568 *habits*
445 *vestes*
512 *pantalons*
0 *caleçons*
329 *capotes*
650 *schakos*

451 *bonnets de police*
408 *gibernes*
408 *porte-gibernes*
196 *baudriers*
8 drum carriages
8 drums

286 musket slings
412 muskets
412 bayonets
196 sabres

Carabinier of the 1ᵉ *Légère* by Martinet. Regimental records imply no bearskins existed in the unit, but the fragmented nature of the archive is not conclusive.

Officer of the 1ᵉ *Légère* during the 100 Days. (*Collection KM*)

Carabinier of the 1ᵉ *Légère* during the 100 Days campaign. (*Collection KM*)

Voltigeur of the 1ᵉ *Légère* as they appeared at Waterloo. (*Collection KM*)

Chasseur of the 1e *Légère* dressed as they appeared at Waterloo. (*Collection KM*)

Regulations in Practice 61

Chasseur of the 1e *Légère* c.1812 by Martinet. The yellow plume may suggest he is actually a *voltigeur*.

The *dépôt* held no stocks of clothing, arms or equipment, neither did it hold any materials for the production of clothing.[4] The lack of any records for the dress of *carabiniers*, *voltigeurs* and drummers means we can offer no statement about the dress of these men or the regiment for most of the Empire period.

2ᵉ *Légère*

We are missing a great deal of archive papers for the regiment. The only paper archive for the regiment we can locate comes from August 1814. The reviewing officer noted:

> Dress: it is very good and well sewn; but it is not uniform.
> Clothing: the cloth that has been sent by the suppliers is to be totally rejected as it is very bad quality, in consequence the clothing of the corps is all entirely bad.
> Equipment: it is complete, but on the whole, it is in bad condition and far from uniform. None exists in the dépôt.
> Items in the Magazine: The items not made in the *dépôt* include blue broadcloth as well as tricot and linen for lining: items that have been made in the dépôt include 135 *capotes*, 168 *habits*, 40 *gilets*. These items are very good.[5]

The inspection report to which the summary was attached is missing from the regiment's archive; therefore, we can say little more about the regiment as it was in summer 1814. The regiment's paper archive is partially complete to allow us to assess if Bardin was implemented or the 1814 regulation changes were carried out. From the accounts of the regiment, we find the following purchases were made:[6]

3rd Quarter 1814
790 pompoms, total 118fr 50
726m 20 linen cording, total 145fr 24
17 sets of cords for grenadier bearskins, total 85fr
5 sets of bearskin cords for *sapeurs*
996 white cockades, total 49fr 80

1st Quarter 1815
952 pairs of chinscales for *schakos*, total 706fr 50

2nd Quarter 1815
50m of silver lace
100 *aigrettes* for *carabiniers*
100 *aigrettes* for *voltigeurs*
121 cockades
Clothing, total 1,130fr 25
Drum major's mace, total 170fr

Chasseur of the 2ᵉ *Légère* as they appeared from 1802 through to summer 1814 by Martinet.

Carabinier of the 2ᵉ *Légère* as they appeared from 1802 through to summer 1814 by Martinet.

Voltigeur of the 2ᵉ *Légère* as they appeared from 1802 through to summer 1814 by Martinet. The scarlet cuffs are unexpected.

Chasseur of the 2ᵉ *Légère* as they appeared during the 100 Days.

360 hunting horns in copper costing 25 centimes each, total 90fr
50 long straps and 20 pairs of *capote* straps for *sacs de peau*, total 75fr
82 pairs of *caleçons*, total 193fr 52
84 new *schakos*, total 873fr 60

The bearskin cords being purchased in 1814, long after bearskins had been abolished under Bardin, shows that *sapeurs* and the *carabiniers* perhaps only of 1ᵉ battalion still retained bearskins. Alas we do not know how many bearskins were in use – presumably sufficient for at least a company. The cording was used according to the accounts to attach the cockade to the *schakos*. The *carabiniers* in bearskins resulted in the regiment being misidentified at Waterloo as the Old Guard by men from the 52nd Regiment of Foot, particularly George Gawler and others.

Of interest, 55 new *gilets manches* for *carabiniers* were made. These required 40cm of scarlet cloth, costing 15fr a metre, the bill coming to 6fr. Presumably the cloth was for piping or some other form of decoration like a scarlet collar or cut out grenade badges for the arms? At the same time a further 1m of scarlet cloth, costing 15fr, was purchased for *gilets manches*. In addition, five new *bonnets de police* were made, the total cost being 18fr 90, and 24fr 50 was spent on seven pairs of grenadiers' epaulettes. The regiment's master tailor produced eight new *habits* at a cost of 71fr 40 for the tailoring. His total tailoring bill for the third quarter of 1814 was 2,647fr 50, a considerable sum, so we assume a large quantity of the regiment's clothing was renewed.[7]

The following amounts of cloth and materials were purchased in the first and second quarter of 1815:[8]

20m beige broadcloth, total 185fr
22m 68 blue broadcloth, total 245fr 14
0m 76 white broadcloth, total 6fr 84
0m 30 scarlet broadcloth, total 4fr 81
8m blue serge, total 14fr 16
15m 64 blue tricot, total 82fr 42
23m 68 linen for lining, total 31fr 97
5 dozen and 4 large buttons, total 1fr 39
236 dozen small buttons, total 4fr 68
TOTAL: 576fr 44

Following Waterloo, the *dépôt* of the regiment was disbanded on 26 September 1815. It held the following materials:[9]

634m 15 beige broadcloth
857m 28 blue broadcloth
19m 12 white broadcloth
4m 93 chamois broadcloth

104m 14 blue serge
175m 01 blue *tricot*
832m 74 linen for lining
182m 28 linen for *caleçons*
11m 10 green serge
11m 10 green *tricot*

The green *tricot* was used to make *pantalons* and the green serge had one purpose: to line *habits*. We assume green broadcloth had existed in *dépôt* and it was used entirely. Was this for drummers to be reclothed in green in 1815 or what remained from green clothing decreed in 1814? The lace used by the drummers is also a mystery. Silver lace was purchased, presumably for rank stripes, but not an inch of Royalist or Imperial Livery seems to have been purchased or remained in *dépôt*. So, we are left to speculate still further about the dress of the drummers. The chamois cloth was also undoubtedly for the collar of *voltigeurs*' *habits*. No *aigrette*s or epaulettes were in *dépôt*.

3ᵉ *Légère*

At the time of writing, few archive sources can be found regarding the dress and equipment of the regiment. Reviewed on 25 July 1805, the men were dressed in 1,658 *schakos* and had 199 *chapeaux*, which is something of a surprise. No bearskins existed for the *carabiniers*, and no chamois broadcloth for the *voltigeurs*. The inspector ordered *schakos* to be adopted, 981 in the first year, the remainder in the next. Of interest, 38 – we assume *voltigeurs* – were armed with light cavalry *mousquetons*, and the drummers and *cornets* were issued the same firearm.[10] Reviewed 25 January 1808, the report makes no mention of *voltigeurs* or *carabiniers*. It does tell us every man carried a sabre, 56 light cavalry *mousquetons* were in use, and that for immediate needs 1,340 *habits* and *gilets*, 2,681 pairs of *pantalons*, 670 *schakos*, 129 *gibernes* and belts were needed.[11]

We know nothing more until the report from 25 September 1815, which gives the contents of stores:

62m 24 white broadcloth that has been bleached white
76m 84 scarlet broadcloth
1,950m 19 beige broadcloth
736m 22 blue serge
285m 84 red worsted lace

In addition, stores had 177 complete uniforms that were cut out and waiting to be sewn together. Made items in stores included 18 bearskins and colpacks – *sapeur* or drum major? – 7 grenadiers' *aigrettes*, 9 *voltigeurs*' *aigrettes*, 150 *schakos*, 220 sets of *schakos* cords, 324 *schako* plates, 1,000 white cockades, 4 pairs of grenadiers' epaulettes and 4 sets of *sapeurs*' equipment. Clearly the *sapeurs* had colpacks, and fairly recently the *carabiniers*

Drummer of the 3ᵉ *Légère* in a naïve sketch copied here by Knoetel, dated to 1809.

Grenadier of the 3ᵉ *Légère* during the 100 Days. The pink facings are totally unexpected. (*Collection KM*)

had worn bearskins. Of note, stores held 60 spare stock buckles, 974 black stocks, 89 pairs of black twill gaiters, 458 pairs of grey linen gaiters, accompanied by 251 pairs of grey linen *pantalons*.[12]

4ᵉ *Légère*

The regiment's paperwork for its clothing is sparse. The bulk of the paper archive that exists deals with the 100 Days. Reviewed on 15 October 1804, the three battalions mustered 1,716 men. Since the last review a year earlier, 157 men had died, 446 had deserted, 91 had been discharged and 70 had been sent home from hospital as unfit for further duty. Indeed, 180 were sick in hospital at the time of the review, and a further 172 would be discharged following it: 978 men left the regiment, and 1,015 joined. The men were noted as being weak and the theoretical knowledge of the officers and men was also weak, and over the previous ten months the inspector was at pains to point out to the War Minister that 'no instruction had been carried out'. In terms of clothing 'the majority of the *habits* are in bad condition' reported the inspector.[13]

Officer of *légère* c.1804. He carries a light cavalry sabre, which may imply a mounted role. (*Photograph and Collection of Bertrand Malvaux*)

Inspected on 13 July 1805, since the last review 54 men had died, 130 had deserted and 206 were in hospital. The three battalions mustered 89 officers and 1,699 other ranks, which included 7 musicians. The men were wearing *schakos*, and no bearskins existed for the *carabiniers*. Stores held 1,456m 84 of beige broadcloth to make *capotes*, but no garments had been made, and 4m 69 of chamois broadcloth had been used to make *voltigeur* clothing. The *voltigeur* company was wholly armed with 326 light cavalry *mousquetons*. Of the 1,702 *habits* in service, 707 needed repairs and 72 immediate replacement. Of the 1,903 pairs of *pantalons*, 869 pairs needed repairs and 647 immediate replacement, as did 290 *schakos*, 45 *gibernes* and 54 *baudriers*. For immediate needs stores held 203 *habits*, 201 vestes, 118 pairs of *pantalons* and 509 *schakos*.[14]

Inspected again on 30 November 1807, the *carabiniers* were wearing *schakos*, just as in 1805, 9m 93 of chamois broadcloth was used to make *voltigeur* clothing and a stockpile of 1,646m 40 of beige broadcloth was held, and had not been used to make *capotes*. Every man had a sabre, and just 40 *mousquetons* were in use, with the officers and *sous-officiers* of the *voltigeur* company.[15] Nothing else is known until we come across a report produced on 18 to 20 June 1815 that gives us some information about what the army was actually dressed like. The review reads as follows:

4e *Légère*

The dépôt comprises 277 men, of which available for service, fully clothed and equipped are 80 men.

The corps has received clothing for 879 men, and have dressed 748 men, there remains available 134 uniforms. The administrative council, in order to equip 1,000 men, has passed marchés [purchase agreements] for the sum of 46,730fr 93 for new items and replacements for the year of 1815, and has received into the *dépôt* the materials to produce:

796 *pantalons*
488 *capotes*
618 *habits*
468 *gilets manches*[16]

This document is one of a mere handful for the regiment for its dress and equipment. The next document for dress was drawn up at the disbanding of the unit in summer 1815. In July 1815, the regiment's *dépôt* held 171 *gibernes*, 168 *porte-gibernes*, 3 drums and carriages, 1 *sapeur's* axe and 174 bayonets.[17] The *dépôt* also held the following amounts of cloth, clothing and equipment:[18]

321m 50 beige broadcloth
237m 34 blue broadcloth
54m 67 white broadcloth
35m 85 scarlet broadcloth
16m 68 green broadcloth
1,021m 28 white serge
403m 37 blue *tricot*
39m 93 linen for linings
1,240m linen for *caleçons*
0m silver lace
81m 40 wool lace for corporals
14m 60 wool lace for chevrons
180m drummers' livery
5 *habits*
35 *gilets manches*
25 *pantalons* de tricot
10 *schakos*

182 *bonnets de police*
60 pompoms
7 pairs of epaulettes for *carabiners*
223 *gibernes*
353 *porte-gibernes*
1 *baudrier*
3 drum carriages
3 drums
315 musket slings
1 drummers' apron
1 *sapeurs'* axe case and belt
22 black stocks
865 pairs of shoes
5 pairs of linen *pantalons*
4 *sacs de peau*
203 *épinglettes*
145 musket worms

The *carabinier* company certainly wore scarlet epaulettes, but do not seem to have had their own-pattern *schakos*. Drummers wore Imperial Livery on green *habits* – alas we cannot tell if this was an innovation of 1815 or if it had been in use since 1813.

5ᵉ *Légère*

At the time of writing the regiment's paper archive housed at Service Historique de la Défense contains no comments on its clothing.[19]

6ᵉ *Légère*

On 10 December 1805 the regiment purchased 115 pairs of *voltigeur* epaulettes, 5 pairs of epaulettes for adjutants, 120 *voltigeur* sword knots, 24 pairs of *carabiniers'* epaulettes, 24 *carabiniers'* sword knots and 24 plumes for *carabiniers*. In the midst of the 1807 campaign Marshal Ney granted the regiment a gratification on 27 January 1807 to buy new epaulettes and plumes for the *voltigeurs* and *carabiniers*. In 1808 lace was purchased for the regiment's *bonnets de police*, which the War Ministry objected to, as the *bonnets de police* of the rank and file had no lace or devices, i.e., they were entirely blue with either white or scarlet piping to the flamme and turban, the latter always being devoid of lace. With the formation of the 4th battalion, 4 *sapeurs'* aprons and 4 pairs of gauntlets were purchased, along with 25 *baudriers*; 3 fanions for the battalion were also purchased. Some 649fr was spent in 1809 buying boots and *culottes de peau* for the regimental artillery drivers.[20]

The regiment's archive is sparse: we do not have either the 1808 or 1814 inspection returns. The notes about the regiment to the War Ministry observed the unit had not adopted the regulations of 19 January 1812, which henceforth were to be strictly observed.[21] Regimental accounts reveal that during the 100 days 60fr was spent on 100 pompoms for *chasseurs* and 240fr of 96 *aigrettes* for *voltigeurs*, while 55fr was spent on a cover for the eagle and *drapeau*.[22]

Disbanded in September 1815, the *dépôt* held 302m 37 blue broadcloth, 30m 52 white broadcloth, 1m 87 red broadcloth, 339m 68 blue tricot, and 193m white serge. The *dépôt* also held 4 *capotes* awaiting disposal, 148 new chasseur *habits* and 5 awaiting disposal, 12 non-regulation drummers' *habits* – these were green with Imperial Livery we assume – 24 *vestes*, 193 brand-new pairs of blue *pantalons de tricot*, 237 *schakos*, 220 *bonnets de police*, 470 *schako* covers, 443 *houpettes* and 67 pairs of grenadiers' epaulettes.[23] In the *dépôt* of 3ᵉ battalion were 77 *chasseur habits*, 145 *vestes*, 134 pairs of *tricot pantalons*, 14 *schakos*, 1,146 *capotes*, 4 muskets, 44 sabres, 2 *gibernes* and *porte-gibernes*, 661 pairs of shoes, 209 pairs of black gaiters, 215 pairs of grey gaiters, 94 *havresacs* and 82 pairs of *pantalons de route*. Sent to the arsenal at Reims were 123 *gibernes* with 118 *porte-gibernes*, 38 *baudriers*, 3 drums and carriages, 1 drumstick holder, 12 musket slings, 105 muskets, 20 dragoon muskets, 41 sabres and 119 bayonets. The dragoon muskets were issued to *voltigeurs*.[24]

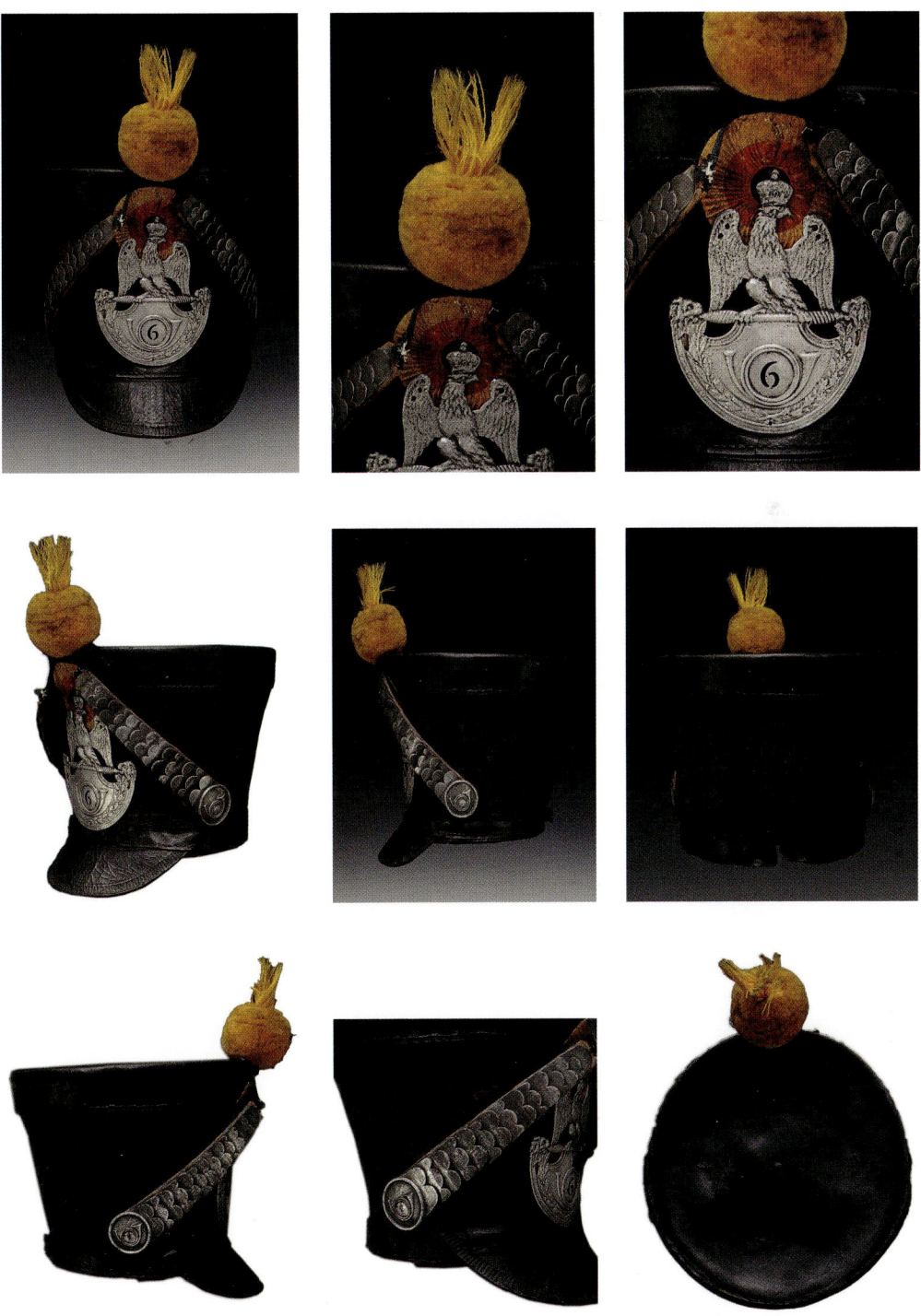

Voltigeur's schako of the 6e *Légère*. (*Collection and Photograph of Bertrand Malvaux*)

7ᵉ *Légère*

At the time of writing the earliest records for the dress of the regiment is from a document of 15 January 1807, which states it issued 1,698 *habits*, 3,078 *gilets*, 3,758 pairs of *pantalons*, 2,151 *capotes* ready-made and a further 953 in kit form, as well as 1,914 pairs of shoes and 143 shirts. Also issued were 284 *marmites* with covers and bags, 2,473 white metal (tin) *petit bidons*, and 146 hatchets with cases and 284 *gamelles*.[25] Following the Battle of Essling, the regiment made good its damaged clothing. The regiment had to buy cloth and materials in Vienna, at prices much higher than allowed for by the War Ministry in Paris. Purchased materials included:[26]

4m 28 white broadcloth
23m 80 red broadcloth
535m 50 blue broadcloth for *pantalons*
164m 22 beige broadcloth costing 10fr 40 a metre

Senior officer's *schako* of the 7e *Légère* dating to the last years of the empire. Martinet implies the embroidered upper band was a common feature of senior officers' *schakos*. (*Collection de l'Office du Tourisme de Pontarlier. Dépôt au Musée municipal de Pontarlier – France*)

974m 01 beige broadcloth costing 12fr 45 a metre
462m 51 blue broadcloth costing 16fr 39 a metre
154m 49 beige broadcloth costing 11fr 35 a metre
160m 25 beige broadcloth costing 12fr 60 a metre
95m blue broadcloth costing 15fr 21

The beige broadcloth was used to make 1,098 new *capotes* costing 2fr 50 each to make, and were made by civilian tailors in Vienna! Remarkably the regiment had broadcloth *pantalons* and not tricot. Other materials purchased included 511m 70 of linen for linings, 63m 07 blue serge to line the tails of *habits*, and 34m 51 red serge to line the *habits* of the regimental artillery, for which 68 *habits* and *vestes* were made. For the *carabiniers* of 3ᵉ battalion, it was estimated to cost 1,024fr to provide them with bearskins. Out of economy, some 461fr 40 was spent buying them 56 *schakos*, with lace embellishments, costing 11fr 50, to accord with the other companies of the regiment, 94 pairs of white *schako* cords costing 3fr 70 a pair for the 2ᵉ and 3ᵉ battalion, and 8 dozen cockades for *schakos*. We assume the *carabiniers* had bearskins in the first two battalions and also epaulettes. The band master was reclothed as well: 2m 40 of super fine *bleu de ciel* broadcloth was purchased as well as silver lace to adorn the *habit*.[27] We assume the band was likewise dressed: the colour of the *vestes* and *pantalons* is not known. Were the drummers so dressed?

Reviewed on 1 May 1811, the inspector noted the regiment had 57 officers, 2,524 men and 78 horses. He added that 13 officers were needed to bring the regiment up to capacity. Clothing wise, 100 *habits*, 182 vestes, 188 pairs of *pantalons*, 88 *schakos*, 510 *capotes*, 59 *gibernes*, 61 *giberne* belts, 27 *baudriers*, 88 infantry muskets, and 21 dragoon muskets for the *voltigeurs* needed repairs. Missing items included 42 *gibernes* and belts, 177 *baudriers* and 109 sabres.[28]

The regiment was inspected on 5 September 1814. The inspector noted that the clothing was well made, but that 119 *habits* were missing, as were 632 *capotes*. The *dépôt* was empty bar 1,244m of beige broadcloth to make *capotes* and a combined total of 255m of blue and white broadcloth.[29]

The 1ᵉ, 2ᵉ and 3ᵉ battalions were wound up on 10 September 1815. Sent to the *dépôt* at Strasbourg were 1,033 *habits*, 722 *vestes*, 1,208 pairs of *tricot pantalons*, 1,222 *capotes*, 1,222 *schakos*, 1,030 sets of braces, 1,495 *gibernes*, 1,491 *giberne* belts, 467 *baudriers*, 30 drums and carriages, 1,540 muskets and 480 sabres.

The regimental *dépôt* was disbanded on 25 September 1815. The *dépôt* held not a single item of clothing, but it did hold 183 pairs of *carabinier* epaulettes, 82 *carabinier schakos*, 467 *chasseur* and *voltigeur schakos*, 6 *schako* covers, 120 red *houpettes*, 100 yellow *houpettes* and 411 fusilier *houpettes*. So we must imagine *carabiniers* had regulation epaulettes and *schakos* but a red-tufted pompom in lieu of an *aigrette*. We also note 127 *porte-gibernes*, 35 musket slings and 186 *baudriers* made from blackened cowhide were held awaiting disposal. Also, in *dépôt* was 720 of drummers' lace, 150m 95 white worsted lace, 82m 03 red worsted lace, no green or chamois broadcloth, but it did hold 0m 11 beige broadcloth,

247m 58 blue broadcloth, 24m 65 white broadcloth, 16m 12 scarlet broadcloth and 1,410m blue serge. Also lodged in stores were 5 shirts, 2 pairs of linen overalls, 1 black stock, 553 pairs linen socks, 322 pairs of wool socks, 439 *épinglettes*, 10 screwdrivers, 24 white cockades, 271 tricolour cockades, 157 pairs of *voltigeur* epaulettes, 37 red plumes, 10 yellow plumes, 2 green plumes, 136 yellow sword knots and 1,293 green sword knots.[30] Were these items in *dépôt* awaiting disposal following the Bardin edict or in store waiting to be issued? Alas we cannot tell. During the 100 Days, regimental accounts record that ordered on 6 April 1815 were 32 *carabinier aigrettes* costing 112fr, 36 *voltigeur aigrettes* costing 98fr, and 114 chasseur *houpettes* costing 68 fr, but these items arrived after Waterloo was lost.[31]

8ᵉ *Légère*

At the time of writing, no archive sources can be found regarding the dress and equipment of the regiment. The relevant document boxes are missing in the archives.

9ᵉ *Légère*

Inspected 14 August 1805, the inspector notes that the peak of the *schakos* was not well placed, so too the plumes. He adds that the soldiers did not have sleeves on their *gilets* (contrary to regulations) and officers did not have the right number of buttons on the *revers* and cuff. No bearskins existed for the *carabiniers*, but since October 1804, 3m 24 chamois broadcloth had been used to make *voltigeur* clothing. We note 160 *mousquetons* were issued, 106 to officers and regimental staff and 54 to drummers, who presumably also had *gibernes* and belts.[32]

Issued under the decree of 15 January 1807, the regiment was issued 1,025 *habits*, 3,010 *gilets*, 3,015 pairs of *pantalons*, 1,191 *capotes* ready-made and a further 926 in kit form, as well as 4,467 pairs of shoes and 1,561 shirts.[33]

Reviewed again on 1 January 1808, we note 3,396 *capotes* were in use, 4 *cornets*, and the majority of the unit's clothing was in desperate need of replacing: of 3,396 *habits*, 368 needed repairs and 1,684 immediate replacement. Likewise, every single pair of *pantalons* had to be replaced. Stores reports 3m 24 chamois broadcloth had been used. Just 36 bearskins were likewise in use, 108 smocks, a mere 206 pairs of *pantalons de route*, and headdress was a mix of *chapeaux* and *schakos*. Stores also reports 179 pairs of *carabinier* epaulettes, and 1,714 pairs for *chasseurs* and *voltigeurs*. Again, we find 144 *carabinier* sword knots and 1,418 for *chasseurs*, as well as 108 *carabinier* plumes and 1,747 *chasseur* plumes, which must have also been used by *voltigeurs*. All bar 43 *mousquetons* had been lost on campaign.[34]

Martinet gives the unit chamois cuff facings.

At the end of the 1814 campaign, the regiment's clothing needed repairing, replacing or was missing – the same story is repeated in every regiment analysed in this book. A staggering 407 *habits* had to be replaced as of the old model and 227 men had no *habit*,

Officer of *carabiniers* of the 9e *Légère* sometime in the first half of 1808. (*Collection KM*)

Carabinier and *chasseur* of the 9ᵉ *Légère* in the first half of 1808. (*Collection KM*)

496 men had no *gilets manches*, while 450 men no *pantalons de tricot* and must have been on parade wearing *pantalons de route*. Some 494 men had no *capote*, and of those *capotes* that existed, 101 needed repairs and 243 needed immediate replacement. Last but not least, 467 men had no *bonnets de police*. Remarkably, 333 men were on parade in *chapeaux*! These were all in the 6ᵉ battalion and had been issued *capotes*, *pantalons de route*, *chapeaux*, and gaiters, as well as a *havresac*, *giberne* and belt. The *dépôt* held very little cloth and materials: 225m 05 beige broadcloth, 515m blue broadcloth, 18m 50 white broadcloth, 7m 60 scarlet broadcloth, 772m blue tricot and 0m 65 of linen. Likewise, clothing in the *dépôt* consisted of 6 *capotes*, 12 *bonnets de police*, 193 pairs of *caleçons*, 1,043 *chasseur houpettes*, 1 *voltigeur cornet* and 2 pairs of grenadiers' epaulettes.³⁵ The inspector noted that everything had to be replaced as it was worn out and not regulation: he noted to the War Ministry that the regiment had not acted upon the decree of 19 January 1812, or the *circulaire* of 23 April 1814, and ordered the regiment to adopt Bardin clothing and to dress the drummers in blue with Royalist Livery.³⁶

A somewhat enigmatic *schako* of the 9ᵉ *Légère*. The green body, with red lace upper band and white lace side chevrons, may indicate a drummer, or in this case a *voltigeur cornet*. (Office de Tourisme de Fontainebleau)

On 24 May 1815 the major reported that the 1ᵉ and 2ᵉ battalion mustered 1,270 other ranks and the 3ᵉ battalion 385 men, with 63 in the 4ᵉ and 136 in the 5ᵉ. To clothe and equip the men in 3ᵉ battalion, the major reported he needed 230 pairs of *pantalons de tricot*, and 244 pairs of black gaiters. Of the men available for service with the 1ᵉ and 2ᵉ battalion, 12 were dressed in *capote*, *gilets manches* and *pantalons de tricot*, 10 were dressed in a *capote*, *habit-veste* and *gilet manches* with *pantalons de route* and grey gaiters, 5 in a *habit-veste* and *gilet manches*, *pantalons de route* and grey gaiters, and 12 in *gilet manches*, *pantalons de route*, and grey gaiters. Every man had a *schako*, *giberne* and belt, musket with bayonet as well as *havresac*, linen, footwear, and *petit equipment*. In the 4ᵉ battalion the major reported that to clothe all the allocated men, 45 *habits-vestes*, 61 *capotes*, 62 pairs of *pantalons* and 62 pairs of black gaiters were needed.³⁷

Disbanded in summer 1815, the *dépôt* held no stocks of clothing or equipment. We do note the unit's *capotes* were made from white tricot. It did itemise *habits* for *carabiniers*, *voltigeurs*, *chasseurs* and drummers, and also *schakos* for *carabiniers*, *voltigeurs* and *chasseurs* – despite none being in *dépôt*, we assume they had existed in use at some point. *Voltigeur schakos* are surprising as in theory these did not exist under Bardin. Cloth in the magazine comprised 390m 86 blue broadcloth, 44m 05 white broadcloth, 13m 47 scarlet broadcloth, 8m 92 chamois broadcloth, 299m blue serge, 2235m 73 linen for linings, 1m

80 silver lace and 56m 50 white worsted lace. *Dépôt* did hold 48 *bonnets de police*, 132 pairs of *caleçons*, 475 sets of braces, and 154 *houpettes*. Equipment held included 100 old *gibernes* and 320 needing repairs, 175 buff *giberne* belts and 70 in blackened cowhide, 122 musket slings, 35 *baudriers*, 11 drums, 11 drum carriages, 3 drummers' aprons, 7 *sapeurs*' aprons, 3 *sapeurs*' axes and 4 pairs of gauntlets for *sapeurs*. In addition, were 100 pairs of grey gaiters, 400 *épinglettes*, 271 shirts, and 270 pairs of linen *pantalons*.[38]

10ᵉ *Légère*

The paper archive for the regiment's clothing is hit and miss for what is preserved. Reviewed on 17 October 1804, not an inch of chamois broadcloth existed, and no distinctions existed for the *carabiniers*. About the appearance of the men, the inspector was aghast that the *sous-officiers* had cropped their hair short, and the inspector reminded the regiment's colonel that the band was to cost no more than one day's pay per officer per year and to establish regimental school as they had been ordered to by General Suchet at the last review but had not acted upon. The colonel and other officers were 'chewed out' for having embroidered epaulettes indistinguishable from a general, for having ordered the officers to cut their hair in the style *a la titus*, and for ordering them to wear a non-regulation épée, and was also reminded that light infantry officers had silver appointments and not gold. The inspector also remarked that the cut of the regiment's clothing was of several models and did not accord to the regulations, while the *schakos* in use were not of regulation model. None of these issues should exist, reported Inspector General Suchet. Perhaps not surprisingly, when we look in detail at the clothing, of 2,226 *habits*, 586 needed repairs and 775 total replacement; also needing replacement were 1,360 *vestes*, every single pair of *culottes* were to be replaced, while 2,226 pairs of *pantalons* and 803 *bonnets de police* were needed, along with *803 schakos*. Suchet added that the master tailor would be sent model items to copy to ensure what he made was according to the regulation.[39] Exactly the same comments can be made of the 13 August 1805 inspection, except we note the 6 *voltigeur cornets* were armed with light cavalry *mousquetons* and were issued *gibernes* and belts.[40] Purchased in 1806 were:

100 pairs green epaulettes
1,000 sword knots
1,750 pairs green epaulettes
500 plumes
200 sword knots

The War Ministry reminded the regiment that the decree of 10 February 1806 authorised only epaulettes for *adjutant-sous-officiers* and grenadiers or *carabiniers*. The expense was considered fraudulent. Five hundred *schakos* were purchased in the same year, along with 385 *schako* plates for men transferred from the 2ᵉ and 4ᵉ *Légère*, along with 55 sets of *schako* cords. The unit also had their black stocks made from fabric produced from woven

Sapeur of the 10ᵉ *Légère* drawn sometime in the first half of 1808. (*Collection KM*)

Study of an officer of the 10ᵉ *Légère* from 1808. (*Collection KM*)

horse, which became formalised under Bardin. During 1809 879 pairs of linen *pantalons de route* were made in Vienna, along with 465 *capotes*.[41]

Nothing else is known until August 1814, when the regiment had the following items of clothing and equipment:[42]

Item	In Good Repair	In Need of Repair	Need Replacing	Items due to be replaced	Items missing
Habits	450	370	480	130	739
Vestes	385	190	410	75	774
Pantalons de tricot			945		854
Caleçons			945		854
Capotes	575	280	235	90	999
Bonnets de police	675	76	273		231
Schakos	515		390		894
Gibernes	875	205	64		777
Porte-gibernes	875	90	64		777
Baudriers	180	10	5		442
Drums	25		25		
Drum carriages	25	10	5		
Musket slings	880		59		777
Muskets	775	175	80		
Sabres	180	29			
Bayonets	Nil				

Worthy of comment is the observation that the regiment had no bayonets at all. It is clear sabres and *baudriers* were issued only to *carabiniers* and *sous-officiers*. Unlike the *voltigeurs* in the line infantry, which were issued the regulation *cornet*, the regiment only had drummers. Likewise, the regiment had no equipment for *sapeurs*, assuming the light infantry had these after 1812. *Dépôt* held only 14m 50 of chamois broadcloth, and 1,047m of linen. Brand-new clothing and equipment ready to be issued in the *dépôt* included 71 *chasseur habits*, 6 drummers' *habits*, 32 *gilets manches*, 1,078 pairs of *caleçons*, 200 *gibernes*, 200 *porte-gibernes*, 52 *baudriers*, 2 drums and carriages, 17 grenadiers' *aigrettes*, 26 *voltigeurs*' *aigrettes*, 563 *houpettes*, 2 *voltigeur cornets*, and 174 pairs of grenadiers' epaulettes.[43] The inspector informed the War Ministry that the regiment had not adhered to the regulation of 19 January 1812, and many 'innovations' in the colour, cut, and dimensions of items of clothing and equipment existed that were to be rigorously corrected.[44]

At disbandment the regiment had in *dépôt* 12m 47 scarlet broadcloth, 14m 40 beige broadcloth and 890m of blue tricot. We also find in *dépôt* 77 *habits vieux modèle*, 5 pairs of *pantalons de tricot*, 237 red and yellow *aigrettes*, 138 *houpettes* for *carabiniers*, 58 sword knots for *carabiniers* and 75 pairs of epaulettes for *carabiniers*. In addition, were 2,312 *gibernes* with 1,895 belts, 1,100 musket slings, 426 *baudriers*, 40 drums with carriages, 21 canteens in white metal, 17 *bidons*, 18 *marmites*, 60 *gamelles*, 21 pairs of linen overalls, 11 *giberne* covers and 14 pairs of shoes. Furthermore, *dépôt* held '*modeles de ministre*' supplied to the regiment at some time after the 1814 inspection – suggesting the regiment only adopted the provisions of Bardin regulation in late 1814 into spring 1815! The *dépôt* held 6 *habits*, 1 *gilet manches*, 1 pair tricot *pantalons*, 1 *bonnets de police*, 1 pair of underwear, 1 *schako* with cover, 1 *aigrette*, 1 *giberne*, as well as 1 pair each of grey short gaiters and black short gaiters.[45]

11ᵉ *Légère*

The unit was created in 1811 from the *Tirailleurs Corses, Tirailleurs du Po, Tirailleurs de la Legion de Midi* as well as the *Valaison Bataillon*. Reviewed at the end of 1811, the inspector noted that for the year 1812 the regiment needed 296 *habits* and *vestes*, 149 pairs of tricot *pantalons*, 182 *capotes* and 27 *schakos*. The inspector noted the *habits, vestes* and *pantalons* in use were in a very bad state of repair across the regiment and, regretfully he commented, did not accord to the regulations.[46] Clearly the regiment was decked out in the uniforms of its constituents' elements with no new clothing yet in use. We know nothing more until the regiment was inspected on 4 August 1814. The *dépôt* held a remarkable array of cloth and materials:[47]

0m 70 beige broadcloth
172m 24 blue broadcloth
256m 18 white broadcloth
283m 38 scarlet broadcloth
16m 11 green broadcloth
13m 73 chamois broadcloth
43m blue serge
125m serge
632m 27 *bleu celeste* serge
308m 95 white serge
977m 16 blue tricot
0m green *tricot*
1,901m 80 *bleu celeste* tricot
558m 61 white tricot
278m 96 linen for lining
55m 80 linen for *caleçons*
493m drummers' lace
1m 50 worsted lace for corporal's stripes
45m 60 red worsted lace

What do we make of the *bleu celeste* tricot and serge? We assume this was left over from the *Tirailleurs du Midi*, who wore *bleu celeste pantalons* and *vestes*. Yet we ask, was this cloth also used by the band and drummers in the replacement unit? It seems a logical use

Fabulous Bardin-regulation *schako* of the 11ᵉ *Légère*. (*Photograph and Collection of Bertrand Malvaux*)

for such a stockpile, but we have no evidence of this. The large amount of scarlet cloth was clearly inherited from the *Valaison Bataillon*, who wore scarlet *habits*. The green serge and tricot, as well as broadcloth, was undoubtedly used to make green light infantry clothing as per the 1814 regulation.

It is clear *voltigeurs* had chamois distinctions and that some drummers at least had green *habits*, presumably with Imperial Livery. The *dépôt* held no new clothing beyond 37 new pairs of *pantalons de tricot* and 32 pairs of *caleçons*, but it did hold 117 carabinier schakos, 22 chasseur schakos, 50 *gibernes* with 36 *porte-gibernes*, 4 drums with carriages, 4 *sapeurs'* axes, aprons and gauntlets, 1,032 *houpette*s, and 129 pairs of carabinier epaulettes.[48]

The inspector noted that the regiment had not acted fully on the provisions of the decree of 19 January 1812, and it was necessary 'to amend the clothing as rapidly as possible' to ensure it was correlated with the dispositions of the regulations.[49]

Disbanded on 3 August 1815, the *dépôt* held stocks of cloth, materials and clothing. Cloth included 960m 07 blue broadcloth, 433m 60 beige broadcloth for *capotes*, 20m 05 chamois broadcloth for *voltigeur habits*, 267m 65 white broadcloth for piping, 306m 87 red broadcloth for facings, 791m 27 blue serge, and 24m 53 *bleu celeste* serge – a far smaller amount than in 1814 with over 600m used, so we ask, what had it been used to make? Bandsmen's clothing? We also note that 100m of green serge had been used, leaving 25m in store, logically used to line green drummers' *habits*. Also in stores was 1,459m 74 blue *tricot* for *pantalons* and *vestes*, 44m 39 green *tricot* for drummers *vestes* and *pantalons* and 27m white tricot. In addition, we find 511m 30 drummers' lace – a large increase on stocks held in 1814 – 24m 70 silver lace and 117m 20 worsted lace. New clothing in *dépôt* included 97 *habits*, 198 *pantalons de tricot*, 232 pairs of *caleçons*, 231 *bonnets de police*, 29 pairs of *carabiniers*' epaulettes, 43 carabinier schakos, 438 *schakos* of *chasseurs*, 1,600 *houpettes*, 5 *capotes* and 346 *schako* covers. Nothing for *voltigeurs*, we note, bar the chamois cloth for collars.[50]

12ᵉ *Légère*

Reviewed on 3 August 1805, not an inch of chamois broadcloth or any distinctions existed for the *carabiniers*; every man was wearing a *schako*. The *voltigeur* companies were issued 336 light cavalry *mousquetons* but it seems carried sabres as for the 1,205 men on parade, 967 sabres were issued. Also in use with the officers and *sous-officiers* of the *voltigeur* companies were 27 *carabines rayé* (rifles).[51] Inspected on 3 December 1807, the regiment had the following items of clothing and equipment in use at the end of the 1807 campaign:[52]

Carabinier schako of the 12ᵉ *Légère*. (Private Collection Switzerland)

Regulations in Practice 87

Martinet shows this *voltigeur* of the 12ᵉ *Légère* presenting regimental distinctions: the scarlet cuff and yellow crescents to the green epaulettes.

Item	In Good Repair	In Need of Repair	To be written off	Total	Total made since 23 September 1804	To be replaced
Habits	468		86	554	1,011	86
Vestes	459		64	523	4,583	64
Pantalons	430		82	512	5,739	82
Schakos	510		43	552	4,687	43
Bonnets de police	386		104	490	3,446	104
Capotes	340		90	430	1,994	90
Gibernes	238		108	418	3,161	180
Porte-gibernes	238		184	418	3,172	180
Baudriers	238		184	422	3,134	184
Musket slings	199		180	379	3,588	180
Drum carriages	4		3	7	27	3
Drums	4		3	7	19	3
Voltigeur cornets					6	

The inspection did not cover the war battalions or the detachments, it was literally just the *dépôt* company under scrutiny. The *dépôt* had produced since 1804 4,011 *habits*, and 58 had been in *dépôt* in 1804, making 4,069, of which 4,050 had been issued. In addition, 502 existing *habits* had been repaired and 19 new ones were in *dépôt*. We know the *voltigeur habits* had chamois collars as in September 1804 *dépôt* held 6m 18 of chamois cloth and a further 9m 72 was purchased up to December 1807, making a total of 15m 90, all of which was used. The *voltigeur* companies of 1e and 2e battalion were detached as *bataillons d'elite*, i.e., the *Grenadiers Renuis*, and had 314 dragoon muskets, with 148 examples remaining with the 3e battalion.[53]

Inspected on 2 September 1814, the *dépôt* was totally devoid of cloth and materials and held very few items of clothing and equipment, just 6 *capotes*, 8 *habits*, 7 *gilets manches*, 12 pairs of *pantalons de tricot*, 4 *bonnets de police*, 36 *gibernes* and 11 *houpettes*. In consequence we can say nothing about the appearance of the regiment's drummers, *voltigeurs* and *carabiniers*. The inspector remarked that 75 per cent of the regiment's clothing was worn out and not a single item was made according to the Bardin regulation except for that worn by the men in the *dépôt* battalion! The leather work was described as 'very old and not uniform', and the inspector further remarked that blackened cowhide was used

Chasseur sous-officer's schako of the 12e Légère. (Private Collection Switzerland)

Battalion officer of the 12ᵉ *Légère*. His *schako* has laurel leaf embroidery to the upper band, matched on extant items.

side by side with buff. The regiment's muskets were all in good repair, he noted, although most men used improvised musket slings as 600 examples were needed. He reported that many men were missing sabres in the *carabinier* company: 202 *baudriers* were issued for just 120 sabres! Some 245 men had no *giberne*, and 216 men no *giberne* belt, and the inspector noted some *gibernes* were held up with string and other similar improvised means of suspension.[54]

When disbanded on 18 September 1815, the *dépôt* held very little: 1m 91 beige broadcloth, 508m 14 blue broadcloth, 24m 35 white broadcloth, 11m 12 scarlet broadcloth, 1m 58 chamois broadcloth, 309m white serge, 73m blue tricot, 1m 35 silver lace, 639m 49 lace for chevrons and 180 drummers' lace. No *aigrettes* or epaulettes are listed.[55]

The lack of archive paperwork concerning the distinctions of drummers, *carabiniers* and *voltigeurs* means we can say nothing conclusive about the appearance of these men. The bulk of the regiment in 1814 wore old-pattern clothing and equipment. We wonder if it was ever replaced with Bardin regulation?

13ᵉ *Légère*

Inspected on 3 October 1804 by General of Brigade LaMartilliere, the men's clothing came in for some critique: of the 2024 *habits* in use, 874 needed replacing and 353 total replacement, or around 50 per cent. Every single pair of *pantalons* had to be replaced as they were 'worn out'. The men all wore *schakos*, but 961 had to be replaced as they were damaged beyond repair and 200 needed repairs. We wonder what exactly the men had been doing with their headdress to damage it so badly in under a year since it was issued? Despite having six *voltigeur cornets*, they had no instruments and carried drums. However, 10m 80 of chamois broadcloth had been used to make collars of *voltigeur habits*. Less than half of the *carabiniers* had bearskins: just 40 were in use for 84 men in 1st battalion, with a 40 brand-new examples in stores with 49 *schakos*. The regiment unusually – perhaps copying the *garde impériale* – used three sizes of buttons on their *habits*, stores holding 329 dozen large regimental buttons, 245 dozen small regimental buttons and 288 dozen medium regimental buttons. LaMartilliere ordered the production of 1,100 *habits*, 2,200 pairs of *pantalons*, 1,100 *schakos*, with 6 horns to be purchased.[56]

Inspected again on 28 July 1805 at Gand by LaMartilleire, he noted that 130 muskets, 130

With its dark green body and matching pompom, this may be a *cornet's schako* of the 13ᵉ *Légère*. (Private Collection Switzerland)

Original *habit* of the 13ᵉ *Légère* dating to *c.*1810. The epaulettes are erroneous, added to complete the garment. The shoulder loops indicate the epaulettes were green. (*Office de Tourisme de Fontainebleau*)

bayonets and 30 sabres needed immediate replacement as they were damaged – how? – beyond economic repair. Regimental accounts report 50,632fr spent on 'clothing for the sea and clogs'. Does this mean 'bathing costumes' or are we missing something in translation? Looking at the men's clothing a matter of weeks before leaving camp, of the 2,148 *habits* in use, 1,214 were *hors de service*, i.e., totally worn out, and 365 needed immediate repairs. In addition, 1,428 *vestes* needed replacing and 1,197 pairs of *pantalons*, 266 *schakos*, 572 *gibernes*, 523 *giberne* belts, 253 *baudriers*, 395 musket slings and 6 drums. Yet for immediate needs stores held 483 *habits*, 451 vestes, 2,311 pairs of *pantalons* and 13 *schakos*, leaving 64 *habits*, 204 *vestes*, 60 pairs of *pantalons*, and 36 *schakos* to make up the shortfall. It is incredibly unlikely that the worn out clothing was replaced before the regiment hit the road to Vienna. For whatever reason, just 13 bearskins were issued – for the *sapeurs*? – to the *carabiniers*, leaving 27 in stores, with a further 24 being ordered to be purchased. The officers, *sous-officiers*, corporals and *fourriers* of the *voltigeur* companies were all issued An XI light cavalry *mousquetons*.[57]

Regimental accounts report the following expenses after the review:[58]

Drum major of unknown *légère* regiment observed sometime in 1806 in Germany.

1806
Production of 2,141 pairs of *pantalons de route* at 95 centimes each
Purchase of effects for adjutant-*sous-officiers*, 4 pairs of boots and epaulettes. Total 558fr 75
190m 65, blue broadcloth, total 2,020fr 89
16m 86 white broadcloth, total 151fr 74
15m 05 red broadcloth, total 217fr 93

1807
4,053m 34 linen, total 368fr 35
698 pairs of green epaulettes at 2fr 50 each
1,000 *schakos* with cords, total 10,500fr
Bearskin cords for *carabiniers*' bearskins, total 1,080fr
Production of 1,149 *capotes*, total 1,725fr 50
12 drums, with drum carriages, drumsticks, total 976fr 80

Inspected on 5 December 1807, we note 250 bearskins existed and 3,237 beige *capotes* were in service. Stores reports that 11m 88 of chamois broadcloth had been used to make *voltigeur* clothing, 7,741m 51 of grey linen had been used to make linen *pantalons* and gaiters. Stores report 27 bearskins had existed in 1805, had been issued, and a further 24 were needed as replacements. The *sous-officiers* and *officiers* of the *voltigeur* company of the 1ᵉ battalion were issued *carabines rayé* (rifles). Every man carried a sabre.[59] Following the inspection, regimental accounts record:[60]

1808
Purchase of cloth, round cording, wool lace and tassel for *bonnets de police*, total 728fr
2,809m linen for linings, total 502fr 39
Purchase of green epaulettes, total 3,847fr 30
1,200 cockades, total 360fr
600 musket works, total 240fr
600 *épinglettes*, total 102fr
82 pairs of grenadiers' epaulettes, total 295fr 30
95 *schako* cockades 237fr 50
Round cord for *bonnets de police*, 28fr
6 pairs of epaulettes for *adjutant-sous-officiers*, total 2,925fr 50
3 sets of cords for *voltigeur cornets* at 32fr each
938 *capotes*, total 1,407fr
25m 25 white broadcloth, total 223fr 28
0m 98 scarlet broadcloth, 14fr 06
35m white serge, total 97fr 55

1809

Purchase of yellow and green plumes, total 4,644fr
Purchase of *houpettes* and cording for *bonnets de police*, total 405fr
3,357m linen, total 839fr 36
Purchase of green epaulettes, green and white lace for embellishment of the epaulettes, total 1,773fr 75
247m blue broadcloth at 13fr 50 a metre, 4m 32 scarlet broadcloth at 17fr 50 a metre, total 564fr 54
2,279m 37 beige broadcloth for *capotes*, 1,212m 98 blue tricot, 194m 19 blue tricot, 1,526m 25 grey tricot for *capotes*, 1,077m 90 blue tricot, total 34,230fr 68
40 aunes [1 aune = 1m 14] of silver lace to decorate the 24 musicians' *habits*, total 312fr
6 sabres for adjutants, total 168fr
6 *chapeaux* for adjutants, total 276fr
6 pairs of epaulettes for adjutants, total 60fr
984 *capotes* at 1fr 50 each, 1,067 *capotes* at 1fr 25 total 2,809fr 75
5 drums, with carriages, total 515fr
Material and labour to repair uniforms, 3,819fr 35

1810

Purchase of 50 *porte-gibernes*
4 pairs of epaulettes and sword knots, total 206fr
2 'garnitures' for *voltigeur cornets*, total 9fr
31 pairs of cords, total 83fr 20
Lace, tassel, cording in *garance* for *bonnets de police*, total 90fr
130 *capotes*, total 32fr 50
4m white broadcloth, total 38fr
11m 34 scarlet broadcloth, total 198fr 45
425m 50 blue tricot, total 2,627fr 88
28m 59 linen, total 38fr 59
202m 86 white serge, total 359fr 06
312m 67 linen, total 432fr 10
57m 12 white broadcloth, total 536fr 64
54m 30 scarlet broadcloth, total 948fr 50
6m chamois broadcloth, total 64fr 80
395m 54 white serge, total 700fr 10
1563m 54 linen, total 2,110fr 77

1811

9,675 pairs of shoes, 200 large straps for *havresac*, 3,780 white stocks.
5 aunes of superfine blue broadcloth cloth for uniforms of adjutants at 40fr a meter
2 pairs of boots for adjutants, total 60fr

108 *habits* relined, total 237fr 60
170 *habits* repaired, total 135fr 50
17m 60 red broadcloth, total 189fr 20
200m blue tricot, total 1,010fr
24m 55 linen, total 33fr 14
Copper to make bayonet scabbard chapes, total 101fr 75
Drum major's mace, total 30fr
6 pairs of broadcloth *pantalons*, total 37fr 86
29 *capotes* at 12fr 12 each, total 351fr 58
34 *bonnets de police*, total 60fr 86
27 pairs of linen *pantalons de route*, total 41fr 04
8 pairs of black gaiters, total 11fr 60
28 pairs of grey gaiters, total 25fr 20
39 shirts, total 87fr 75

1812
27m 30 white broadcloth, total 245fr 70
0m 74 blue broadcloth, total 8fr 32
7m 65 red broadcloth, total 78fr 50
20m beige broadcloth, total 180fr
10m 31 blue serge, total 16fr 01
700m 50 linen, total 943fr 67
221m 24 fine linen, total 349fr 36
180 dozen and 8 small buttons, total 32fr 50
1,000 large straps for *havresacs*, total 1,500fr

The accounts are interesting in several points. Firstly, the regiment had a band, it mustered eight men, and their uniforms were decorated with silver lace. The costly scarlet cuffs of the *habits* were replaced by cheaper *garance*. The epaulettes of the *chasseur* companies were green, the boards ornamented with white or green braid – presumably denoting *voltigeur* and *chasseur*? The accounts also show that the *schakos* of the regiment sported green and yellow plumes – green for *chasseurs* and yellow for *voltigeurs*, we presume. The inspector noted that since 1808 green epaulettes were forbidden for *chasseurs* and *voltigeurs*. The adjutant's *habits* had embroidered silver hunting horns to the tails and *bonnets de police*, the *bonnets de police* also having silver lace, silver cording and silver tassel.

Reviewed on 1 May 1811, the inspector noted the regiment had 64 officers, 2,185 men and 93 horses. He added 9 officers were needed to bring the regiment up to capacity. Clothing wise, 565 *habits*, 246 vestes and 665 *capotes* needed repairs. Needing replacing immediately were 571 *habits*, 832 vestes, 633 pairs of *pantalons*, 1,130 *schakos*, 1,235 *bonnets de police*, 65 *capotes* and 170 baudriers. Missing equipment included 96 bearskins for the *carabiniers*, 30 drums and carriages and 66 sabres. We also note 63 An XI light cavalry *mousquetons* needed repairs, as did 15 infantry muskets and bayonets and 62 sabres. The regimental artillery harness also needed repairs. Also needing repairs were 180 bearskins and 741 *capotes*.[61]

Sadly, we know nothing more until summer 1814, when the regiment was wearing:[62]

Item	In Good Repair	In Need of Repair	Need Replacing	Items due to be replaced	Items missing
Habits	410	114	55	75	130
Vestes	408	71	104	28	132
Pantalons de tricot	299		152	89	241
Caleçons	299		152	89	241
Capotes	432	45	106	2	108
Bonnets de police	361		38	141	179
Schakos	459		48	33	81
Gibernes	451	20	56		56
Porte-gibernes	451	20	56		56
Baudriers	58		103		100
Drums	20				
Drum carriages	20				
Musket slings	456		81		81
Muskets	400	51	56		
Sabres	50	8	103		

The inspector remarked that the colonel had not acted upon the decrees of 1812 regarding the new uniform regulations, and the regiment was entirely dressed in short *habits*. Items of clothing and equipment in the *dépôt* comprised:[63]

Item	New	Need Repair	To be replaced	Comment
Capotes	245		2	
Carabiniers' *habits*			None	
Voltigeurs' *habits*			None	
Fusiliers' *habits*	458		21	
Drummers' *habits*			26	Green with Imperial Livery
Gilets manches de fusilier	99			
Gilets manches de tambour			None	
Pantalons	121		10	
Bonnets de police	382			
Caleçons	589			
Braces	547			
Carabiniers' *schakos*	263			
Fusiliers' *schakos*	427		50	

Item	New	Need Repair	To be replaced	Comment
Schako covers	432			
Gibernes	107		279	
Porte-giberne	168	3	227	242 in black cow leather
Musket slings	50		125	152 in black cow leather
Baudriers	126			
Drums		5		
Drum carriages	3			
Sapeurs' apron		2		
Houpettes	149			
Voltigeurs' cornet	None			
Grenadiers' epaulettes				

The black cross belt for the *giberne* and musket sling were authorised in June 1813, therefore it is not a surprise to find them in use. In 1814 the regiment had a huge stockpile of cloth in the *dépôt*.[64]

243m 95 beige broadcloth for *capotes*
2713m 81 blue broadcloth
158m 59 white broadcloth
71m 52 scarlet broadcloth
114m 60 green broadcloth
12m 47 chamois broadcloth
192m blue serge
3,659m 28 blue tricot
404m grey tricot for *capotes*
35m green serge
69m 85 green tricot
34m 368 silver lace for *sous-officiers*
46m 36 wool lace for corporals
134m 55 scarlet wool lace
450m livery for drummers

The drummers' lace is described as all of the old model, it is therefore Imperial Livery. We can be certain therefore that the regiment had drummers in Imperial Livery. The appearance of the *habit* is open to question.

On 24 February 1814, the light infantry officially went into green clothing: green *pantalons de tricot*, green broadcloth *habits* with red collars piped white, green serge tail facings piped white, green revers and cuffs piped white. The large amount of green broadcloth, 114m 60, the 69m 85 green tricot and 35m green serge points towards the existence of light infantry in green *habits*. The green tricot was certainly used to make green *pantalons* and perhaps also green *gilets manches*. The green serge had no other purpose than to face the tails of *habits*. But what of drummers? Undoubtedly the *habits* were green with Imperial Livery, which from April 1813 had white tail facings. The black leather work confirms that the directives from 1813 regarding the shortages of buff leather were put into practice, yet the inspector remarked that the regiment had not acted upon the decree of 19 January 1812 or later circulars from the War Ministry. The regiment's council of administration was ordered to replace the clothing, but for matter of economy all the pre-Bardin clothing in use that was serviceable or brand new and unissued was to remain in use, and the unit would inherit pre-Bardin clothing from the 27ᵉ and 28ᵉ *Légère*. So, we have to imagine some men in green *habit-vestes* with black leather work, others in old-pattern kit with white and black leather work![65]

We know nothing else until after Waterloo. The *dépôt* held very few items of clothing and equipment, clearly what had existed in stores was issued to the men of the 6ᵉ battalion and we also suppose to the war battalions:[66]

5 *habits*
29 *vestes*
47 pairs of *pantalons de tricot*
26 *chapeaux*
5 *capotes*
52 *carabiniers' schakos*
192 *bonnets de police*
19 pairs of *carabiniers'* epaulettes
33 pairs of braces
101 *schako* covers
627 *schako* plates
62 *gibernes*
313 *porte-gibernes*
10 *baudrier*s
10 drum carriages
19 drums
3 drummers' aprons
10 sets of drumsticks and holders
297 *gibernes* to be disposed of
169 *porte-gibernes* in blackened cowhide to be disposed of

The *chapeaux* are most interesting as in theory they had been removed from use in 1801, yet we note 181 men were wearing *chapeaux* in 1814: we assume due to shortages these items were pressed into service. Were the *schako* plates hastily taken off *schakos* after Waterloo and placed into stores? Perhaps so, unless they were the Royalist pattern that had been placed into store with the start of the 100 Days. Cloth and materials in the *dépôt* tell us a great deal about the appearance of the regiment at Waterloo. Cloth remaining at the time of disbandment was:[67]

0m 48 beige broadcloth
103m 13 blue broadcloth
11m 98 white broadcloth
4m 22 scarlet broadcloth
48m 30 green broadcloth
3m 75 Chamois broadcloth
1,399m 75 grey tricot for *capotes*
422m 25 blue tricot
339m 71 blue serge
8m green serge
45m scarlet wool lace for chevrons
120m 95 white wool lace for corporals
0m 52 silver lace for *sous-officiers*

A mix of beige broad cloth *capotes* and grey tricot *capotes* were in use, and had been since 1814 if not earlier. More green *habits* were made prior to disbandment as over 100m of the green broadcloth was used – sufficient to make 50 *habits* – along with just over 20m of the green serge. The presence of *chapeaux* and tricot for *capotes* clearly tells us that the dress regulations were not strictly adhered to, so green drummers' *habits* with green tail linings seems perfectly acceptable. The 450m livery for drummers in the *dépôt* in 1814 was described as the *Anciene modèle* in October 1814, so clearly this was Imperial Livery as Royalist Livery would undoubtedly be new model. The *dépôt* held 38 drummers' *habits* in green with Imperial Livery in October 1814, which were it seems reissued in the 100 Days, and the green cloth used up, no doubt repairing these *habits*, which by 1814 were at least two years old. The regiment also had 12 drummers' *gilets manches* in green tricot. The *dépôt* also held 509 black leather *porte-gibernes*, along with 152 musket slings. Black leather work would have made the regiment highly distinctive at Waterloo. It would also have helped conceal the men in the scrub around Hougoumont far more than white cross belts would have done.[68]

14ᵉ *Légère*

The regiment was primarily based in Italy and served on Saint Domingo and Corfu until 1814. A document dated 9 January 1811 informs us that the regiment supplied from its *dépôt* to the *regiment de la Méditerranée* 182 pairs of shoes, 137 shirts, 90 pairs of black gaiters, 62 pairs of grey gaiters, 166 *habits*, and 4 muskets of the non-regulation type. The *habits* had been taken from old soldiers when they had been given new-issue *habits* and had been taken into the regiment's reserve stock. The regiment was also to supply 150 *capotes* and 125 pairs of *pantalons*.[69]

Officer of unknown *légère* regiment *c.*1812 by Martinet.

The Light Infantry   101

On 21 November 1812 the cadre of the newly raised 7ᵉ battalion was reviewed. For the 1,641 men on parade, 343 *habits* were in use, of which 156 were in desperate need of replacement and leaving just 187 in good condition. Every single one of the 324 *gilets manches* were to be replaced, as were every single pair of *pantalons de tricot* – 222 pairs. Also to be thrown out were 276 *bonnets de police*. Interestingly, just 3 *baudriers* and sabres were issued to the drummers.⁷⁰

Reviewed in summer 1814, the inspector noted 'nothing is uniform', adding that 'the decrees of 19 January and 7 February 1812 have not been enacted … nor have the modifications to the dress as authorised 23 April 1814'.⁷¹ Re-formed during the restoration, the regiment's workmen were hard at work making new clothing when the Empire fell. Stores at the time of disbandment were bursting at the seams, holding 1,049 *habits*, 1,048 *gilets*, 1,049 pairs of *pantalons*, 1,047 pairs of underwear, 1,049 *bonnets de police*, 1,049 *capotes* and 1,048 *schakos*, as well as 995 *gibernes* and belts, 159 *baudriers*, 19 drums and carriages, 1,012 musket slings, 5 *sapeurs'* axes and 2 *sapeurs'* aprons.⁷²

15ᵉ *Légère*

Inspected on 8 December 1807, not an inch of chamois broadcloth existed in stores in 1805 or had been purchased since that date. Every man was wearing a *schako*. Despite not have any distinctions, the *voltigeurs* were armed with 326 dragoon muskets, with the officers and *sous-officiers* being issued 31 rifles. Only *carabiniers*, *sous-officiers*, drummers and *cornets* carried sabres.⁷³ Interestingly, in 1805 the *voltigeurs* had been issued 327 light cavalry *mousquetons* and 24 rifles – it is clear the firearms had been exchanged on campaign, and the *voltigeurs* had lost their sabres, and had no chamois distinctions.⁷⁴ This is maybe because the elite companies were detached, but this would not explain the different armament as all the companies were *chasseurs*.

Reviewed on 1 May 1811, the inspector noted the regiment had 653 officers, 2,242 men and 92 horses. He added that 15 officers were needed to bring the regiment up to capacity. Clothing wise, 260 *habits*, 298 *vestes*, 1,082 pairs of *pantalons*, 265 *schakos*, 58 bearskins for *carabiniers*, 260 *bonnets de police*, 222 *capotes*, 129 *gibernes*, 4 *giberne* belts and 144 musket slings needed immediate replacement.⁷⁵

Reviewed on 28 March 1813, the 2ᵉ battalion mustered 19 officers and 680 other ranks. The clothing, the inspector noted, was of good quality for the *habits* and *gilets manches*, but the *pantalons* were made from inferior-quality tricot. Some 56 *capotes* were needed to give every man a *capote*, and others needed to be replaced that had been supplied from the *dépôt* brand new but were very mediocre due to shortages of affordable quality materials to make clothing from. The equipment was of good quality except the *gibernes*, which were in the most part badly made from cheap materials. Only the *carabinier* company carried sabres, and needed three more of these and two more *gibernes* to complete the battalion's equipment. We note further that 10 muskets were not French and 108 needed repairs.⁷⁶

Martinet presents this *voltigeur* officer wearing the Bardin-regulation uniform.

Inspected in summer 1814, the *dépôt* held virtually nothing in terms of cloth: 11m 15 scarlet broadcloth, 8m 75 chamois broadcloth, and 375m 95 linen. New clothing and equipment in the *dépôt* included 904 *capotes*, 45 *chasseur habits*, 4 drummers' *habits* that were green with Imperial Livery, 315 pairs of *caleçons*, 214 *gibernes* with belts, 9 drums and carriages and 417 *houpettes*. *Voltigeurs* clearly had chamois collars to the *habits*. We have no details at all about the dress of the *carabiniers*. The clothing in use had been issued for 18 to 20 months. The broad cloth used to make the clothing of the first two battalions, the inspector noted, was very good, but the linings needed total replacement. The *pantalons de tricot* supplied from the government reserves were of different quality to those supplied by the regiment. The *schakos* in use were all described as life expired and in need of replacement despite having been in service for just two years, remarked the inspector rather incredulously.[77]

Disbanded on 25 September 1815, the *dépôt* held 1,278m 01 blue broadcloth, 33m 82 scarlet broadcloth, 9m 11 blue tricot, 18m 05 silver lace, 98m 75 worsted lace, 37 *habits*, 37 *gilets manches*, 65 pairs of *pantalons de tricot* accompanied by 33 pairs of *caleçons*, 39 *capotes*, 98 *schakos*, and 18 *bonnets de police*. For *carabiniers*, the *dépôt* held 96 *aigrettes* and 179 pairs of epaulettes – none of which existed in 1814 so clearly had been purchased either before or during the 100 Days – and 96 *voltigeur aigrettes*.[78]

16ᵉ *Légère*

Reviewed on 12 October 1804, the regiment was wearing a mix of *chapeaux* and *schakos*, and not an inch of chamois broadcloth had been purchased or used: this is not a surprise as the *voltigeurs* and *carabiniers* were detached to the *Grenadiers Réunis*.[79] Inspected again on 27 July 1805, the regiment had 4 battalions, each of 8 *chasseur* companies.[80]

At the time of writing the earliest records for the dress of the regiment is from a document of 15 January 1807, which states the 16ᵉ was issued 1,001 *habits*, 1,986 *gilets*, 1,954 pairs of *pantalons*, 1,082 *capotes* ready made and a further 1,026 in kit form, as well as 3,084 pairs of shoes and 1,925 shirts. Also issued were 312 *marmites* with covers and bags, 2,476 white metal *petit bidons*, 161 hatchets with cases and 312 *gamelles*.[81]

Inspected on 27 January 1808, the regiment mustered 3,723 men and 108 officers. The regiment had 303 *carabiniers*, 353 *voltigeurs*, 53 drummers, 8 cornets and 11 *enfant de troupe*, 8 musicians and no *sapeurs*. From the inspection, the regiment wore *schakos*. Some 1,092 new ones were needed and 476 had been lost in the recent campaign from men killed or wounded taken to hospital; not a single bearskin existed for the *carabiniers*. A total of 1,308 new *habits* were needed. Between 1805 and 1808 a staggering 6,618 *habits* had been made, of which 6,305 had been issued and 313 remained in the *dépôt*. Likewise, 8,049 vestes had been made, 1,195 remained in stores, 9,902 pairs of blue tricot *pantalons* had been made, with 596 pairs remaining. Remarkably, 61 *capotes* had existed in 1805 and a further 2,119 had been made, making 2,135 *capotes* in total, all bar 72 being issued, and these had required 6,254m of broadcloth to make. For *habits*, 7m 25 of chamois broadcloth had been used out of 18m 72 purchased.[82]

Naïve study of a sergeant of *chasseur*s of the 16ᵉ *Légère*. Contrary to what re-enactors and artists imply, he has green *chasseur* epaulettes and white *schako* cords. He is wearing the 1806-pattern *schako*. (*Private collection France*)

In order to purchase replacement equipment and materials – the inspecting general had authorised the production of 1,941 *habits* and *vestes*, 3,883 pairs of tricot *pantalons*, 971 *schakos*, and 1,294 *capotes* – the regiment compiled a price list of government set prices for items and the local prices. Materials wise, white broadcloth, blue broadcloth, scarlet and chamois are listed along with cloth specifically for *capotes*, black twill for

Drum major of the 16ᵉ *Légère* drawn from life in the first half of 1808. (*Collection KM*)

Sapeur of the 16ᵉ *Légère* drawn from life sometime in the first half of 1808. No archive evidence confirms or denies this elaborate uniform. (*Collection KM*)

Carabinier and *voltigeur* of the 16ᵉ *Légère* drawn from life in 1808. (*Collection KM*)

Chasseur of the 16ᵉ *Légère* drawn sometime during 1808. (*Collection KM*)

gaiters, grey linen for gaiters, linen for linings, white serge and blue tricot. Not an inch of drummers' livery is noted, only silver lace at 7fr 50 a metre, white at 60 centimes a metre and red at the same price. Among the items of equipment, we find plumes costing 2fr, pompoms 90 centimes, white metal hunting horn badges for *gibernes* costing 70 centimes each, grenades for *gibernes* costing 75 centimes, *carabinier* epaulettes costing 2fr 50 a pair, and sword knots for *carabiniers* costing 1fr. Nothing was purchased for *sapeurs*, no *schako* cords, no *voltigeur* epaulettes, nor *chasseur* epaulettes.[83]

Following the inspection on 27 January 1808, the major reported to the Minister of War in a letter dated 23 March 1808 that the regiment had four battalions, had 3,650 men under arms, needed 529 conscripts, 73 men had been kicked out of the regiment for bad behaviour, and 56 had been proposed for retirement. The clothing was described as in good condition, and that the regiment needed 65 pairs of shoes and 208 muskets.[84]

On 1 October 1808 the elite companies of the regiment that had been detached to form the *Grenadiers Réunis* were inspected when the provisional formation was disbanded, some five officers and 185 other ranks. A total 156 men returned to the 16e, which included 42 from the 9e *Légère*, one man from the 27e *Légère* and also one from the 8e *Légère*. The inspector noted that 54 *habits* needed replacing within a year, and 102 within two years; of the *vestes*, 66 likewise needed to be replaced in a year and 90 had 2 years' use left in them; every pair of *pantalons* needed replacing within 6 months. The *carabiniers* from the 16e had 71 bearskins, the *voltigeurs* wore *schakos*.[85]

We know nothing else until the regiment was disbanded on 2 September 1814. On this date the *dépôt* held 2m 03 scarlet broadcloth, 18m green broadcloth, 1m 29 chamois broadcloth, 50m white serge, 75m 09 blue tricot, 4m of drummers' '*galons de liveree en N*', 10m 37 silver lace, 73m 96 worsted lace for corporals and 616m 99 red lace for service chevrons. Clothing in the *dépôt* included 47 *capotes*, 1 *voltigeur habit*, 155 *chasseur habits*, 1 green drummers' *habit*, 27 *chasseur gilets manches*, 63 pairs of *pantalons de tricot*, 20 *bonnets de police*, and 102 pairs of *caleçons*. Also held were 313 grenadier *aigrettes*, 407 *voltigeur aigrettes*, 1,379 *chasseur houpettes* 7 pairs of epaulettes for *adjutant-sous-officiers* and 500 pairs of grenadier epaulettes for *carabiniers*. A single pair of linen *pantalons* were in *dépôt*, along with 6 pairs of drumsticks, 370 crowned 'N' *giberne* ornaments and 99 copper grenade badges. Lodged in stores were also 191 shirts, 6 pairs of *pantalons de toile*, 171 black stocks, 1,235 white stocks, 400 pairs of linen stockings, 121 pairs of linen ankle socks, 289 pairs of black gaiters, 116 pairs of grey gaiters, 140 *sacs à distribution*, 145 *havresacs* and 597 waxed linen *giberne* covers.[86] We know nothing else about the regiment.

17e *Légère*

Inspected on 7 October 1804 in Strasbourg, the major reported that the regiment mustered three battalions, and 2,612 men, of which 73 were sick. Since the previous year's review, 36 men had died and 353 had deserted. This despite the barracks being clean, in good repair and food plentiful and of good quality. The men were 'a good type' but 'had very weak constitutions'. Despite this the accommodation was very good, so too the blankets, mattresses and food. Clearly the men were heading home for other reasons. The men recruited from the Dordogne in rural south-west France, the inspector noted, 'showed no intelligence and absolutely no spirit for the military'. Basically, being far from home, resenting conscription and with language barriers, the men simply went back to their farms. The inspector ordered the regiment to make *capotes* with all urgency. Of the men's *habits*, 2,598 existed, some 1,014 examples needed replacement and 449 repairs. Since 1803, 1,190 *schakos* had been issued, replacing the largely useless *chapeau*.[87]

Reviewed on 16 August 1805, the grenadier companies had 244 bearskins, with the *voltigeurs* and *chasseurs* wearing 2,606 *schakos*. We assume the *voltigeurs* had chamois facings as the inspection notes 'scarlet broadcloth and other colours', of which almost 70m had been used. In stores were 28 additional

Officers' *habit* of a *voltigeur* company of the 17ᵉ *Légère* made reflecting the Bardin regulation. (*Musée de l'Empéri, Collections du Musée de l'armée, Anciennes collections Jean et Raoul Brunon*)

bearskins. The men were also issued white and black stocks. Armament wise, the *voltigeurs* were issued 312 sabres and dragoon muskets, with the officers and *sous-officiers* being issued 27 *carabines rayé*. The drummers, *cornets*, *fifre* and *sapeurs* were issued 91 An XI light cavalry *mousquetons*.[88] Inspected in Strasbourg on 1 November 1807, no bearskins existed, the 6 horns with the *voltigeur* companies had been lost and all bar 18 *mousquetons*.[89]

Disbanded on 16 July 1814, the *dépôt* of the regiment held a cross section of cloth and materials, including 42m 23 of drummers' lace, 430m of blue broadcloth, 46m of white broadcloth and 37m of scarlet broadcloth. Brand-new unissued clothing in the *dépôt* included 17 *capotes*, 76 *chasseur habits*, 145 *gilets manches*, 19 pairs of blue *pantalons de tricot*, 39 *bonnets de police* and 21 pairs of *caleçons*, 1 *carabiniers' schako de modèle*, 20 *chasseur's schakos*, 205 *carabiniers aigrettes*, 202 *voltigeurs aigrettes*, 180 pairs of *carabiniers'* epaulettes and 65 *chasseur houpette*s. The *dépôt* also held 564 *giberne* covers. Also lodged were 2,185 pairs of *pantalons de route* made from linen or cotton, 2,185 *gilets* made from linen or cotton, 2,185 pairs of gaiters made from linen or cotton, 148 red or green sword knots, 53 pairs of green *chasseur* epaulettes, 6 sets of drumsticks and holders, and 177 *gibernes* with 175 belts made from blackened cowhide, and 57 *giberne* covers.[90] Clearly the men had linen *gilets* and *pantalons* rather than blue tricot at some stage.

18ᵉ *Légère*

Inspected on 12 October 1804, the most remarkable aspect of the review was the presence of men wearing white uniforms in the 3rd battalion: 283 white *habits* and 283 blue were in use side by side. We also report 4 axe cases and axes for the *sapeurs*. We remark further than the stores held nankeen for making gaiters and *pantalons*, as well as holding 3 pairs of *carabinier* epaulettes, with 3 sword knots and 4 plumes and for *chasseurs*, 5 pairs of epaulettes, and 19 sword knots. *Carabiniers* and *sapeurs* had *schakos* for headdress.[91] We know nothing else until the inspection report dated 16 July 1814 reveals that the clothing in use was as follows:[92]

Item	In Good Repair	In Need of Repair	Need Replacing	Items due to be replaced	Items missing
Habits	82	12			5
Vestes	52	4			37
Pantalons de tricot	78	20			9
Caleçons	3				84
Capotes	74	11			13
Schakos	84	6			3
Bonnets de police	42	1			45

The 87 men under arms possessed 182 shirts, 62 pairs of *pantalons de route*, 62 black stocks, 181 pairs of shoes, 70 pairs of black gaiters, 57 pairs of grey gaiters and 4 *sacs a distribution*. The *dépôt* held 65 *gibernes* and belts needing repairs, 1 sabre belt needing repairs, 5 life-expired drums and carriages, and 6 *sapeurs*' axes and cases needing repairs. Passed to the 14ᵉ *Légère* was just over 36m blue broadcloth, 10m 24 scarlet broadcloth, 13m 70 chamois broadcloth and tellingly 10 green drummers' *habits* adorned with Imperial Livery and 4 drummers' *gilets* as well as 145 grenadier *aigrettes* and 81 for *voltigeurs*.[93]

19ᵉ *Légère*

No regiment of this designation existed during the 1st Empire.

20ᵉ *Légère*

No regiment of this designation existed during the 1st Empire.

21ᵉ *Légère*

Like most regiments of *légère*, the paper archive is sparse for its clothing. Reviewed on 3 December 1807, we note the *carabiniers* had no distinctions, and the *voltigeurs* had chamois collars and were armed with 397 dragoon muskets. The *sous-officiers* and

Sergeant major of the 21ᵉ *Légère* carrying a battalion eagle. Improbably, he is wearing a bearskin and a *voltigeur habit*. (*Collection KM*)

corporals of the regiment were armed with light cavalry *mousquetons*, and the officers of the *voltigeur* company were armed with rifles, as was the band. Amazingly, the regiment was wearing *chapeaux*.[94] Every one of the 2,554 *schakos* in existence in 1805 had been lost on campaign, and out of necessity replaced with infantry *chapeaux*![95] Drawn up for inspection on 1 August 1814 prior to disbandment, the 2ᵉ battalion's clothing and equipment was as follows:[96]

Item	In Good Repair	In Need of Repair	Need Replacing	Items due to be replaced	Items missing
Habits		65	2	2	8
Vestes		65	1	3	8
Pantalons de tricot			38	31	8
Caleçons					77
Capotes	68			8	8
Schakos	67			2	8
Bonnets de police					77
Gibernes	66				8
Porte-gibernes	66				8
Baudriers	44				2
Drum carriages	2				
Drums	1				
Musket slings	66				7

Of interest, the regiment had two *mousquetons* in use, 65 muskets and 44 sabres, 111 shirts, 61 pairs of linen *pantalons* – not enough of either type of *pantalons* existed for each man to have a pair, it was either or. The same situation arose with gaiters: 70 pairs of black gaiters were in use and 68 of grey – again a mix and match situation. Likewise, 66 black stocks were in use and 11 white. Just 70 *sacs de peau* were in use, so 7 men had no means of stowing their equipment. No materials existed in the *dépôt*, but 11 *capotes* needing repair and 17 waiting to be sold off as rags were in *dépôt*, along with 11 *bonnets de police* needing repairs. New items in the *dépôt* included 37 *gibernes*, 38 *porte-gibernes* and 24 muskets sling, accompanied by 21 *gibernes* needing repairs, 20 *porte-gibernes*, 10 musket slings, 3 drums all needing repairs and 3 drum carriages to be written off. We can say nothing else about the dress of the regiment.[97]

22ᵉ *Légère*

The regiment's archive is incredibly sparse for dress and equipment. The 1805 inspection notes the men were wearing *chapeaux* and not *schakos*.[98] Reviewed on 7 March 1808, the *voltigeurs* had no distinctions and the *carabiniers* had no bearskins.[99] The inspection report dated 16 July 1814 reveals that the clothing in use was as follows:[100]

Chasseur wearing Bardin-regulation uniform. (*Collection KM*)

Item	In Good Repair	In Need of Repair	Need Replacing	Items due to be replaced	Items missing
Habits	79	26			1
Vestes	70	25			10
Pantalons de tricot	75	18			5
Caleçons	73	17			7
Capotes	31	9			59
Schakos	73	20			7
Bonnets de police	47	17			33
Schako covers	55	17			25

The *dépôt* held no stocks of cloth and materials and held no clothing, therefore we can say nothing else about the regiment's clothing.

23ᵉ *Légère*

Inspected in October 1804, no *carabinier* or *voltigeur* distinctions existed: this is no surprise as they were detached to the *Grenadiers Réunis*.[101] The same observations are applicable to the November 1804 inspection.[102] Inspected again on 18 September 1805, we note 12 *sapeurs*' aprons were in use, 17m 04 of chamois broadcloth had been used to make *voltigeur* clothing, yet the *carabiniers* wore *schakos*.[103]

Reviewed on 23 March 1808, the detached 3ᵉ battalion had used 4m 29 of chamois broadcloth to make *voltigeur* clothing. We also report 1,000m of black mohair lace was in stores to bind the top edge of the men's gaiters, but none had been used. We also report the *sapeurs* had 13 bearskins, every man had a *schako* with cords, the *voltigeurs* had 146 green plumes, the *chasseurs* had 600 green plumes with red base and the *carabiniers* 135 red plumes. We also report 1,576 pairs of green epaulettes existed – for both *chasseurs* and *voltigeurs* – and 100 red for *carabiniers* accompanied by 78 green sword knots for *voltigeurs* and just 8 red examples for *carabiniers*.[104]

The two war battalions were inspected on 25 May 1808: they possessed no epaulettes, no plumes, no sword knots and every man was dressed as a *chasseur*.[105] Clearly the detached battalion was dressed flamboyantly.

In 1814, the regiment was disbanded into the 4ᵉ *Légère*, at which time it drew up comprehensive accounts. From these we note on 25 October 1813 567m of blue broadcloth, 15m white broadcloth, 7m 60 scarlet broadcloth and 480m beige broadcloth was purchased from M. Flaze, clothier, for 11,064fr 33. More cloth was obtained in December 1813 and January 1814, but none was green or chamois. Stores in August 1814 held 531m 25 of Imperial Livery: as this came in rolls of 560m, very little had been used – unless it was more of the same already in use – no more than two garments being made.[106] This and other items were passed to the 4ᵉ:[107]

640 dozen large buttons

Chasseur of an unknown *légère* regiment drawn from life around Dresden in summer 1813. (*Collection KM*)

127 dozen small buttons
219m 42 of white lace
204m 79 lace for chevrons
531m 23 drummers' livery
961m 50 black mohair lace
169 pairs of *caleçons*
2,760 pompoms
121 pairs of *carabiniers*' epaulettes
8 *sapeurs*' aprons
67 Sabres
375 musket worms
229 shirts
226 black stocks
119 pairs of linen socks
230 pairs of shoes
153 pairs of black gaiters
90 pairs of grey gaiters
183 *sac de peau*
902 *sac à distribution*
124 *giberne* covers
61 old cockades
326 musket worms
313 *épinglettes*
73 sets of *habits* and shoe brushes

We must wonder why so many items from the 23ᵉ *Légère* remained unused. Certainly, the buttons were not transferable to the 4ᵉ *Légère*, but all the items of clothing presumably were. The black mohair lace is clearly all that remained from stocks held in 1808, with a tiny amount used. The presence of large numbers of pompoms suggests the use of these items in lieu of *aigrettes*. The *carabiniers* clearly had scarlet epaulettes and the drummers were decked out in Imperial Livery – the lace was not used by the 4ᵉ *Légère* and remained in *dépôt*, unused in summer 1815 along with the tricolour cockades.

24ᵉ *Légère*

Reviewed on 20 November 1807, the men were wearing infantry *chapeaux* – 891 being in use, with the 1,220 *schakos* issued by 1805 being lost on campaign it seems – as well as 534 greatcoats, all that remained from 2,000 made since 1805. Some 9m 48 of chamois broadcloth had been used to make *voltigeur* clothing, and the *sapeurs* had 24 axes with belts and 13 aprons. The aprons were all in store, along with 11 axes. The drummers were armed with light cavalry *mousquetons*.[108] In 1805 the *carabiniers* and *sapeurs* had had 73 bearskins and these were seemingly lost in action.[109]

The regiment's newly raised 4ᵉ battalion was inspected on 10 January 1812, when it mustered 765 all ranks. The inspecting officer praised the quality of men, saying they were 'a good sort'. However, he condemned their clothing, noting that the conscripts of year 1811 were all badly dressed, the clothing was old and had reached the end of its service life, and the *vestes* and *pantalons* needed total replacement. All the new short *habits*, *gilets manches* and *pantalons* destined for the battalion had gone instead to the 1ᵉ and 2ᵉ battalion as replacements, and the old uniforms from the veterans was passed to the new battalion. The same was true of the conscripts admitted to the other three battalions: the conscripts were dressed in what was left over in *dépôt* and clothing taken off serving soldiers.[110]

The 1ᵉ to 4ᵉ battalions were reviewed again in July 1813, the clothing was all brand new and in good condition, but not yet of the new regulation. The inspector noted that 146 sabres and *baudrier*s were missing from the *carabinier* companies.[111] Purchased for the 3ᵉ battalion in 1813 were 75 *aigrettes* for *voltigeurs*, 50 pairs of epaulettes for *carabiniers*, and 183fr 25 was spent on 'garnitures' for *carabiniers*' *schakos*.[112] We have been unable to locate any further archive paperwork for the dress of the regiment.

25ᵉ *Légère*

The regiment's paper archive is minimal concerning the dress of the regiment. Reviewed in 1805, the elite company had 250 bearskins and 2,450 *schakos* were in use. Interestingly, 83 *gibernes a la corse*, i.e., ammunition boxes worn on a waistbelt,

Voltigeur – presumably – of an unknown *légère* regiment. Oddly the cuff facings are scarlet.

were in service, of which 83 waistbelts were in use. Further, 7m 07 of chamois broadcloth had been used to make *voltigeur* clothing. We also note the *voltigeurs* were armed with 324 dragoon muskets, 74 light cavalry *mousquetons* were in use, 11 were issued to *voltigeur sous-officiers*, 33 to the drummers and *cornets* as well as 30 to grenadiers. Thirty-six rifles were in use, 12 with the staff, 20 with *sous-officiers* and 4 with *fourriers*.[113] The 4ᵉ battalion was inspected on 24 May 1812, when it mustered 529 other ranks. The clothing was described as new and reasonably well made. The inspector noted that many of the *pantalons de tricot* were in bad condition, many had faded badly and lost their colour because the dye used was cheap and substandard.[114] Disbanded in 1814, the *dépôt* held no stocks of cloth or materials, no clothing, but it did hold 4 fusilier *schakos*, 249 *gibernes* with belts, 108 musket slings, 11 drums, 12 drum carriages, 27 *marmites*, 26 *bidons*, 68 *gamelles* and 15 drummers' aprons. We can say nothing about the appearance of *carabiniers*, *voltigeurs* or drummers.[115] We have been unable to locate any further archive paperwork for the dress of the regiment.

26ᵉ *Légère*

Inspected on 26 September 1804, every man was wearing a *chapeau*, no distinctions existed for *voltigeurs* or *carabiniers*.[116] Moving on to 24 July 1805, 2,235 *schakos* were ordered and 781 *habits* and *vestes manches* had been made for new entrants to the regiment. Nothing is reported for *carabiniers* or *voltigeurs*. We do note 74 light cavalry *mousquetons* were in use: 48 with the drummers and cornets, 14 with *voltigeurs*, 1 with a *fourrier*, 1 with a sergeant and 10 with the band. Also in service with the *voltigeurs* were 27 rifles: 9 with the officers and 18 with the *sous-officiers*. Clearly officers had *gibernes* issued.[117]

The 1808 review is missing from the regiment's archive and we know nothing more until 1 May 1813. At the time of the review, the 1ᵉ battalion mustered 861 all ranks, and the clothing was described as entirely new and of the new model. The battalion lacked 10 *habits* and *vestes*, 13 pairs of blue *pantalons de tricot*, 8 *capotes* and 30 *schakos*. The 2ᵉ battalion was inspected on 2 May 1813 and mustered 671 rank and file. The *capotes*, rather than being made of beige broadcloth as in 1ᵉ battalion, were made from grey tricot. The battalion needed 8 *habits*, 8 *vestes*, 13 pairs of *pantalons*, 9 *capotes*, 6 *schakos* and 10 *bonnets de police*. Equipment wise, it was lacking 8 *gibernes*, 115 *baudriers*, 6 musket slings, 2 bayonet scabbards as well as 63 shirts, 315 pairs of shoes, 17 stocks, 13 pairs of black gaiters, 10 pairs of grey gaiters, 17 *sacs à distribution* and 16 pairs of linen *pantalons de route*. The regimental artillery had 1 *sous-lieutenant*, 1 sergeant, 1 corporal and 11 gunners.[118] No other clothing records can be located at the time of writing.

27ᵉ *Légère*

The paper archive for the 27ᵉ tells us a great deal about the dress of the regiment. At the time of the 1805 review, 39m 39 of chamois broadcloth had been used on *voltigeurs'* distinctions: a huge amount, so we wonder if the cornets had chamois *revers* to the *habit*

Carabinier of unknown regiment *c.*1808.

to account for this? Of note, the men were wearing *chapeaux*.[119] Regimental accounts show that in 1806 the regiment spent 4,342fr 50 to purchase 1,466 green plumes, 800 pairs of green epaulettes for *chasseurs*, 350 green sword knots and 1,000 stock buckles. Also purchased were 359 pairs of black gaiters with white piping to the top edge and with a white tassel at the front, and 209 pairs of grey gaiters. In the spring and summer of 1806, 1,010 *habits* were repaired, which needed 53m 64 of white broadcloth, 12m 30 of scarlet broadcloth and 0m 50 of blue tricot. The large purchase of white cloth was to change all the regiment's piping to white; it had all been in scarlet, as had been the cuffs to the *habits*!

Purchased in 1807 were an additional 1,300 pairs of green epaulettes, 741 green plumes and 1,400 stock buckles for the sum of 4,454fr, and 576 new-model *schakos* were purchased costing 10fr 50 apiece. Also purchased in 1807 were 2,240 fusilier *houpettes*, 450 *havresacs*, 200 black stocks, 2,000 white stocks, 2,000 pairs of grey gaiters, 2,000 pairs of black gaiters, and 1 pair of adjutant's epaulettes.[120]

Inspected on 28 November 1807, the report shows the men were all wearing *schakos*, not an inch of chamois broadcloth had been purchased or used since 1805, and no distinctions existed for *carabiniers*. In addition, 27 light cavalry *mousquetons* had been issued to drummers and cornets, 18 being lost on campaign.[121]

The 1808 purchases included 750 pairs of green epaulettes – no red ones or for *carabiniers* ever seem to have been purchased: does this mean *carabiniers* had green epaulettes at this date? – 280 plumes, 100 sets of *schako* cords, 100 stock buckles and 1,030 *schakos* to replace the non-regulation items in use, some two years after the new model had been introduced! Epaulettes, it seems, were an innovation of 1808 and later. Clothing repaired in 1808 included 1,485 *habits*, 1,485 *vestes* and 498 pairs of blue tricot *pantalons*. Some 1,3068fr 96 was spent on cloth, which comprised 53m 83 blue broadcloth, 9m 05 chamois broadcloth to replace the collars on *voltigeurs' habits*, 10m 58 blue serge and 56m 93 blue tricot.

The first reference we have to *carabiniers* having epaulettes comes from 18 March 1811, when 160 pairs of red epaulettes were purchased along with 212 red pompoms, 722 pairs of green *chasseur* epaulettes, 100 stocks and 70 *havresacs*. Included in the March contract was the repair of 47 *habits* and 78 pairs of blue tricot *pantalons*.

The regiment's paper archive tells us that in 1812 the Administrative Council authorised the production of 3,426 pairs of blue tricot *pantalons*, 301 *habits*, 300 *vestes*, 300 *capotes* and 150 *bonnets de police* as well as the purchase of 2,073 *houpettes* to dress new entrants to the regiment in summer 1812. In spring 1813 the administrative council agreed to the production of 620 *habits*, 620 *vestes*, 1,000 pairs of blue tricot *pantalons*, 1,000 pairs of *caleçons*, 1,000 *capotes* and 97 *bonnets de police*. Purchased or made in 1814 were 1 *capote*, 31 *vestes*, 23 pairs of tricot *pantalons*, 295 *bonnets de police*, 251 pompoms, 54 sets of braces, 8 pairs of *caleçons*, and 557 pairs of linen *pantalons*.

Inspected on 1 September 1814, the *dépôt* held 14m 70 of beige broadcloth, 841m 35 of blue broadcloth, 7m 80 of scarlet broadcloth, 2m 70 of chamois broadcloth, 18m 50 of blue serge, 3 *capotes* that were to be disposed of, 13 worn-out *chasseur's habits*, 10 new

Naïve coloured sketch of a *voltigeur cornet* – albeit with a trumpet – from the 27ᵉ *Légère* observed in Germany sometime in 1806. It is possible this figure is from the regimental band, of which the regiment had eight musicians at the time the image was created.

pair of *pantalons*, 101 chasseur *houpette*s and very little else beyond 79 *schako* covers, 202 new *gibernes* with belts and 65 *gibernes* with belts needing repairs – all the *porte-gibernes* were black cowhide, as were 267 musket slings. Of the men on parade that day, 130 men had blackened cowhide *baudriers* and *porte-gibernes*. The regiment presented a very mixed look indeed. The inspector remarked that the unit had not acted upon the decree of 19 January 1812 or later circulars from the War Ministry. The regimental band had one trumpet, one horn, five clarinets, one bass drum and one pair of cymbals.[122] We are totally ignorant of how the bandsmen were clothed!

28ᵉ Légère

When inspected on 1 September 1814, the regiment's *dépôt* held a considerable amount of cloth and materials, which included 301m 30 of beige broadcloth, 745m 30 of blue broadcloth, 33m 80 of white broadcloth, 1,132m 79 of blue serge, 1m 60 of blue tricot, as well as 44 brand-new *chasseur habits*, and 2 needing repairs, and 12 green drummers' *habits* with Imperial Livery, listed as 'old model'. Also held in the *dépôt* were 337 brand-new *chasseur gilets manches* and 12 green drummers' *gilets manches*, 104 pairs of *pantalons de tricot*, 292 new *bonnets de police*, 478 pairs of *caleçons* and 277 pairs of grenadiers' epaulettes for the *carabinier* company. No *aigrettes* were listed as in use by the *carabiniers* or *voltigeurs*. Indeed, the inspector remarked that the regiment had not acted upon the decree of 19 January 1812 or later circulars from the War Ministry regarding the dressing of the drummers in blue with Royalist Livery. The regiment's council of administration was ordered to replace the clothing, but for matter of economy all the pre-Bardin clothing in use that was serviceable or brand new and unissued was to remain in use.[123] The regiment's band was rather larger than the regulation 8 bandsmen. Instruments owned by the officers comprised eight clarinets, two horns, two pairs of cymbals, one serpent, two Chinese pavilions, one tenor drum, one bass drum, one trumpet and one triangle.

29ᵉ Légère

Disbanded in 1803, the regiment was re-formed with the decree of 1 April 1811. Several months passed before the regiment was activated on 16 August 1811. The regiment was formed around a nucleus of men drawn from various line regiments. This had one drawback, as the men were all clothed as line infantry; the men arrived with the new regiment wearing their newly issued clothing. All that was retained by the 29ᵉ *Légère* was the men's equipment. Sent back to the parent regiments was:[124]

Regiment	*Habits*	*Vestes*	*Culottes*	*Capotes*	*Schakos*	*Gibernes*	*Porte-gibernes*	Musket slings
114ᵉ de Ligne	188	188	188	188	188	188	188	188
115ᵉ de Ligne	170	170	170	170	170	170	170	170
117ᵉ de Ligne	164	164	164	164	164	164	164	164
118ᵉ de Ligne	216	216	216	216	216	216	216	216
119ᵉ de Ligne	176	176	176	176	176	176	176	176
120ᵉ de Ligne	195	195	195	195	195	195	195	195
TOTAL	1,109	1,109	1,109	1,109	1,109	1,109	1,109	1,109

Officers of an unknown *légère* regiment observed in Dresden during summer 1813. (*Collection KM*)

The men retained their shoes, *bonnets de police*, muskets, shirts, stocks, gaiters, linen *pantalons*, *sacs de peau* and other small items from their parent regiments, and were dressed as new. Clothing issued and in use on 25 February 1812 was as follows:[125]

	Habits	*Vestes*	*Pantalons*	*Capotes*	*Bonnets de police*	*Schakos*
Received from War Ministry	5,013	4,904	4,992	4,631	5,833	5,332
Lost	325	519	566	860	843	1,429
In use	3,165	3,162	3,165	3,165	3,165	3,903
Remaining in *dépôt*	1,523	1,223	1,261	606	1,325	738

The administrative council of the regiment allowed to the 3ᵉ, 4ᵉ and 5ᵉ battalions 442 *habits*, 900 *bonnets de police*, 359 *baudriers*, 564 musket slings, 4 *mousquetons* for *sapeurs*, all that remained from the 14 the regiment had, 9 being issued already to *sapeurs*, 10 sabres, 22 drums with carriages, 2 *voltigeur cornets*, along with silver lace and all other items of passementerie needed for the battalions. The *dépôt* had also furnished the 10ᵉ *Légère* with 200 *habits*, 387 *vestes*, 376 pairs of blue *pantalons de tricot*, 400 *capotes*, 400 *bonnets de police*, 269 *schakos*, 400 muskets with bayonets, 400 *gibernes* with belts and 400 musket slings. In addition, the 76ᵉ *de Ligne* had been passed 123 *capotes*, 132 *bonnets de police*, and 65 *schakos* – proof positive that line and light infantry had identical items.[126]

A report regarding the 29ᵉ *Légère* describes on 24 January 1813 the problems the regiment faced clothing and equipping new entrants:

> On the 11th day of this month … this regiment had numbered 1,210 men, of which 334 were in uniform and 876 were in civilian clothing. Since then, 150 men have been put into uniforms. We are constantly working on clothing by use of regimental craftsmen and outside contractors.[127]

Inspected on 4 August 1814, the 451 men under arms were entirely dressed in almost brand-new clothing 'according to the regulation of January 1812'. The *dépôt* held 195m 93 blue broadcloth, 6m 31 of chamois broadcloth, and 632m 36 of blue tricot. It did hold brand-new clothing and equipment, which included 23 *habits*, 570 *habits*, 144 *gilets manches*, 105 pairs of *pantalons de tricot*, 180 *bonnets de police*, 4 pairs of *caleçons*, 60 fusilier *schakos*, 60 *gibernes* and belts, 100 *baudriers*, 2 drums and carriages, 12 *sapeurs'* axes, aprons and pairs of gauntlets, 42 grenadier *aigrettes*, 62 *voltigeur aigrettes*, 606 *houpettes* and 80 pairs of grenadiers' epaulettes. Also, in *dépôt*

Officer of *voltigeurs* of an unknown *légère* regiment observed in Dresden during summer 1813. He is wearing Bardin-regulation uniform. (*Collection KM*)

30ᵉ Légère

No regiment of this designation during the Empire.

31ᵉ Légère

Formed on 23 September 1803 from Piedmontese troops and reviewed on 8 October 1804, the elite company was detached, and the men were all newly clothed in the French manner.[129] Reviewed on 20 July 1805, we note 13 *sapeurs*' aprons, axes and cases and 2 *baudriers* to carry the regiment's eagles. We also report 8m 74 of chamois broadcloth had been used for *voltigeurs*' distinctions. A single bearskin existed for the sergeant *sapeur*; every man had a *schako*. In addition, 27 light cavalry *mousquetons* were in use, 9 with officers and 18 with the *sous-officiers* of the *voltigeur* company.[130] Reviewed again on 24 February 1808, the *carabiniers* had 103 bearskins, and 6 horns were issued to the voltigeur company.[131] During 1808, 100 copper grenades for the *carabiniers*' *gibernes* were obtained.[132] During 1813 60 pairs of grenadiers' epaulettes were purchased and 140m of Imperial Livery and a mace for the drum major costing 36fr.[133] At disbandment on 6 October 1814, stores held almost nothing: 11 *habits*, 205 muskets and not much else.[134]

32ᵉ Légère

Raised on 14 July 1805, the regiment was reviewed on 26 November 1807. We note 1,549 *schakos* were in use and 440 greatcoats made from beige broadcloth. Just 86 sword knots and epaulettes existed, presumably for the elite company. The *voltigeur* company was armed with 160 light cavalry *mousquetons*, the *officiers* and *sous-officiers* being armed with rifles. No chamois cloth existed.[135] At the end of the Empire it had battalions in Spain and the Campaign of France. The regiment was disbanded in summer 1814 into the 9ᵉ *Légère* and just 45 men from the *dépôt* battalion were admitted to the 14ᵉ. The men were all equipped with Bardin-regulation clothing, including the drummers, who wore Imperial Livery on green clothing.[136]

33ᵉ Légère

Formed in 1810 with the decree of 9 July from the 1ᵉ *regiment Chasseurs a Pied* and the 1ᵉ *bataillon* of the 6ᵉ *de Ligne* of the former army of King Louis. The regiment had four battalions, each battalion having six companies, two elite companies and four *chasseur* companies. Regiment accounts reveal that between 1 January 1811 and 15 April 1814, the following amount of cloth had been purchased:[137]

8,025m 60 beige broadcloth
13,666m 96 blue broadcloth
317m 97 white broadcloth
212m 59 scarlet broadcloth
158m 07 green broadcloth
18m 50 chamois broadcloth
7,122m 41 blue serge
55m green serge
17,270m 13 blue tricot
164m 05 green tricot for *pantalons*
25, 397m 10 linen for lining
2,372m 42 linen for *caleçons*
177m 93 27mm wide silver lace
239m 30 27mm wide white worsted lace
1,772m 60 drummers' lace

Of note, not an inch of red worsted lace was bought, ergo service chevrons were clearly in white if any were worn. The archive paperwork also shows drummers had green *pantalons de tricot*. The green serge had one use only, to line *habits*, arguably of the drummers or 1814-model *habits*. We note, of the drummers' lace, 1,073m 10 remained in *dépôt* in April 1814, some 390m being used, and 63m 69 green broadcloth being used to produce drummers' clothing. Indeed, regiment accounts record that clothing made between 1 January 1812 and 15 April 1814 was as follows:[138]

2,579 *capotes*
3,879 *habits de chasseurs*
26 *habits de tambour*
3,818 *gilets manches de chasseurs*
26 *gilets manches de tambour*
5,558 *pantalons de chasseur*
26 *pantalons de tambour*
2,460 *bonnets de police*
1,913 pairs of *caleçons*

The following items were passed to the 64ᵉ *de Ligne*:[139]

45 beige *capotes*
65 *chasseur habits*
45 blue *gilets manches*
423 pairs of linen *caleçons*
150 blue *bonnets de police*
340 new *gibernes*
340 *porte-gibernes*

Voltigeur of an unknown *légère* regiment drawn from life in summer 1813 observed in the Dresden area. Cords and plumes had been abolished at the end of 1810, yet our soldier has both. If we look closely he has the 1806 model *schakp* three years after this type was abolished. We know regiments, and army level stores, had thousands of these items which were given priority issue over new items. What ever regulations said, pragmatism was "the order of the day." We note he appears to have dragoon musket. (*Collection KM*)

The Light Infantry 129

Drawn from life in 1808 is this sergeant major of *voltigeurs* of the 31ᵉ *Légère*. (*Collection KM*)

Drawn from life is this *sapeur* of the 31ᵉ *Légère*. (*Collection KM*)

An officer of the 27ᵉ *Légère* wearing Bardin uniform with a group of *chasseurs* and *voltigeurs* from unknown regiments of *légère* observed in the Dresden area in summer 1813. (*Collection KM*)

200 musket slings
260 *baudriers*
14 new drums, 9 needing repairs and 1 to be written off
9 sets of *sapeurs'* equipment (apron, axe and axe case with belt, gauntlets)
9 new *voltigeur cornets* and 2 to be written off
1 eagle on pole
1 *drapeau* with cravat with gold embroidery

When the *dépôt* was emptied in summer 1814, the regiment had 47 new *chasseur habits* in *dépôt*, 71 needed repairs and 20 were life expired. Also, in *dépôt* were 28 *bonnets de police* and 115 pairs of braces, 100 *chasseur schakos* needing repairs and 66 of the old model. Also in *dépôt* were 15 pairs of worn out *carabiniers'* epaulettes.[140] Cloth in the *dépôt* included 448m 80 beige broadcloth, 85m 65 blue broadcloth, 9m 70 white broadcloth, 3m 85 scarlet broadcloth, 71m 33 green broadcloth, 6m 44 chamois broadcloth, 173m 91 white

Chasseur of an unknown *légère* regiment in full dress *c.*1812.

serge, 3,034m 42 blue tricot, and 309m 40 drummers' lace, which was presumably Imperial Livery. Brand-new clothing in the *dépôt* ready to be issued included 31 *capotes*, 59 *chasseur habits*, 1 drummers' '*habit*, with 2 needing repairs recorded as green with Imperial Livery, 24 *chasseur gilets manches*, 17 drummers' *gilets manches*, 68 pairs of *pantalons de tricot*, 290 *bonnets de police*, 193 pairs of *caleçons*, 340 *gibernes* with belts, 260 *baudriers*, and 242 pairs of green *schako* cords.

The regimental band possessed one pair of cymbals, one trumpet, one trombone, one flute, one 'small clarinet', one horn and two clarinets.[141]

34ᵉ *Légère*

Created in 1811, we have been unable to locate any archive paperwork for the dress of the regiment, alas we can say nothing about the regiment's appearance.

35ᵉ *Légère*

Formed from the 1ᵉ *regiment de Mediterranean* in 1812, it drew its manpower from the line infantry, notably the 35ᵉ *de Ligne*. A total of 301 officers and men were passed to the 1ᵉ *regiment de Mediterranean* from the 35ᵉ *de Ligne*, who were wearing on 7 May 1812:[142]

Item	Total	Good condition	Bad Condition	To be written off	Observations
Habits	241	73	121	47	The clothing comprises 161 *habit-vestes* and 80 *habits*-long. The blue *pantalons* and *gilets manches* are of the new model delivered to the regiment on various dates in 1811.
Gilets manches cut round	222	160	34	28	
Pantalons de tricot	239	149	85	5	
Schakos	240	13	218	9	
Bonnets de police	209	97	73	39	
Capotes	None				
Gibernes	241	231	10		
Porte-gibernes	241	237	4		
Musket slings	217	217			
Bayonet scabbards	237	217	19	1	
Muskets	241	338	2	1	
Bayonets	241	239	1	1	
Épinglettes	128	119	9		
Musket worms	162	157	4		
Shirts	546	392	119	35	
Pairs of shoes	320	193	82	45	
Stockings	None				
Black stocks	227	199	23	5	
Black half gaiters	115	105	23	5	
Grey half gaiters	216	183	22	11	
Linen *pantalons*	209	200	7	2	

All items were of the October 1811 regulation, most notably the round-cut *gilets manches* and short *habits*. The regiment must have looked very odd indeed wearing infantry *habits* of two models, along with blue *pantalons de tricot*.

We know nothing more about the dress of the regiment until it was disbanded in 1814. *Dépôt* held in summer 1814 12 green drummers' *habits*, yet no green cloth or lace for drummers existed in the *dépôt*. Clearly it had all been used to produce clothing. Also in *dépôt* were 724 brand-new *chasseur habits*, 1 *sapeurs*' apron and 2 pairs of gauntlets, 855m of blue broadcloth, 424m of blue serge and 430m of linen.[143] We have been unable to locate any further archive paperwork for the dress of the regiment, so alas we can say nothing else about its appearance.

36ᵉ *Légère*

Raised in 1812 from the *Belle Isle* infantry regiment. Inspected on 26 September 1814, the inspecting officer noted the bulk of the regiment's clothing was either in need of repair or total replacement:[144]

Item	In Good Repair	In Need of Repair	Need Replacing	Items due to be replaced	Items missing
Habits	448				
Veste	488				
Pantalons de tricot	351			97	
Caleçons	351			97	
Capotes	422			36	
Bonnets de police	448				
Schakos	448				
Schako covers	448				
Houpettes	448				

At disbandment the *dépôt* held a broad range of clothing: 150 *capotes* made from white broadcloth, 140 needing repairs and 16 that were *hors de service*. Also in that category were 7 *chasseurs*' *habits*. A single *sapeurs*' bearskin was in *dépôt*. Perhaps due to shortages of cloth and clothing in 1814, the regiment had been issued line infantry clothing; 56 new fusilier *habits* were in *dépôt* with 143 *gilets manches*, 100 pairs of white *pantalons de tricot* and 120 fusiliers' *schakos*. Needing repair were 24 fusilier *habits* and 67 pairs of white *pantalons de tricot*.[145] The *dépôt* of the regiment held 208m 71 beige broadcloth, 930m 63 of blue broadcloth, 79m 05 scarlet broadcloth and 344m 45 of blue serge. The inspector noted that of the blue broadcloth:

276m 38 was captured from the English and used to make clothing
52m 60 of blue broadcloth was French
46m 25 was English Kersey used to make *capotes*
555m 50 was English blue common broadcloth to make *capotes* and *bonnets de police*

Drum major of an unknown *légère* regiment at the end of the Empire.

Sapeur of unknown *légère* regiment at the end of the Empire.

Regulations in Practice 137

Officer of *légère* at the end of the Empire.

Carabinier wearing Bardin-regulation uniform at the very end of the Empire. He appears to be from the 1ᵉ *Legere*.

Regulations in Practice 139

Regimental adjutant of presumably 7ᵉ *Légère* at the end of the Empire.

Of the scarlet broadcloth, 36m 05 was actually English madder red common broadcloth. The *dépôt* held stocks of brand-new clothing, notably 21 *capotes*, 86 fusilier *habits*, 257 fusilier *gilets manches*, 231 pairs of blue *pantalons de tricot*, 398 *bonnets de police*, 295 pairs of *caleçons*, 53 sets of braces, 697 fusilier *schakos*, 519 *gibernes* with the same number of *giberne* belts in blackened cowhide, 429 blackened cowhide musket slings, 4,341 fusilier *houpettes*, 0m 72 silver lace, 41m 20 white worsted lace and 425m 45 red worsted lace.[146]

Conclusion

The partial regimental records mean we cannot make any overriding conclusions about the dress of the *légère*. It seems on balance of probability – as with the *ligne* – that *porte-aigle* with halberds and pistols did not exist. Not one halberd, pistol or helmet appears in any late empire inspection report for the *légère*. *Sapeurs* appear in 18 regiments, judging from extant archive documents. Not one grenadier *schako* was in use, at least officially, and 15 regiments out of 33 had *aigrettes*, or less than half. Likewise, 21 regiments used epaulettes of one form or another. We note 18 regiments had chamois broadcloth across the period, meaning *voltigeurs* did not universally have chamois collars and distinctions. Concerning bearskins for *carabiniers*, we note:

2ᵉ *Légère* in 1814–1815, presumably earlier.[147]
3ᵉ *Légère* bearskins and colpacks in 1815.[148]
7ᵉ *Légère* unknown number in use 1809.[149]
9ᵉ *Légère*, 36 bearskins in 1808.[150]
13e *Légère*, 53 bearskins in 1805.[151] All three grenadier companies equipped 1811.[152]
15ᵉ *Légère* all companies equipped 1811.[153]
16ᵉ *Légère*, equipped from 1808.[154]
17ᵉ *Légère*, 244 bearskins 1805, all lost by 1807.[155]
23ᵉ *Légère*, 13 for *sapeurs* in 1808.[156]
24ᵉ *Légère*, 73 bearskins lost in action 1805.[157]
25ᵉ *Légère*, 250 bearskins in 1805, all lost by 1807.[158]
31ᵉ *Légère*, 103 bearskins in use 1808.[159]
36ᵉ *Légère*, *sapeurs* only in 1814.[160]

Clearly, they were not in universal use, and very few after 1808. The 2ᵉ *Légère* retained theirs into 1815. Concerning drummers, we record green drummers' *habits* with Imperial Livery in use in 1813–14 were with the following units:

11ᵉ *Légère*[161]
13ᵉ *Légère*[162]
15ᵉ *Légère*[163]
16ᵉ *Légère*[164]
18ᵉ *Légère*[165]
28ᵉ *Légère*[166]
29ᵉ *Légère*[167]
32ᵉ *Légère*[168]
33ᵉ *Légère*[169]
35ᵉ *Légère*[170]

Some units only adopted Imperial Livery in 1815:

2e *Légère*[171]
4e *Légère*[172]
6e *Légère*[173]
13e *Légère*[174]

Prior to the 100 Days, some regiments applied Imperial Livery to blue (?) *habits*:

17e *Légère*[175]
23e *Légère*[176]

Therefore, it seems, most drummers wore a variation on the standard *légère* uniform. The 27e seem to have dressed in sky blue, with dark blue facings and a quasi-Imperial Livery, if – this is a big if – a *habit* noted by Bucqouy in the 1920s is a genuine garment. No one has ever seen this, and its location is unknown in 2024.

Further archive work is needed in the correspondence files of the army of Germany, Spain, Portugal and others if we are to say more about the dress of the *légère*, particularly supply on campaign. Because of the fragmented nature of regimental archives, we can say little about how and when the *légère* adopted Bardin with any degree of precision.

One of the key findings of this research is that it shows that the 1812 regulations as imagined by Vernet never made it off the drawing board. When an author says 'Bardin' or '1812 regulation' it is clear that they have no awareness about the complexity of the so-called Bardin regulation and its implementation across the army only beginning in reality from summer 1814. 'Bardin' was not a single, comprehensive regulation: it evolved to suit the economic realities that France found herself in. Rather than simplifying the dress of the army, it created chaos. With three versions of Bardin all in use side by side, often contradicting the other collations, no one really knew what was, or was not, regulation. This was only 'nailed down' with the 1814 collation, which was the first time that the Bardin regulation was enacted en masse to reclothe the army, an exercise that cost 6.5million fr and was not yet finished when the 100 Days began. The Bourbons during the first restoration spent vast sums of money in remaking the army in its own image and creating order from chaos by vigorously imposing the 1814 collation with no hesitation or deviation. A few regiments slipped through the net, of course, metaphorically speaking, because of the sudden appearance of the Emperor on French soil, which resulted in administrative chaos. We know from archive sources that the 1808, 1811 and '1812' model *habit* and other items were used side by side in 1814 with three different patterns of plate in the same company. This was common sense: the regulations only set in stone what was to happen in the future. For example, if a battalion was wearing the 1806 *schako* with cords and plumes, and these items still had years of life left in them, with the introduction of the new 1810 *schako*, the men would wear their old-pattern kit till it was life expired. Replacement would be piecemeal as kit would wear out at different

Cornet dressed with Royalist Livery observed at the very end of the Empire. The scarlet cuffs are a recurring theme in period iconography. The chamois cuff flap is matched by an original *habit* of a *voltigeur* officer of the 1ᵉ *de Ligne*.

Drummer of *carabiniers* wearing Royalist Livery at the very end of the Empire.

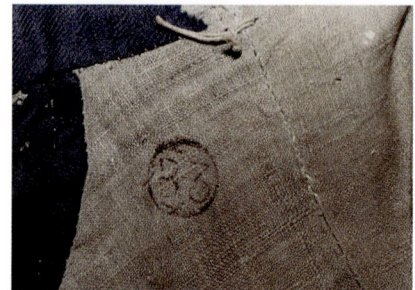

Unique drummers' *habit* of unknown *légère* regiment dating to the 1813–15 period. How typical this garment was can only be guessed at.

rates depending how careful the soldier was. Bardin as a decree on 19 January 1812 is a myth – it never could have been adopted in full given the army was at war and the state was in economic freefall. As long as a soldier had a *schako*, *capote*, *pantalons*, gaiters, shoes, *giberne* and belt and musket, that was all he needed and no one really cared if the kit he was wearing was old, new, or worn out.

Regulations in Practice 145

Chapter 6
Other Regiments

As well as forming regular army regiments, the French army had a multiplicity of other regiments, which fell partway between an ad hoc police force and a territorial army. In addition, the navy required artillerymen to man its guns and each ship had its own garrison of infantry. They all had to be clothed and equipped by the state.

Following the disasters of the Russian campaign, the French army was rebuilt around a hard core of veterans from Spain. As well as drawing in hundreds of thousands of raw conscripts to the army, in spring 1813 thousands of already trained men filled out the ranks of the National and Municipal Guards as well as reserve units. Realising that these men could be better employed on active service, Napoléon issued a *senatus-consulte* on 11 January 1813, calling for the recruitment of 350,000 additional men, of which 100,000 were to be drawn from the National Guard, 100,000 men drawn from the reserves of the classes of 1809, 1810, 1811 and 1812 and 150,000 from the class of 1814. These men became the 134^e to 156^e *de Ligne*.

Ships' Garrisons

In addition to newly levied conscripts, some 7,244 men all clothed and equipped, from over 20 different regiments of *ligne*, were on board the warships of the French Navy kicking their heels. On shore, their duties were to guard the ports, and at sea to defend their ships from boarding parties when in action, as well as to provide musketry from the fighting tops. The French Navy following Trafalgar barely put to sea. These men could be better used, reasoned the Emperor.

To this end he ordered them to re-join their regiments on 5 October 1812.[1] To do so, the Minister of the Navy proposed to return 5,063 men by November, with the remainder during February 1813. Minister of War Henri Clarke reported to the Emperor on 14 November 1812 that orders had been given to land the Antwerp infantry companies and form the *régiment de marche de l'Escaut*, commanded by a major. We know from archive documents that this regiment was hastily formed and left Antwerp on 20 November bound for Wesel, where it arrived on 25 November. Inspected in Berlin on 5 January 1813, the report tells us the regiment had had 41 officers and 1,577 *sous-officiers* and men when it left Antwerp but it had lost 3 officers and 212 men on the route march to Berlin. The inspector noted the men were 'of bad quality and insubordinate in the extreme; we are ignorant of their military discipline as we have never seen them drill'. The major in charge of the regiment lamented that he lacked battalion commanders and that the insubordination existed because the officers were not sure of themselves. He added that most of the officers were reluctant, crippled old soldiers, and reported that the clothing of the regiment was fairly good, 'even though many *habits* and *gilets* were totally worn out', adding that 'the equipment is fairly good but many *schakos* are lacking their chinscales and the muskets had been badly maintained'.[2] One assumes sending men to garrison duty on board ship was a good way for a colonel to rid himself of 'bad pennies'! We lose track of this regiment, and the regiment raised in Texel, once they arrived in Berlin.

Naval Artillery

The naval artillery had been consolidated with the decree of *18 Brumaire An XII* (10 November 1803) from 21 battalions formed into 7 *demi-brigades* into 12 battalions, which in turn were formed into 4 regiments. Under the decree of *2 Frimaire an IX* (23 November 1800) each man was issued a *havresac*, 3 shirts, a pair of black gaiters, 1 pair of linen gaiters, 2 pairs of shoes, and 3 pairs of stockings. The An XII decree stated that the clothing was to be a *habit* and *veste* in blue broadcloth with the collar, cuffs, revers and lining of the *habit* to be the same colour, piped scarlet. The cuff flap was scarlet piped blue. The *veste* and *pantalons* were made from blue tricot. In undress they were allowed a *patelot* or double-breasted fatigue coat. Headdress was a *chapeau* and *bonnet de police*. For working duties the men were allowed a pair of linen *pantalons*. Scarlet wool-fringed epaulettes were worn at the shoulder. The sabre belt and *giberne* belt were to made from whitened buff leather.[3] From 1807 they replaced the *chapeau* with the *schako*.

The Emperor realised that the usefulness of his navy was limited, and that the gun crews on board ship were a clothed and trained body of artillery who were, like the infantry garrison, doing nothing in particular and could be sent to the army. To this end, he stripped the ships of their gunners, as he explained in a letter of 23 January 1813 to the Minister of War:

> I have written a decree which transfers the twelve marine battalions to your ministry and, since there are many old soldiers within them, I have taken the liberty of doubling these battalions and, instead of having twelve, there will be twenty-four. These battalions, of 840 men each, will give me 20,000 men. However, I only have 16,000 so I need to find 4,000 more, of which 2,000 have to be conscripted from the 100,000 men and the other 2,000 from the conscripts of 1814.[4]

Rather than being used as artillery, these gunners found themselves being used as ad hoc infantry. These naval regiments were formally taken into the Army on 1 February and were ordered to assemble at Brest, Toulon, Cherbourg and Antwerp. It marked the end of any naval ambitions for the Emperor, and can be seen as a tacit acknowledgement of the failure of French naval policy.

Supplied with greatcoats and three pairs of shoes, the first six battalions of the 1ᵉ Regiment, the first eight battalions of the 2ᵉ and the first three battalions of the 3ᵉ and 4ᵉ, a total of 16,895 men, were formed into 20 battalions and were ordered to Mainz to join the 2nd Observation Corps of the Rhine under the command of Marshal Marmont. The other battalions were ordered to stay at the *dépôts* until they had received their drafts of conscripts.[5] Some of the men, passing through Paris, were inspected at Saint Denis by General Mouton, Count of Lobau and ADC to the Emperor. Mouton reported to the Emperor on 21 February that:

> The column I saw on the 19th was about 1,500 men strong. They belonged to all four of the regiments. There were, however, about three battalions present that were from the 3rd Regiment, numbering 1,200 men. This troop had a lot of new recruits, some of which were quite frail and others that have only joined their units recently and, consequently, lack any military training. These battalions are unable to drill or manoeuvre together and this is due, in part, to the sort of service that they had undertaken up until now. The 2nd lieutenants requested were all present, some *sous-officiers* and corporals were missing, which were replaced immediately, but quite a few officers and *sous-officiers* were absent and had left word that they were on their way and would be able to join the unit at Mainz. It is said that the gunners that are to complete these three battalions are old. This troop really needs to be assembled in order to begin its instruction, work together and improve their clothing. They say that this will be done by the time they reach Mainz. The old gunners still have the old uniform, that is to say the long-tailed coat, no greatcoat and the newly arrived men are, for the most part, with waistcoats and greatcoats. They say that the dress will be completed when they get to Mainz. Their equipment isn't tended to and needs to be renewed, while their linen and shoes are serviceable. These men are not used to marching. There are two well-presented companies that are not part of the 3rd Regiment, one of which Your Majesty saw at the Cherbourg seawall.[6]

Upon arrival in Mainz, the manpower of these battalions was 9,640 men, who were now organised into two brigades. The 1ᵉ and 3ᵉ Regiments would form Cacault's brigade of the 1st division of the corps and the 2ᵉ and 4ᵉ Regiments would form Buquet's brigade of the 2nd division.[7] Marmont was far from impressed at the poor condition of these men, and outlined to the Emperor the realities of not only the naval artillery corps but also the state of the military stores in Mainz. He lamented that:

> Once I had arrived in Mainz, I became aware of the situation regarding the men that had recently arrived in my army corps … The naval troops have arrived, or are arriving today or tomorrow, but neither their strength nor training match the reports given by the Minister of War. There must have necessarily been a mistake or omission in the orders. In any case, I have to bring this to Your Majesty's attention in order to tell you the reality regarding these troops […] Generally, the naval troops

appear to be in good spirits but they lack many items of equipment needed for their service.

These units lack drums and drummers. There are approximately 250 missing from the four regiments. There are none in the stores in Mainz and Strasbourg and the means with which to make them here are extremely limited. The only way of providing these units with what they need is by supplying the items from France.

Furthermore, these units are totally devoid of any campaign equipment: in this regard are all the other units stationed here. The stores at Mainz do not contain a single item of campaign equipment and the delivery of these items from manufacturers is delayed. The items we were hoping to get from Frankfurt haven't arrived yet […] the 1st Observation Corps must be fully supplied before the second, and the former is far from having everything it needs […] The weaponry of these units needs to be changed but the arsenal in Mainz doesn't have the resources to do so […] The 1st Regiment also needs *gibernes* and belts but there are none here […] With respects to the clothing of the Corps, almost all the conscripts here are wearing a *capote* over a *gilet*: other items are still coming up from the rear. I do not know when these items will arrive.[8]

Blackened cowhide equipment was issued to replace missing or defective buff items. Despite lacking arms and clothing, the naval artillery contributed to the campaigns of 1813, and had won the admiration of their commander. The impression given by this report of the officers and soldiers was supported by Jean-Louis Rieu, a lieutenant in the naval artillery based at Antwerp, who recalls that:

the naval artillery no longer provides men to the warships. Instead, infantry is used to man them and the artillery is only used to guard the ports, arsenals and colonies. The naval crews now man the ships' guns themselves […] The officers, almost all of whom are issued from the ranks, married and old, only had little practical experience acquired during the rare moments they were on board but absolutely no theoretical knowledge and even less education […] I was therefore going to war at the head of a company, with only two young officers fresh out of the St-Cyr academy to act as lieutenants. Despite what our regimental title might have suggested, we were only to be used as infantry and since we were in the process of completing the training of our long-neglected officers and *sous-officiers*, our shortfalls would be provisionally corrected by the presence of infantry officers.[9]

He describes his lieutenant's uniform as:

a simple blue coat with red collar and cuffs, yellow piping, blue woollen breeches, top-boots and leather sword belt. Our colonel added golden grenades on the collar, replaced the sword belt with a broader one in white buff leather, fitted with a fabulously big gilded plate, embossed with huge cannon, that would fasten on the waistcoat and, what was even more beautiful, replaced our top-boots with big *écuyère*-style boots garnished with silver spurs.[10]

As well as finding themselves as ad hoc infantry, many naval gunners were also transferred to the *Garde Imperiale* but this time as artillery: a detachment of 150 men was sent to reinforce the artillery of Bonet's division. The situation report of 15 April in the 2nd Observation Corps of the Rhine indicates that there were 20 naval battalions amounting to 12,080 men, of which at least 4,000 were conscripts from the army. The real number of ex-naval gunners was therefore approximately 8,000 men.[11] The use of naval artillery as infantry was a desperate act of short-term needs, as Marmont explains:

> the naval artillery regiments, which made up most of my corps, deserve much praise for their bravery and their good spirits. Never have soldiers exposed themselves to the enemy's cannon with such good grace and held with such resolution. But these troops were clumsy and completely lacked experience fighting on land.[12]

The navy was an ideal recruitment source for the army to make up its losses.

Another source of manpower were the men who were on shore making rigging, and conducting general militance of the ships, as well as production of munitions. On January 23, Napoléon asked Clarke to choose, among the naval artisans, men of 22 years of age with more than two years of service to join the workers' battalion used by the artillery, engineers and miners. He believed that 1,200 men could be found without any difficulties. Afterwards, the same method was used to complete two engineer battalions by drafting in naval conscripts of 22 years of age who had served on board ship for at least two years and able to swim: yet in this second draft of men just 590 men from the warship and flotilla crews would be transferred into the army.[13]

Garde de Paris

Formed with the decree of 4 October 1802 as the 'Municipal Guard of Paris' from apparent veterans, it consisted of two infantry regiments and a squadron of dragoons, under the control of the very much civilian regional administration of the *Département du Serine*. Each battalion comprised a grenadier company and three of *chasseurs*. With the decree of 18 May 1806 Napoléon renamed it the *Garde de Paris* and made it s definite part of the French Army. The establishment was now six companies per battalion, one of grenadiers, one of *voltigeurs* in lieu of the *chasseurs*, and four of fusiliers. The dragoon contingent, dressed in *bleu de ciel* with scarlet facings, mustered two companies, forming a single squadron.

In new year 1805 a detachment was sent to the *Armée de Hollande*, consisting of the dragoons under Colonel Goujet and the first battalion of each regiment under Colonel Rabbe and Chef de Bataillon Etienne Bardin respectively. The two battalions returned to Paris, having seen no action, following the Treaty of Pressburg.

Martinet presents a suit of images of the 1st regiment of *Garde de Paris* in its first green uniform. We have a grenadier, *chasseur*, fusilier and *voltigeur*.

Other Regiments 153

Grenadier and fusilier of the 1st regiment of *Garde de Paris* in the second white uniform.

Drum major and grenadier of the 1st regiment of *Garde de Paris* in its first green uniform. (*Collection KM*)

On 22 December 1806 the first battalion of each regiment under the overall command of Colonel Rabbe was sent to Mainz as the Régiment de Paris, where it arrived on 1 January 1807. Originally tasked with garrisoning Cassel, Napoléon sent orders after Eylau that the two battalions were to march to Berlin and the regiment was ordered to join Lefebvre's corps at Danzig on 11 April. Casualties at Friedland were 1 officer and

Other Regiments 155

Grenadiers of the 2nd regiment of *Garde de Paris* in the first scarlet uniforms with green facings. (*Collection KM*)

37 other ranks killed, with 5 officers and 200 men wounded. The regiment returned to Paris on 28 October 1807. In November 1807 two battalions under Major Estève were sent to join Dupont's corps, which crossed into Spain on 19 November. Part of Barbou's division, the *Garde de Paris* distinguished itself at the bridge of Alcolea and at Baylen. In June 1808 a single battalion of six companies was sent to reinforce the army in Spain. The two regiments were combined into a single entity, the *Régiment d'infanterie*

de la Garde de Paris, with the decree of 12 February 1812. The *dépôt* was established on 1 April 1812. The decree of 12 February dressed the regiment in white *habits*, with green collar – chamois for *voltigeurs* and scarlet for grenadiers – *revers*, tail facings and cuffs. Grenadiers were allowed scarlet epaulettes, bearskins with cords and plume, to wear the *sabre briquet* and have grenade *giberne* ornament. Fusiliers were authorised to use a crowned 'N' and *voltigeurs* a hunting horn. All metal work was in white metal.

The guard was viewed with suspicion by Napoléon: all bar the dragoon squadron, the *Garde de Paris*, had not opposed General Mallet's aborted coup of 1812. The dragoons found themselves transferred to the *Garde Imperiale* and incorporated into the red Lancers. Perhaps to get the officers and men away from Paris, as well as to solve manpower needs, the Emperor ordered on 6 January 1813 for the regiment to march to Erfurt, where it

Sapeur and Grenadier of the 2nd regiment of *Garde de Paris* in full dress.

Officer, *chasseur* and fusilier of 2nd regiment of *Garde de Paris*.

was to be disbanded to provide the cadre of the new 134ᵉ *de Ligne*. The disbandment on 21 January of the 125ᵉ and 126ᵉ *de Ligne* provided manpower to bring the regiment up to strength. The 4ᵉ battalion of the 125ᵉ, which was locked up in Stettin, was on paper at least transferred to the 134ᵉ de *Ligne* along with the *dépôt* battalion of the 125ᵉ. These, together with the 4ᵉ and 5ᵉ battalions of the 126ᵉ, became the 5ᵉ and 6ᵉ battalions of the 134ᵉ. On 1 March 1813 the new regiment had 1,829 men under arms.[14]

The decree of 6 January 1813 transformed the white-clad regiment into the 134ᵉ *de Ligne*. The regiment was mobilised on 2 February 1813 and then dissolved on 19 July 1814. No clothing records can be found.[15]

Chasseur of the 2nd regiment

Officer of the dragoon contingent of the *Garde de Paris*.

Dragoon and (opposite) trumpeter of the dragoon contingent of the *Garde de Paris*.

Departmental Reserves

Among the troops readily available to rebuild the army following the Russian campaign were different Departmental Reserve Companies. The latters' duties primarily involved internal police work, and they had been formed on 18 August 1805. About their duties, the decree reports:

> Article 1 – In each département, an infantry company shall be raised, which shall be designated the 'Reserve Company of the département'.
>
> Article 2 – These companies shall be assigned to guard the prefectures, the archives of the départements, the penitentiaries, the homeless shelters and poorhouses as well as the police cells and the prisons, however on no account shall their service interfere with the work of the Gendarmerie.[16]

Their *habits* were *bleu de ciel* with white *veste* and *pantalons*, each unit being distinguished with its own combination of piping and facing colours.[17] Headdress was originally a *chapeau*, but the *schako* was introduced by the circular of 27 November 1807:

> Effective immediately, the *schako* shall replace the bicorn, however those bicorns which are already in use shall be worn until they are completely dilapidated.[18]

A more dramatic change occurred just over six months later, when the prefects received the following decree, penned in Bayonne on 12 July 1808:

> Article 6 – The reserve companies of the départements [...] shall wear the white coat, while retaining the old facing colours. However, for the moment only the new recruits to the companies shall be supplied with the white coat.[19]

The companies with the old facing colour white were now to be distinguished by the colour sky blue. The circular of 1 October 1812 informed the prefects that they were to:

> ensure that the uniforms of the reserve company of your *département* are altered according to the decree of 19 January 1812. These changes become applicable, without the colour of the uniforms, lapels, turnbacks, cuffs, etc. being affected.[20]

Since the creation of the reserve, Napoléon had used it as a source of men: 600 men were transferred to the cavalry in 1808: the 1ᵉ and 2ᵉ *Legion de reserve* became the 121ᵉ *de Ligne* bulked out with men from the 117ᵉ *de Ligne* on 25 April 1809.[21] Dressed in white, they would have stood out from the bulk of the blue-clad line. Inspected on 24 March 1809 at the siege of Saragossa, the unit was missing 100 *habits*, 1,000 *capotes*, 200 pairs of shoes, 150 pairs of black gaiters and 700 pairs of long grey gaiters.[22] A *dépôt* was established at

Other Regiments 163

Fusilier of *Legion Departmental de Paris* in full dress *c.*1808.

Fusilier of *Legion Departmental de Paris* in full dress *c*.1812.

Tudella on 28 April 1809. It had proved largely impossible for the unit to be reclothed and march to Spain. All effort was to be made to harmonise the dress with the *ligne*.[23] Inspected at the end of October 1809, all the clothing was described as new: clearly, they were now in blue.[24]

Disbanded in August 1814, the unit's stores held the following materials:

480m 69 beige broadcloth
11,010m 04 white serge
1m 52 yellow worsted lace
627m 20 Imperial Livery

Stocks of clothing included 235 *habits* and *vestes* of the old model, 198 *habits-vestes*, 2,335 pairs of *culottes* in good condition and 233 pairs needing repair, and 1,402 *capotes*. Other items included 395 *gilets manches*, 448 pairs of *pantalons en tricot*, 451 pairs of underwear, 5 *sapeurs'* aprons, 3 *sapeurs'* axes with cases, and single pair of gauntlets for *sapeurs*. We note 1e and 2e battalion were wearing pre-Bardin clothing, complete with long gaiters, and the 3e battalion and *dépôt* were wearing a mix of Bardin and earlier regulations.[25]

The 122e *Regiment d'infanterie de Ligne* was formed on 1 June 1809 from the 3e and 4e battalion of the 3e *Legion de reserve* as well as elements from the 119e *de Ligne*, plus the 4e battalion from the 4e and 5e *Legion de reserve*.[26] How quickly the uniform changed over is very hard to judge. The regiment's paperwork says nothing on clothing.[27]

As war plans developed against Russia, the reserves were once more a source of men for the regulars. In March 1812, 4,000 men were sent to the National Guard to replace the guardsmen who had been mobilised into the *ligne*. Aware that the army being regenerated following the massive losses in Russia lacked trained *sous-officiers* and cadre, on 15 February 1813 Napoléon ordered that 1,020 men from the reserve companies and 976 from the National Guard were to head to Hanover by 1 April to act as *sous-officiers* in the companies being formed there.[28] How effective these men were is open to judgement.

As well as transferring men from the reserve to the regular army piecemeal, Napoléon ordered the 116 departmental reserve companies to provide 4,000 men to form a new 37e *Légère*. Created by the decree of 7 February 1813, the new regiment was to be organised at Mainz. The strength of the new regiment would be 3,307 men on 1 March 1813, divided into four field battalions. Two weeks later, a fifth (*dépôt*) battalion was added on 15 March, taking the regimental strength up to a theoretical 4,060 men. Yet on 15 April, the three war battalions could only muster 2,851 men, with the last two battalions only having 305 each. As the departmental reserves were mostly composed of former soldiers who were more used to the duty of policing rather than the rigours of campaign, one can easily realise why the strength of the regiment quickly diminished. We wonder as to the effective capabilities of the regiment. Ultimately, the 37e was disbanded on 12 May 1814 into the 5e *Légère*.[29] Sadly, no archive papers can be found for the clothing of the regiment at the time of writing.

Chapter 7

The National Guard

The National Guard had existed since 1790 and had been organised as a sort of militia by successive laws until enshrined in the constitution of 1800. Following the decree of 30 September 1805, the National Guard was to be comprehensively reorganised, in each department of the Empire. Although this was only carried out in a few departments, it still meant 60,000 men were under arms.

Whatever the Emperor's intentions, it was not until 1812 that a formal reserve was created that would have the tasks of guarding the borders, policing and the safeguard of the maritime *dépôts*, arsenals and fortresses, therefore freeing the army for other tasks. This reserve or territorial army was sanctioned by a *senatus-consulte* dated 13 March 1812. Henceforth the National Guard was now organised into three categories called *bans*.

The first *ban* was formed from able-bodied men aged between 20 and 26 of the classes of 1807 to 1812 that were not called up to the army. The second was comprised of able-bodied men aged between 26 and 40 and the third included all able-bodied men aged between 40 to 60. The *senatus-consulte* also stipulated that the *bans* would be organised into a hundred cohorts, of which 88 belonged to the first *ban* and 12 to the second and third. Each cohort was formed by a battalion of six companies, each with 140 fusiliers, an artillery company with 100 men as well as a *dépôt* company, also of 100 men: in total each cohort would thus have 1,040 men. The officers and *sous-officiers* were either to be appointed from retired soldiers or from National Guardsmen who had served in the regular army.

Napoléon, in a further decree dated 14 March 1812, stipulated that there would only be 88 cohorts instead of 100, which would sidestep the need to call up the older men of the second and third *bans*. The decree stated that each cohort was to muster six companies of fusiliers, and a company of artillery. Six cohorts were to form a brigade, and were to be accorded eagles.

In order to man the 88 cohorts, it was necessary to call up 91,520 men, a number that was never reached: in reality only 78,000 men were enlisted. In order to clothe and equip these men, the National Guard was ordered to adopt Bardin clothing with a decree of 14 March 1812.[1] The uniform was to be of fusiliers of the line, with white metal buttons bearing the Imperial Eagle and the text '1ᵉ *Ban de la Garde Nationales*'. The decree makes mention of white lace for corporals' stripes, that the artillery had blue *habits* and *pantalons*, and that their white metal buttons bore crossed cannon. Drummers were accorded green *habits* and Imperial Livery, and the band green *habits-vestes* and *pantalons*.[2] The National Guard were unaffected by later amendments to Bardin until 1814, when they were ordered to remove Imperial iconography.

National Guardsman in parade dress *c.*1806 by Martinet, accompanied by men wearing the Bardin regulation.

In order to fill the shortfall in men, a second *senatus-consulte*, dated 1 September 1812, followed up by a decree of 22 September 1812, assigned 17,000 conscripts called up in 1813 to the cohorts. However, despite Imperial ambition, this levy of conscripts was so slow that application of the decree was only carried out in the first days of 1813. As a consequence, only 6,937 conscripts had arrived at the *Cohortes dépôt*s by 15 January 1813.

To clothe the men, a decree was issued 27 November, which acted upon the decree of 26 June 1812. The conscripts were to be issued a *capote*, *bonnet de police*, a pair of *pantalons*, a pair of underwear, two shirts, a pair of stockings, a pair of shoes and a pair of linen gaiters.

The *habits* were second hand: they were to be collected from those *Cohortes* selected to receive the new Bardin regulation, and given to the conscripts. Clothing was to be taken back from men on leave, in hospital or who had died. The *Cohortes* were to provide the remaining items of uniform and equipment through the same means.[3] The men must have looked far from uniform, wearing a mix of Bardin and pre-Bardin clothing.

Officer's *habit* of National Guard. It differs from those of the *Garde Imperiale* by virtue of the silvered buttons and silver embroidered eagles to the tails. (*Private Collection UK*)

Grenadier *schako* according to the Bardin regulation for an unknown cohort of National Guard. (*Collection and Photograph of Bertrand Malvaux*)

On 5 November 1812, Napoléon instructed Clarke to prevent the mobilised National Guard *Cohortes* in the Pyrenees from entering into Spain, and passed orders for them to be deployed to guard the border. By new year 1813, over 70,000 men had been trained, clothed and equipped: a vast pool of men, ostensibly with little to do.[4]

At the close of December 1812, the government enacted a propaganda exercise to rally the people to the eagles, as well as to calm nerves after the Malet plot as much as to show the allies that, despite the losses of the Russian campaign, France was not defeated.

On 27 December 1812, the *Monitor* newspaper declared that the 87ᵉ National Guard *Cohorte* (at Groningen), the 51ᵉ to 54ᵉ *Cohortes* (at Hamburg), the 71ᵉ (at Brussels), the 67ᵉ (at Dieppe), the cohorts raised in the departments beyond the Alps and the 13ᵉ (at Le Havre) had spontaneously asked to be able to serve in the Grande Armée. This 'wish' to defend the Empire did not fall on deaf ears. On 5 January 1813, Minister of War Clarke wrote to Napoléon:

> Your Majesty had ordered that each cohort provide 60 men to strengthen the second regiments of *Tirailleurs* and *Voltigeurs*, representing a total of 4,800 men. On the 2nd of the current month, 3,734 of these men arrived in Paris. Of these, 980 men have been judged as being unable to carry out military duties and replaced with 400 substitutes, which gives a total of 1,380 men. Therefore, the number of men having the necessary criteria to serve in the Guard amounts to 2,354. Every time that I've been forced to send back men that are unable to serve back to their cohorts, I have also advised the commanders of these cohorts that these men had to be replaced by soldiers of a strong constitution and willing to be enrolled into the Young Guard. I have written on a number of occasions about this very subject to the generals in command of brigades of the 1st *ban* of the National Guard and those in command of military districts.[5]

Furthermore, the Emperor realised that the National Guard would be the cadre of a revitalised Grande Armée and on 6 January ordered that 'the Elbe Observation Corps must be entirely made up of cohorts', the following day announcing that 48,000 National Guardsmen were to be mobilised and sent to Germany. Two days later Napoléon wrote to Marshal Louis-Alexandre Berthier, advising:

> I have converted the 48 cohorts into 22 regiments of the line, each with four field battalions and a *dépôt* battalion. Each regiment will have an artillery company and with the rest of the cohort companies, I will form three new artillery regiments, each with 20 companies.[6]

Codifying this decision, on 11 January 1813, a *senatus-consulte* stipulated that the cohorts of the first ban would cease being part of the National Guard and would be transferred to the regular army.[7]

Irrespective of the quality of the officers, which was sometimes mediocre or poor, it is undeniable that the men in the cohorts were better soldiers than recently called-up conscripts. Transferring the National Guard to the regular army made a lot of sense, as the guardsman had at least eight to nine months' military experience. Between 15 and 25 January, 68 cohorts (including those at Rome, Turin, Florence, Genoa and Alexandria) marched off to their rendezvous points, where they were to arrive between 27 January and 26 March. The *Cohortes* from Antwerp and Breda were held up at Nijmegen due to ice on the River Waal.

The artillery companies were stripped from some of the cohorts and were to serve as field artillery. To this end, on 18 January 28 artillery companies received orders to march to Magdeburg, where they were to arrive between 6 February and 26 March. A further two companies were sent to Wesel and another two were sent to Frankfurt. Three days later, on 21 January, the remaining 24 artillery companies were issued orders to also head to Magdeburg, where they were expected to arrive between 11 February and 11 March. These guardsmen became the cadre of the re-formed foot artillery. On 20 January, a detachment from the 47ᵉ *Cohorte*, which were guarding Spanish prisoners of war, received orders to head to Calais to re-join their parent unit as it made its way to Mainz.[8]

The process of mobilisation is outlined in a letter from the War Administration to the Emperor:

> by a letter dated 27th January, Your Majesty informed me of your intention to call into service 60,000 men of the 1st *ban* of the National Guard during the months of April and May, to gather them in large towns, preferably the chief towns of the military districts where they are to be dressed and formed into regiments. Your Majesty wishes that shirts, waistcoats, breeches, gaiters, shoes, leather accoutrements, headdress and greatcoats be given to them at once. Your Majesty believes that by providing these basic necessities, they will be able to wait for the jackets until June or even July. I therefore propose the following process as being the most appropriate:
>
> 1° That all clothing articles be in accordance with that specified in the Decree of January 19th and that the buttons of the *habits-vestes* and *gilets manches*, as well as the *schako* plates, be of yellow metal and without any regimental numbers;
>
> 2° That all clothing articles be manufactured by the Prefects in the chief towns where the men will be assembled;

French prisoners of war *c.*1814. The silver distinctions of officers and men, like the former National Guard *Cohortes*, are obvious in this period image.

3° That the Prefects also be responsible for acquiring the lining fabric, the drawers, part of the headgear and the leather accoutrements that the governmental stores are incapable of supplying. Bearing in mind the high cost and scarcity of buff leather which can now almost only be purchased from the English […] the Prefects should be given the option to use black cowhide if they are unable to acquire buff leather;

4° That in order to establish uniformity among all parts of the uniform, headdress and leather accoutrements, it is necessary for patterns and estimates to be sent to the chief towns […];

5° That all fabrics, linings, leather accoutrements and headgear left in the stores and that are apt for service, and not earmarked to be sent to the Grande Armée or to Spain, shall be sent to the Prefects to issue to the men;

6° That the value of leather equipment issued from stores will be taken from the 40fr granted by the Decree of 9 March 1811;

7° To authorise me to issue captured Nankin coats and trousers to the troops gathering beyond the Alpes, in Provence or in Languedoc, as well as other captured articles that could be used for their clothing.

The scarcity of woollen fabrics makes this a necessary measure to take.⁹

On 23 February 1813, the War Ministry advised the Council of Administrations of these 22 new line infantry regiments that under the terms of the Decree of 21 February 1813 each soldier had been granted by the Emperor the sum of 16fr to renew their linen shirts

French prisoners of war *c*.1814. The silver distinctions of officers and men like the former National Guard *Cohortes* are obvious in this period image. We know many regiments did not have time to change to copper buttons and other devices before mobilisation as *ligne* regiments.

and underpants, as well as shoes. A War Ministry circular of 23 February 1813 accorded to the regiment funds to purchase:[10]

2,500 dozen yellow metal buttons
56 drums
89m 55 gold lace
201m 60 yellow worsted lace
2,500 *schako* plates and chinscales in copper
400 pairs of grenadiers' epaulettes
400 grenadiers' *aigrettes*
400 *aigrettes* for *voltigeurs*
400 *baudriers* for grenadiers
2,500 numbers or other devices to ornament the *giberne*
400m red worsted lace to decorate *schakos* of the grenadiers
16 *sapeur* axes
16 *sapeurs'* axe cases
16 *sapeur* aprons
16 pairs of *sapeur* gauntlets
8 *voltigeur* cornets
Instruments for the band

The War Ministry ordered 2,500 pairs of shoes to be issued to each of these regiments as well as 20,000fr to cover the uniform costs of these units and the changes associated

Schako of grenadiers of a mobilised National Guard *Cohorte*. The plate, as per regulation, lacks a number. (*Collection de l'Office du Tourisme de Pontarlier. Dépôt au Musée municipal de Pontarlier – France*)

with their new designation.[11] Thanks to that funding, the *havresac* of each soldier was to immediately be completed with appropriate equipment, three shirts, two pairs of shoes (not including the pair covered by the Emperor's generosity) and the *sac à distribution* to be used for carrying rations.

On 23 January, the 135ᵉ *Ligne* received its orders to leave Paris for Mainz. The first battalion left the following day, the second the day after, the third on the 26th and the fourth on the 27th. The first battalion arrived at its destination on 16 February and the three others at one-day intervals.[12]

Five days later, on 28 January, marching orders were given to the 136ᵉ and 144ᵉ *Ligne*. The first set off from Paris and the other from Lyon and both headed off for Mainz. On 8 February, the 138ᵉ *Ligne* left Paris for Mainz, followed by the 139ᵉ *de Ligne* on the 11th and by the 140ᵉ and 141ᵉ Regiments on the 15th, although the latter would have their orders changed the following day to postpone their departure to the end of February or beginning of March. On 22 February, orders were given to many of the cohorts' *dépôt* companies that now belonged to the new line infantry regiments to head to Utrecht in order to be formed into six provisional march battalions for the observation corps of the Elbe.[13] The *dépôt*s of the 144ᵉ to 156ᵉ *Ligne* received the same orders on 27 February.[14]

One of the key questions to ask is how many of the converted National Guard units ever adopted their new unit designations beyond changing buttons and badges? What follows is a review of the 134ᵉ to 156ᵉ *de Ligne*.

135ᵉ *de Ligne*

The 135ᵉ *Regiment d'infanterie de Ligne* was formed on 12 January 1813 and was mobilised two days later, the 14th, in Paris by mobilising the 1ᵉ, 8ᵉ, 9ᵉ, and 11ᵉ *Cohortes*, *Garde Nationale* into a line infantry regiment. We know very little about the dress of the regiment. The *Journal Militaire* reports the decree of 14 March 1812, under article 29 of which the *Garde Nationales* were to be dressed in the clothing and equipment of the recent model and patterns sent to the regiments by the minister for war, i.e., the Bardin regulation for the *ligne* infantry. One difference was that buttons were to be white metal, along with the chinscales, *schako* plates and stripes for corporals and *fourriers*. The decree stated the battalions were to comprise solely of fusiliers and drummers.[15]

The *dépôt* of the regiment on 22 August 1814 held no stocks of cloth whatsoever from which to make uniforms. It did hold 500m of drummers' livery plus 120 brand-new *capotes*, 124 brand-new fusilier *habits*, 303 *gilets manches*, 228 pairs of *pantalons*, 291 *bonnets de police*, 310 pairs of *caleçons*, 280 fusilier *schakos*, 342 *schako* covers, 216 *gibernes* with belts and 508 *houpettes* for fusiliers. Not a single grenadiers' *schako*, *aigrette* or pair of epaulettes were in use or existed in *dépôt*. It is likely the drummers wore Imperial Livery, and the lace in *dépôt* was indeed Imperial Livery but very little had been used given the amount present. Likewise, no *voltigeurs' aigrettes* existed. This leaves us to suppose all ranks were dressed as fusiliers as per the National Guard uniform decree of 1812.[16]

Some of the mobilised National Guard units did have the chance to adopt their new regimental numbers, as this extant *schako* for the 136ᵉ *de Ligne* implies. (*Collection de l'Office du Tourisme de Pontarlier. Dépôt au Musée municipal de Pontarlier – France*)

136ᵉ *de Ligne*

Mobilised in Paris on 26 January 1813, the regiment existed for little over 18 months as on 1 July 1814 the 3ᵉ, 4ᵉ, and 5ᵉ battalions passed to the 12ᵉ *de Ligne*, and the 1ᵉ and 2ᵉ passed to the 55ᵉ *de Ligne*.[17] The regiment was mobilised before the 23 February decree came into force, ergo we wonder if the regiment ever changed its National Guard uniform. We know very little about the regiment's appearance until it was inspected in summer 1814. The men of the regiment from the 1ᵉ battalion were wearing the following clothing and headdress:[18]

Item	In Good Repair	In Need of Repair	Need Replacing	Items due to be replaced	Items missing
Habits	11	24	50	27	48
Vestes	5	9	34	4	108
Pantalons de tricot	9	2	18	4	127
Caleçons	9	2	18	4	127
Capotes	8	15	17	32	88
Bonnets de police	13		11	74	62
Schakos	3	2	19	44	92
Schako covers					160
Grenadier *aigrettes*					12
Voltigeur *aigrettes*					21
Fusilier *houpettes*					127

Chasseur of the National Guard during the 1st Restoration. (*Collection KM*)

The battalion was missing 2 pairs of epaulettes for adjutants and 12 pairs of grenadiers' epaulettes – none were in use. Of interest, 10 drummers' *habits* with livery were needed, along with 41 pairs of gold stripes and 52 pairs of yellow rank stripes. Does this mean that the corporals and *sous-officiers* still used silver and white lace? Very likely. Does this also mean the drummers had no lace and were dressed as fusiliers? Very likely, ergo it seems the 23 February 1813 decree was not enacted in the regiment. The battalion also possessed 283 shirts, just 7 pairs of linen *pantalons de route* – so we wonder if the 127 men with no *pantalons de tricot* were wearing civilian legwear. Also in use were 105 black stocks, 160 pairs of shoes i.e., enough for every man. We also note 42 men had black gaiters and 15 wore grey gaiters, meaning over 100 men had no gaiters at all, and just 51 men had a *sac de peau*.[19]

137ᵉ *de Ligne*

Raised in spring 1813 by the decree of 12 January by mobilising the 2ᵉ, 84ᵉ, 85ᵉ, and 86ᵉ *Cohortes, Garde Nationale*. The 4ᵉ, 5ᵉ and 6ᵉ battalions of the regiment were inspected on 3 August 1814:[20]

Item	In Good Repair	In Need of Repair	Need Replacing	Items due to be replaced	Items missing
Habits	55	2	1		4
Vestes	44	1		11	6
Pantalons de tricot	43		10		9
Caleçons	15			39	8
Capotes	33	5		18	6
Bonnets de police	42			15	5
Schakos	53			5	4
Schako covers					62
Braces					62
Houpettes de fusiliers					40
Aigrettes de grenadier					19
Aigrettes de *Voltigeur*					1
Grenadiers' epaulettes			19		
Adjutants' epaulettes			2		
Gold lace			14		
Yellow worsted lace			14		
Red worsted lace	None				
Drummers' lace					

The *dépôt* held 43m 96 of blue broadcloth, 9m 72 of white broadcloth, 13m 97 of scarlet broadcloth, and 40m white serge.

Grenadier of the National Guard during the 1st Restoration. (*Collection KM*)

The *dépôt* of the regiment was packed to the rafters with clothing, all brand new and waiting to be issued, comprising 253 *capotes*, 438 fusilier *habits*, 481 fusilier *gilets*, 473 pairs of *pantalons de tricot*, 376 *bonnets de police*, 484 pairs of *caleçons*, 797 pairs of braces, 260 fusilier *schakos*, 364 *schako* covers, 1,022 *gibernes* with 831 belts, 688 musket slings, 5 drums and carriages and lastly 759 *houpettes* for fusiliers. Of the leather work and equipment, 566 out of 831 *porte-gibernes* were made from blackened cowhide, accompanied by 632 musket slings made from the same. Not an inch of green cloth or drummers' livery was to be found, or drummers' *habits*, so we guess these men were dressed the same as the rank and file.[21] The decree of 1812 forming the National Guard had allowed Imperial Livery, so we assume its absence in July 1814 was from green clothing being hastily taken from use. An extant *schako* plate for the regiment is white metal and is a National Guard example crudely re-stamped. We suppose the regiment had white metal *schako* fittings.

138ᵉ *de Ligne*

Formed with the decree of 12 January 1813 from the 44ᵉ, 45ᵉ, 46ᵉ, and 64ᵉ *Cohortes, Garde Nationale*. Mobilised in Paris on 1 February 1813, the *dépôt* was established at Cherbourg on 1 April 1813.

Disbanded under the terms of the decree of 23 April 1814, the regiment was wound up at Tours on 1 August 1814, the men and equipment passing to the 27ᵉ *de Ligne*.[22] We wonder if the regiment ever exchanged its National Guard items as it was mobilised before the February decree came into force. Clothing in use at time of disbandment was as follows:[23]

Item	In Good Repair	In Need of Repair	Need Replacing	Items due to be replaced	Items missing
Habits	271	8	17	10	11
Vestes	232	4	8	35	38
Pantalons de tricot	241		7	41	28
Caleçons	241		7	41	28
Capotes	194	6	17	17	83
Bonnets de police	234	14	5	20	44
Schakos	243	21	4	25	24
Schako covers					
Braces					
Houpettes de fusiliers			None		
Aigrettes de grenadier *ou voltigeur*					
Grenadiers' epaulettes					
Sword knots					

Sapeur, drum major and drummers of the National Guard during the 1st Restoration. (*Collection KM*)

The regiment was armed with 292 muskets, of which 35 were dragoon muskets for *voltigeurs*, 48 were foreign and 209 were old model, i.e., the 1777 model that had not been updated in An XI, so too the sabres!

The regimental *dépôt* held huge quantities of brand-new clothing on 1 August 1814, namely 265 *capotes*, 351 *habits*, 455 *gilets manches*, 452 pairs of *pantalons de tricot*, 352 *bonnets de police*, 450 pairs of *caleçons*, 321 pairs of braces, 670 fusilier *schakos*, 28 *schako* covers and 1,366 fusilier *houpettes*. Cloth and materials held included 925m 81 of blue broadcloth, 178m 74 of white broadcloth, 86m 78 of red broadcloth, 2m 94 of green broadcloth, 1,092m 60 white serge, 221m 80 white tricot, 205m 87 linen, 45m of drummers' lace, 19m 56 of red serge, 36m 79 of blue tricot, 26m silver lace, and 17m 10 white linen lace.[24]

The white lace was clearly for corporals' stripes pre-conversion to line infantry, as the National Guard had white lace for corporals as well as white metal buttons.

139ᵉ *de Ligne*

Formed from the 16ᵉ, 17ᵉ, 65ᵉ, and 66ᵉ *Cohortes, Garde Nationale* in Paris on 6 February 1813. It was disbanded at Lisieux on 8 June 1814.[25] As the regiment was mobilised before the 23 February decree on clothing for the former National Guard regiments, we assume its men went to war dressed as National Guardsmen.

We know little about the regiment's appearance. Inspected in September 1814, the men of the 1ᵉ battalion were wearing a mix of rags and clothing in good condition:[26]

Item	In Good Repair	In Need of Repair	Need Replacing	Items due to be replaced	Items missing
Habits	85	3	11	88	
Vestes	55	2	6	57	36
Pantalons de tricot	85	2	7	87	5
Caleçons	18	11		39	60
Capotes	94		5	94	
Bonnets de police	73		26	73	
Schakos	None				

The total lack of *schakos* comes as a surprise! What exactly were the men wearing on their heads? Clearly not every man had a sleeved waistcoat, and a mix of linen *pantalons* and *pantalons de tricot* were in use, just 41 pairs of the former being in existence! A mix of gaiters were in use, 92 pairs of black and 65 of grey. No cloth, materials or clothing was in the *dépôt*, so we can say little else about the regiment's appearance.[27]

140ᵉ de Ligne

Raised in 1813 from the 40ᵉ, 41ᵉ, 42ᵉ, and 43ᵉ *Cohortes, Garde Nationale*. The first four battalions were formed in Paris on 12 February 1813 and the *dépôt* was created at Brest on 21 March 1813, where the regiment was disbanded on 16 September 1814 into the 15ᵉ and 65ᵉ *de Ligne*.²⁸

Arguably the regiment did not adopt the February 1813 decree on clothing as it was mobilised before this was enacted. The only inspection report we have for the regiment that existed for just a matter of months is from September 1814. The *dépôt* of the 1ᵉ and 2ᵉ battalion held 2,176m 86 blue broadcloth, 269m 67 white tricot, 70m of drummers' lace, 82 brand-new fusilier *schakos* with 79 covers, 206 *houpettes*, 2 pairs of adjutants' epaulettes, 0m 5 of 27mm wide gold lace, 70m of 27mm wide red worsted lace, 50m 65 of white worsted lace, which was arguably for rank stripes as the National Guard had white metal buttons and white lace, 736 pairs of chinscales and 107 *schako* plates in yellow metal waiting to be issued. Beyond reasonable doubt, the men were still wearing their National Guard uniforms, and the *schakos* had white metal chinscales and plates. The inspecting general remarks that the King would allow each man a new *habit*, as well as a sabre appropriate to their rank, and that all the old, wounded and infirm National Guardsmen would be released from further military service.²⁹

The 5ᵉ battalion, some 73 men and 16 officers, was disbanded at the end of September 1814, with its clothing mostly worn out or missing. For example, 8 men had no *habit*, and of those in use 7 needed total replacement; 43 men had no *gilets manches* and 10 needed total replacement; 67 men had no *pantalons de tricot*, 33 men no *capote* and 28 *capotes* were life expired. In addition, 8 men had no *schakos* and 38 no *bonnet de police*. No *aigrettes* or epaulettes existed for grenadiers or *voltigeurs*, and as no chamois broadcloth existed, we assume these men were dressed as fusiliers.³⁰

141ᵉ de Ligne

Created on 12 January 1813 from the 37ᵉ, 38ᵉ, 39ᵉ et 61ᵉ *Cohortes*, the regiment was mobilised on 14 February 1813 and disbanded on 23 April 1814.³¹ A report of 23 February 1813 informs us:

> The 141ᵉ is entirely dressed, equipped and armed. The changes associated with the new uniform are not yet finished. Around twelve hundred men are still awaiting the new *schako* plates, chinscales and buttons. The grenadier and *voltigeur* companies have all received their *aigrettes*. However, the epaulettes for the grenadiers and *voltigeurs* of the 3ᵉ and 4ᵉ battalions are still missing but we are working actively to remediate these issues and expect that everything will be resolved in a few days.³²

The *dépôt*, when disbanded into the 43ᵉ *de Ligne*, held an odd assortment of items: 272m 71 of linen, 18 dozen large buttons, 51 dozen small buttons and 11m 20 of red worsted lace. Also, in *dépôt* were a whole cross section of '*items de modèle*', notably 1 *capote*, 1 *habit de tambour*, 1 fusiliers' *gilets manches*, 1 pair of *pantalons de tricot*, 1 *bonnet de police*, 1 pair of *caleçons*, 1 set of braces, 1 fusilier *schako*, 1 *giberne* and belt, 1 *baudrier*, and 1 musket sling. *Dépôt* also held 12 new fusilier *habits*, 10 fusilier *habits* needing repairs and 59 that were life expired, 108 life-expired *capotes*, 73 life-expired fusilier *gilets manches*, 84 worn out *bonnets de police*, and 89 life-expired *schakos*. The *dépôt* held 419 *gibernes* needing repair, accompanied by 419 *giberne* belts needing repairs, 12 *baudriers*, 7 drums and carriages and 2 drummers' aprons, again all needing repairs. The presence of *items de modèle* implies that in theory at least drummers had Imperial Livery.[33]

142ᵉ *de Ligne*

Formed in 1813 from the 5ᵉ, 36ᵉ, 38ᵉ and 61ᵉ *Cohortes Garde Nationale*. Mobilised in Paris on 22 February 1813, the *dépôt* was formed at Tours on 1 April 1813. It was disbanded with the decree of 23 April 1814 into the 36ᵉ *de Ligne*.[34] A report of 23 February 1813 reads:

> The 142ᵉ was organised yesterday. It is stationed at Vaugirard, Issy and the surrounding areas and will be able to parade with the 141ᵉ on Thursday if Your Majesty wishes to see these two regiments. Epaulettes and *aigrettes* will be distributed to the grenadiers and *voltigeurs* of the 1ᵉ and 2ᵉ battalions of the 142ᵉ. The plates, chinscales and buttons will be distributed in a few days.[35]

Inspected in summer 1814, the 391 other ranks of the regiment's 1ᵉ and 2ᵉ battalion were wearing a mix of good clothing and rags. Of the 391 men on parade, 313 men had a *habit* in good condition, 25 *habits* needed repair and 75 men had no *habit*. The vast majority of the regiment had no *gilet manches*, some 323 men, just 60 were in good condition and 10 needed repairs. The *pantalons de tricot* were likewise sparse, just 55 pairs in use, all in good condition – the regiment was drawn up on parade wearing their linen *pantalons*. The *capotes* of the regiment were overall in good condition, some 132 examples, 42 needed repairs and 219 men lacked a *capote*, 129 men had no *schako*, 338 men had no *caleçon* and 135 no *bonnet de police*. Cloth in the *dépôt* included 113m 64 of blue broadcloth, 11m 36 of white broadcloth, 5m 65 of scarlet broadcloth, 2,314m 73 of linen, and oddly 117 chinscale bosses. New clothing in the *dépôt* included a single *capote*, 44 fusilier *habits*, 1 *habit de tambour de modèle*, 1 *gilet de fusilier de modèle*, 23 *bonnets de police*, 509 pairs of *caleçons* – more than enough to make up for the shortfall – 1 fusilier *schako de modèle*, 144 *gibernes*, and 145 *porte-gibernes*. The drummers' *habits* were undeniably green with the Imperial Livery, but had others been made? Other items in the *dépôt* included 1 *capote* needing repairs, 11 fusilier *habits* needing repairs and 41 *habits* to be written off as life expired and old model, as well as 24 blackened cowhide *porte-gibernes*.[36]

143ᵉ de Ligne

Created in 1813 from the 28ᵉ, 29ᵉ, 30ᵉ and 31ᵉ *Cohortes Garde Nationale*. The regiment was mobilised at Puigcerdá in Spain on 1 March 1813. A 6ᵉ battalion was raised on 22 November 1813 at Alès and disbanded with the decree of 23 April 1814.[37]

The regiment we assume adopted the provisions of the 23 February 1813 decree respecting the conversion of National Guard regiments, and in theory had grenadiers decked out in fringed epaulettes, *aigrettes* and grenadier-model *schakos*, and had *voltigeurs* with *aigrettes*. Yet given the regiment was in Spain, we wonder if this act was actually acted upon.

The lack of archive paperwork hampers any firm conclusions that this was actually put into practice. Presumably it was given the March date of mobilisation.

Reviewed on 16 August 1814, we can say nothing beyond the fact the men had *habits-vestes, veste manches, pantalons de tricot, capotes, caleçons, schakos* and *bonnets de police* all made to the Bardin regulation.[38] The regiments *dépôt* held some stocks of cloth and materials, notably 1,066m 43m blue broadcloth, 30m 40 white broadcloth, 0m 12 green broadcloth, 5m 80 chamois broadcloth, 465m white serge, 1,0714m 09 white tricot, and 21m 06 linen. The green broadcloth was no doubt all that remained from making Imperial Livery *habits*. Clothing in the *dépôt* that was brand new included 1 *capote de modèle*, 61 fusilier *habits*, 49 *gilets manches*, 29 pairs of *pantalons de tricot*, 49 *bonnets de police*, 431 pairs of *caleçons* and 35 sets of braces. New equipment included 680 *schako* covers, 184 *gibernes* with 155 belts, 831 musket slings, 141 *houpettes* and 313 *baudriers*. Clothing and equipment needing repairs included 451 *capotes*, 152 *habits*, 48 *gilets manches*, 55 pairs of *pantalons de tricot*, 23 *bonnets de police*, 8 pairs of *caleçons*, 256 fusilier *schakos*, 1,937 *gibernes*, 1,725 *porte-gibernes*, 51 musket slings and 6 *baudriers*.[39]

144ᵉ de Ligne

Raised in 1813 from the 32ᵉ, 33ᵉ, 34ᵉ and 35ᵉ *Cohortes Garde Nationale*, the regiment was mobilised on 14 March 1813 at Metz, and the *dépôt* was formed at Châlons on 19 April 1813. It was disbanded on 23 April 1814.[40] The regiment we assume adopted the provisions of the 23 February 1813 decree respecting the conversion of National Guard regiments, and in theory had grenadiers decked out in fringed epaulettes, *aigrettes* and grenadier-model *schakos*, and had *voltigeurs* with *aigrettes*. Clothing and equipment in use at the time of disbandment comprised:[41]

Item	In Good Repair	In Need of Repair	Need Replacing	Items due to be replaced	Items missing
Habits	36	17	15	1	88
Vestes	5	3	7	1	141
Pantalons de tricot	20	7	12	1	117
Caleçons	12	3	8		136

Item	In Good Repair	In Need of Repair	Need Replacing	Items due to be replaced	Items missing
Capotes	18	3	4		132
Schakos	10	15	23		109
Bonnets de police	19	5	2	13	118
Gibernes	77	2		3	62
Porte-gibernes	77	2		2	62
Baudriers	33				25
Drum carriages		1			
Drums		1			
Musket slings	1				144

Given the lack of regulation musket slings, one can only presume that the muskets had a motley collection of string musket slings. The regiment was a total shambles at the end of the 1814 campaign, yet remarkably the regiment's *dépôt* was filled with clothing ready to be issued, which included 230 fusilier *habits*, 2 drummers' *habits*, 120 *gilets manches*, 409 pairs of *pantalons de tricot*, 262 *bonnets de police*, 146 pairs of *caleçons* and 284 *schako covers*. Cloth in the *dépôt* included:[42]

0m 23 beige broadcloth
332m 26 blue broadcloth
39m 20 of green broadcloth
52m 28 chamois broadcloth
244m 75 white serge
595m 65 of white tricot
266m 64 of linen
112m of drummers' livery

The presence of green broadcloth strongly suggests the regiment had drummers in green *habits* with imperial livery and a minimum of two such *habits* existed. *Dépôt* also held 230 brand-new fusilier *habits*, 120 fusilier *gilets manches*, 409 pairs of *pantalons de tricot*, 262 *bonnets de police*, 146 pairs of *caleçons*, 224 *schako covers*, 23 *gibernes* with 22 belts, and 44 *baudriers*.[43]

145ᵉ de *Ligne*

Levied in 1813 from the 6ᵉ, 23ᵉ, 24ᵉ et 25ᵉ *Cohortes*, the regiment was assigned to the first observation corps of the Rhine. The newly formed regiment was to leave Lyon on 7 February and arrive at Mainz on 8 March 1813, yet the *dépôt* was not raised until 19 March 1813 – ergo the men marched to war wearing their National Guard uniforms. Indeed, on 8 March 1813 the inspector of the 19th Military District at Lyon advised the Minister of War:

> I have the honour of providing the following report regarding the first three battalions of the 145ᵉ *Ligne* Regiment (6ᵉ, 23ᵉ and 24ᵉ Cohortes) on the eve of its departure for Mainz on the 6th of this month. I was unable to have more than 90 men in the grenadier companies because it was not possible to find properly sized men and it is hoped that we will be able to complete these companies with the many conscripts to arrive. The men are of good and fine quality, the clothing and equipment is good, the muskets are old, of different models and it would be good to have the change in time for the campaign. Some of the officers have advised that they will be asking to be retired due to their advanced age or their disabilities, which do not allow them to soldier properly.[44]

As the letter highlights, a large number of officers within the cohorts were physically incapable of going to war, or too old. Despite this, the regiment was mobilised on 19 March 1813 and disbanded on 16 July 1814.[45] As the regiment was mobilised before the February decree on clothing for the former National Guard regiments, we assume it went to war dressed as National Guardsmen.

The only inspection return we can locate for the regiment is for a small detachment taken into the 93ᵉ *de Ligne*, which had 22 *habits* in good condition and 2 needing repairs. The 24 men had no *caleçon*, every man had a pair of *pantalons de tricot*, a *capote*, *schako*, *veste* and only 17 had a *bonnet de police*. No other records exist for the dress of the regiment.[46] The *dépôt* of the regiment was absorbed into the 16ᵉ *de Ligne* and was packed to the rafters with materials and clothing. Cloth held included 185m 84 white broadcloth, 5m 30 green broadcloth for drummers, 5m 24 white tricot, 970m 58 linen for lining, not an inch of drummers' lace, and 21m 50 of red serge – this had one use only, to line the tails of the *habits* of the regimental artillery.

Brand-new clothing and equipment in the *dépôt* included 8 *capotes*, 151 fusilier *habits*, 1 *habit de tambour de modèle*, 181 fusilier *gilets manches*, 198 *bonnets de police*, 68 pairs of underwear, 995 [!] grenadier *schakos* – arguably none were issued based on such a huge number in *dépôt* – 363 fusilier *schakos*, 870 *gibernes*, 866 *giberne* belts, 440 musket slings, 1 sabre belt, 11 drum carriages, 119 *houpettes*, 6 *voltigeur cornets*, which were clearly never issued as none were in use, 16m 80 gold lace 27mm wide, and 158 bayonet scabbards. *Dépôt* also held 4 fusilier *habits* needing repairs, 8 non-regulation drummers' *habits*, 29 pairs of life-expired *pantalons de tricot*, and 26 *bonnets de police* needing disposal. The inspector noted all the *giberne* belts and the musket slings were made from blackened cowhide.[47] The presence of green broadcloth, although none remained as it had all been used making clothing, as well as the inventory of the regiment listing and drummers' *habits* strongly suggests drummers wore green, no doubt with Imperial Livery. It seems every man was dressed as a fusilier, drummers excepted.

146ᵉ de Ligne

Created with the decree of 12 January 1813, the 146ᵉ *Regiment d'infanterie de Ligne* was formed from the 3ᵉ, 76ᵉ, 77ᵉ, and 88ᵉ *Cohortes, Garde Nationale* on 1 February 1813. It was disbanded in September 1813 into the 153ᵉ *de Ligne*.⁴⁸ As the regiment existed for just six months, it is no surprise that at the time of writing no archive paperwork can be located about clothing and equipment. As the regiment was mobilised before the February decree on clothing for the former National Guard regiments, we assume it went to war dressed as National Guardsmen.

147ᵉ de Ligne

Created in 1813 with the decree of 12 January from the 15ᵉ, 71ᵉ, 78ᵉ, and 87ᵉ *Cohortes, Garde Nationale*. It was disbanded in September 1813 into the 154ᵉ de *Ligne*.⁴⁹ Reviewed in February 1813, the grenadiers had no sabres or other distinctions. The *schakos* were of 'low quality', and we note 21m 88 blue broadcloth, 3m 74 red broadcloth and 2m 50 of green broadcloth was purchased for the drummers.⁵⁰

148ᵉ de Ligne

Created with the decree of 12 January 1813 from the 72ᵉ, 73ᵉ, 74ᵉ and 75ᵉ *Cohortes, Garde Nationale*, it was disbanded 17 October 1813 into the 25ᵉ *de Ligne*.⁵¹ No archive paperwork can be located about clothing and equipment.⁵²

149ᵉ de Ligne

Formed in 1813 from the 47ᵉ, 48ᵉ, 49ᵉ and 88ᵉ *Cohortes, Garde Nationale*. Mobilised on 1 March 1813, it was disbanded on 21 July 1814 into the 107ᵉ *de Ligne*.⁵³ The regiment we assume adopted the provisions of the 23 February 1813 decree respecting the conversion of National Guard regiments, and in theory had grenadiers decked out in fringed epaulettes, *aigrettes* and grenadier-model *schakos*, and had *voltigeurs* with yellow *aigrettes*. We cannot prove this.

The clothing of the regiment in summer 1814, as with all the army, was in shreds. A total of 179 *habits* were in good condition, 67 needed repairs, 63 needed immediate disposal and 97 men had no *habits*. Likewise, 214 men out of the 379 men under arms had no *gilets manches*, 205 men had no *pantalons de tricot*, 264 men had no underwear, 91 men had no *capote*, 135 had no *schakos* and 84 men had no *bonnet de police*! The *dépôt* of the 149ᵉ *de Ligne* held on 21 July 1814:⁵⁴

Item	New	Good	To be repaired
Capotes	505	1	1
Grenadiers' *habits*			19
Voltigeurs' habits		Nil	
Fusiliers' *habits*		1	1
Drummers' *habits de modèle*	2		
Grenadiers' *gilets de modèle*	1		
Voltigeurs' gilets de modèle	1		
Pantalons		2	1
Bonnets de police	405	12	
Caleçons	603		
Braces	468		
Grenadiers' *schakos*		Nil	
Fusiliers *schakos*	546	27	
Schako covers	442		
Gibernes	495	94	54
Porte-gibernes	495	110	38
Musket slings	305		
Baudriers		1	
Drums	2		
Drum carriages	2		
Yellow wool lace		9m	
Giberne plates	628		

The regiment had sufficient stocks of clothing to replace most of the items listed as *hors de service*, i.e., they had to be replaced as they were worn out and of no further use. The grenadiers' *gilets manches*, based on the Bardin manuscript illustrations by Vernet, either had red grenade arm badges, or based on the November 1812 decree a scarlet collar and shoulder straps. The *voltigeurs' gilets manches*, based on an extant garment and the same decree, would have had a chamois collar. Grenadiers lacked both *aigrettes* and grenadier-pattern *schakos*, and presumably the epaulettes were counted with the *habits*. The listing of *voltigeur habits*, although none existed at the time of inspection, suggests that at some stage these had existed, and they also seem to also have lacked *aigrettes*. The '*plaque du giberne*' we assume to be the conjoined crowned N. Cloth in the magazine comprised the following:[55]

16m 80 beige broadcloth
1,013m 34 blue broadcloth
167m 58 white broadcloth
99m 08 scarlet broadcloth
0m 50 white serge

919m 83 linen for linings
91m 80 linen for *Caleçons*

The lack of further paperwork means that we cannot make any further observations on the dress of the regiment.

150ᵉ *de Ligne*

Created in 1813 from the 68ᵉ, 69ᵉ, 80ᵉ and 81ᵉ *Cohortes, Garde Nationale*. The war battalions were mobilised on 21 February at Mayence (Mainz) and the *dépôt* battalion was mobilised at Liege on 14 April 1813. It was dissolved into the 29ᵉ *de Ligne*.[56] As the regiment was mobilised before the 23 February decree on clothing for the former National Guard regiments, we assume it went to war dressed as National Guardsmen.

Inspected in August 1814, the grenadiers of the regiment had no epaulettes or *aigrettes*, the *voltigeurs* had no *aigrettes* either. The *dépôt* was well stocked with materials, comprising 182m 80 of beige broadcloth for *capotes*, 311m 86 of white broadcloth, 165m 10 of scarlet broadcloth, 661m 60 of white serge, 1,158m 60 white tricot and not an inch of green or chamois broadcloth or drummers lace existed. Also, in *dépôt*, absolutely brand new and ready to be issued were 3 *capotes*, 67 fusilier *habits*, 73 fusilier *vestes*, 12 pairs of *pantalons de tricot*, 26 *bonnets de police*, 44 pairs of braces, 12 fusilier *schakos*, 16 *gibernes* and belts, 59 musket slings, 6 drums with carriages, and 521 fusilier *houpettes*. Therefore, we assume all ranks wore fusilier *schakos*, fusilier *habits*, and it seems drummers wore the same *habit* as the rank and file with no distinctions whatsoever.[57]

151ᵉ *de Ligne*

Formed in 1813 from the 7ᵉ, 50ᵉ, 51ᵉ and 52ᵉ *Cohortes, Garde Nationale*, the regiment was mobilised on 12 February 1813. The 1ᵉ, 3ᵉ, 4ᵉ and 5ᵉ battalions were taken into the 21ᵉ *de Ligne* on 21 June 1814.[58] As the regiment was mobilised before the February decree on clothing for the former National Guard regiments, we assume it went to war dressed as National Guardsmen. Reviewed on 16 August 1814, the 2ᵉ battalion passed to the 76ᵉ *de Ligne*:[59]

Item	In Good Repair	In Need of Repair	Need Replacing	Items due to be replaced	Items missing
Habits	90	39	15	2	10
Vestes	79	11	49		26
Pantalons de tricot	134	17	36	10	29
Caleçons	55	2	1	50	111
Capotes	83	60	33	50	
Bonnets de police	115	9	72	5	25
Schakos	69	10	39	96	12

The battalion had a solitary *sapeur*, with just one set of equipment in use. To make up for the lack of *pantalons de tricot*, 54 pairs of linen *pantalons de route* were in use. Clearly very few men were lucky enough to have a pair of each; ditto 44 pairs of black gaiters were in use and 206 pairs of grey gaiters.

152ᵉ *de Ligne*

Raised in 1813 from the 18ᵉ, 19ᵉ, 53ᵉ and 54ᵉ *Cohortes*, it was mobilised on 1 March. The regiment, we assume, adopted the provisions of the 23 February 1813 decree respecting the conversion of National Guard regiments, and in theory had grenadiers decked out in fringed epaulettes, *aigrettes* and grenadier-model *schakos*, and had *voltigeurs* with *aigrettes*. When inspected on 16 July 1814, the 3ᵉ, 4ᵉ and 5ᵉ battalions' clothing was in tatters:[60]

Item	In Good Repair	In Need of Repair	Need Replacing	Items due to be replaced	Items missing
Habits	564	46	66	13	149
Vestes	556	33	35	23	191
Pantalons de tricot	539	25	54	27	193
Caleçons	482	48	59	61	188
Capotes	515	56		104	163
Schakos	538	20		83	197
Bonnets de police	603	13	17	53	152
Gibernes	456	50			311
Porte-gibernes	456	50			311
Baudriers	133	20			98
Drum carriages	13				
Drums	13				
Musket slings	45				669

Of note, the grenadiers did not carry sabres, and virtually no man had a musket sling. The 618 men on parade also had 1,769 shirts, 640 pairs of *pantalons de route*, 618 black stocks, 854 pairs of linen socks, 1,236 pairs of shoes, 618 pairs each of grey and black gaiters, 587 *sacs à distribution* and 618 *havresacs*.

The *dépôt* held some stocks of materials, notably 3m 60 of beige broadcloth for *capotes*, 663m 83 of blue broadcloth, 101m 85 of white broadcloth, 63m 60 of scarlet broadcloth, 8m white serge, 1,701m 99 white tricot, 199m 49 of linen for linings, and 992m 33 of linen to make *caleçon*. Ironically, the *dépôt* held stocks of clothing to issue men lacking *habits* and *gilets manches* with brand-new items. It held 88 brand-new fusilier *habits*, and a further 50 'just like new', as well as other brand-new items comprising 11 fusilier *gilets manches*, 626 pairs of *pantalons de tricot*, 72 *bonnets de police*, 543 pairs of *caleçons*, 1,334 pairs of braces, 8 *gibernes*, and a further 236 'like new', 11 *porte-gibernes* and 240 'like new' 50 musket slings and 103 fusilier *houpettes*. The *dépôt* did hold a huge stockpile of

496 brand-new white cockades, 300 *schako* plates, and 156 pairs of chinscales both in white metal.[61] Clearly the regiment was still adorned as National Guardsmen, the men still having white metal *schako* plates and chinscales: or were those in store proof that new yellow metal items had been issued and these were the left-over items? Very likely.

153ᵉ *de Ligne*

Formed in 1813 from the 55ᵉ, 56ᵉ, 57ᵉ and 58ᵉ *Cohortes*, the war battalions were mobilised on 22 February 1813 and the *dépôt* on 1 April 1813. As the regiment was mobilised before the 23 February decree on clothing for the former National Guard regiments, we assume it went to war dressed as National Guardsmen. The 1ᵉ battalion was passed to the new 52ᵉ *de Ligne* on 4 August 1814, the 2ᵉ battalion passed to the 88ᵉ *de Ligne* on 21 July, and the *dépôt* was taken into the 51ᵉ *de Ligne* on 31 July 1814.[62]

Inspected on 1 August 1814, the *dépôt* battalion had 98 *habits* in good condition, 13 needed repairs, 20 were in need of total replacement and 11 men had no *habit*. Indeed, no man had every item of uniform, so men with *habits* clearly wore a *gilet manches* or a *capote*, but not every man had these so the battalion must have presented a very mix and match appearance. Indeed, 12 men had no *gilets manches*, 26 no *pantalons de tricot*, 18 no *capote*, 1 had no *schako* and 21 no *bonnet de police*. *Petit equipment* in use included 269 shirts, 52 pairs of *pantalons de route* made from brown twill, 136 black stocks, 12 pairs of linen stockings, 137 pairs of black gaiters, 96 pairs of linen gaiters, 7 *sacs à distribution*, 139 *sacs de peau*, 184 pairs of shoes and 143 pay books. In the *dépôt* were 30 shirts, 39 pairs of brown twill *pantalons*, 170 black stocks, 161 pairs of socks, 8 pairs of shoes, 176 pairs of black gaiters, 465 pairs of grey gaiters, 200 *sacs de peau*, 41 new fusilier *habits*, 26 *bonnets de police*, 21 pairs of *caleçons*, 57 fusilier *schakos*, 270 *gibernes* and belts, 424 musket slings, 7 sabre belts and 1 drum with carriage among other items. Cloth in the *dépôt* was minimal, holding just 267m of blue broadcloth, 28m scarlet broadcloth and 1,041m of white serge.[63] As no epaulettes, *schakos* or *aigrettes* are listed in *dépôt* or in use by grenadiers, we assume they were dressed as fusiliers, as also we assume the *voltigeurs*, so too drummers: had the regiment changed its uniforms since being raised as National Guard? No. Yellow metal *schako* plates exist, but they are far easier items to replace than buying chamois broadcloth, drummers' livery, green broadcloth etc. Adopt, adapt, improvise was clearly the rationale for converting the National Guardsmen's uniforms into that of regular soldiers.

154ᵉ *de Ligne*

Created in 1813 from the 4ᵉ, 20ᵉ, 21ᵉ and 22ᵉ *Cohortes*. Mobilised at Münster on 9 February 1813, the *dépôt* was created at Besançon on 19 March the same year. The 3ᵉ and 4ᵉ battalions were disbanded into the 1ᵉ and 2ᵉ battalions in June 1813, and new 3ᵉ and 4ᵉ battalions formed in September 1813 when the 147ᵉ *Regiment d'Infanterie de Ligne* was disbanded. The 154ᵉ was disbanded on 1 August into the new 42ᵉ *de Ligne*, the *dépôt* passed to the 36ᵉ *de Ligne* on 4 August 1814.⁶⁴ Of the 333 men under arms, 105 had no *habit*, and of the men with *habits*, just 78 *habits* were in good condition, 86 needed repairs and 71 were listed for immediate replacement! Tellingly, 265 men had no *gilet manches*, 244 had no *pantalons de tricot*, just 7 men had *caleçons*, 125 men had no *capote*, 105 no *schako* and 298 no *bonnet de police*. The *dépôt* held virtually no cloth and clothing, just 572m of serge, 1,699m of linen, 38 new *capotes*, 2 new fusilier *habits*, 1 *habit de tambour de modèle*, 2 *gilets manches*, 2 pairs of *pantalons de tricot*, 741 pairs of *caleçons* – more than enough to make up for the shortfall – 1 grenadier *schako* 'de modèle', which was it seems never copied, 1 fusilier *schako* 'de modèle', 2 new *gibernes* 'de modèle' – presumably *sous-officier* and regular soldier pattern – 290 *gibernes* needing repairs and 74 to be disposed of, 522 fusilier *houpettes*, and remarkably 290 *porte-gibernes*, 68 of which were made from blackened cowhide!⁶⁵

155ᵉ *de Ligne*

Formed in 1813 from the 10ᵉ, 59ᵉ, 60ᵉ and 70ᵉ *Cohortes*. Mobilised on 11 February 1813, before the February decree on clothing for the former National Guard regiments, so we assume it went to war dressed as National Guardsmen. When disbanded in 21 July 1814 into the newly formed 50ᵉ *de Ligne* the regiment had a mere 279 *sous-officiers* and men under arms.

The *dépôt* held stocks of cloth and materials to make new clothing and offers one or two surprises. The cloth held included 10m 75 white broadcloth, 8m 35 scarlet broadcloth, 17m 48 green broadcloth, and 39m 24 red serge, clearly left over from the regimental artillery. No drummers' lace existed, so did the drummers have green *habits* with no lace? More likely all the lace had been used to make drummers' and *cornets*' *habits*. Clothing in the *dépôt* included model examples of a *capote*, grenadier, fusilier, *voltigeur* and drummer *habits* and *gilets manches*! Of ready to use clothing, just 5 fusilier *habits* were held! The *dépôt* did hold 25m of white linen lace for rank distinctions.⁶⁶

156ᵉ *de Ligne*

Formed on 16 February 1813 from the 26ᵉ, 27ᵉ, 82ᵉ et 83ᵉ *Cohortes*, the 1ᵉ battalion was disbanded into the 30ᵉ *de Ligne* on 21 July 1814, the 2ᵉ battalion was taken into the 12ᵉ *de Ligne* on 1 July 1814, with the 3ᵉ, 4ᵉ and 5ᵉ battalions passed to the 20ᵉ *de Ligne* on 16 August 1814.

The remaining 93 men of the 1ᵉ battalion had 81 *habits* in good condition, 7 needing repairs and 4 men had no *habit*. Just 72 *vestes* were in use, ditto 77 pairs of *pantalons de tricot* and *caleçons*, 85 men had a *capote*, 82 men had a *schako* and 50 men a *bonnet de police*. The men also had 296 shirts between them, 71 pairs of linen *pantalons*, 56 black stocks, 255 pairs of shoes, sufficient to give each man 2 pairs, 78 pairs of black gaiters, 73 pairs of grey gaiters: very much a mix and match situation as not enough of either existed for a man to have a pair of both, as with the tricot and line *pantalons*. Just 78 *sacs de peau* were in use.⁶⁷

The 2ᵉ battalion was wearing 77 *habits* in good condition, 76 good *gilets manches*, 77 good pairs of *pantalons de tricot*, 68 pairs of *caleçons*, 53 *capotes* were serviceable and 24 needed repairs. Every man had a *schako* in good condition, and 74 men had a *bonnet de police*. They also had had 235 shirts, 74 pairs of linen *pantalons* for 77 men. Seventy-two men had a black stock, 77 men had black gaiters and 74 had a pair of grey gaiters. Every man had a *sac de peau*. *Dépôt* held 53 brand-new *gibernes* with belts and 27 sabre belts.[68]

The *dépôt* held stocks of cloth and materials:[69]

1,645m 96 beige broadcloth
48m 80 blue broadcloth
106m 64 white broadcloth
110m 80 white serge
534m white tricot
1,784m 88 linen for lining
1,487m linen for *caleçons*
17m 25 drummers' lace

Arguably the drummers' livery was Imperial Livery, and what we are seeing in *dépôt* is all that remained from making new drummers' *habits* in 1813 and perhaps 1814 also. That none was in use is no surprise, as we assume the offending items in use with Imperial Livery were simply dumped in a back corner of the stores with the 1st Restoration. The *dépôt* was literally bursting at the seams with clothing. Brand-new unissued clothing comprised:[70]

740 *capotes*
769 fusilier *habits*
1,003 fusilier *gilets manches*
1,916 pairs of *pantalons de tricot*
287 *bonnets de police*
1,638 pairs of *caleçons*
240 sets of braces
812 fusilier *schakos*
861 schako covers
776 *gibernes*
689 *porte-gibernes*
900 musket slings
541 *houpettes*

The *porte-gibernes* and musket slings were made from blackened cowhide rather than buff, reported the inspector. Nothing existed for grenadiers or *voltigeurs*, whose companies also used drummers, so we suppose the regiment never fully adopted the 1813 provision for conversion from the National Guard.

The National Guard Re-formed

Despite a huge transfer of personnel, this was not the end of the National Guard.

On 3 April 1813, a *senatus-consulte* called for a new levy of 180,000 men. Known as the 'six-class levy', it included 10,000 mounted Guards of Honour to be formed into four cavalry regiments and attached to the Imperial Guard, 90,000 conscripts from the 1814 class and 80,000 from the classes of 1807 to 1812. On 5 April 1813, a decree instructed 49 departments to assist in coastal defence, which were those within the maritime districts of Texel, Antwerp, Cherbourg, Brest, Rochefort and Toulon. These new formations stated that each cohort was to have two companies of grenadiers and two of *chasseurs*, each of 150 men, the men to be aged from 20 to 40.[71] At the same time, new urban *Cohortes* were formed in 19 major towns along the Atlantic coast, each to muster 1,000 men. Out of a total of 167,600 National Guardsmen, the decree called up 16,200 men, which were promptly gathered and formed into provisional regiments before being placed under the orders of senator-generals.[72] From June, they were allocated blackened cowhide leather equipment.

The decree of 17 December 1813 made it clear that the men who filled the position of grenadier, *chasseur* and artillerymen of the urban *Cohortes* were to clothe and equip themselves at their own expense. The *chasseurs* were not required to be uniformed, but were issued a musket, *giberne* and belt and *houpette* for their hat. The men were hastily equipped with antique muskets and pikes taken from store houses across the Empire.[73]

In January 1814, with the National Guard being mobilised to serve alongside the army, a new Parisian National Guard formed replacing the *Garde de Paris*, which had been stood down in 1813 when it transferred to the regular army. The Comte d'Artois was named nominal commander of the National Guard during the restoration. Clothing was codified according to the Bardin regulation, grenadiers being allowed bearskins, *chasseurs* wore the *chapeau*, as did fusiliers and gunners.

During the 100 Days a decree of 10 April obliged all Frenchmen aged 20 to 60 to serve in one of the 326 battalions of National Guard. Such were the shortages that by April 1815, a blue linen smock was considered appropriate uniform. The National Guard was stood down on 20 July 1815.[74]

Chapter 8

Foot Artillery

Behind the glamour of the hussars or *cuirassiers* came the support troops: the artillery, engineers, the wagon drivers. We look at their uniforms here. As with all historical research, we are limited by the paper archives that exist in 2024, which is a very small proportion of the paperwork that was generated in the epoch. What follows is a discussion of the paperwork that the author has been able to track down in various French archives for the dress of 'those who also served'.

The 1ᵉ *Artillerie à Pied* was formed on 25 February 1720, as were the 2ᵉ, 3ᵉ, 4ᵉ and 5ᵉ Regiments. The 6ᵉ was formed on 1 January 1757, the 7ᵉ on 8 December 1762, and the 8ᵉ on 24 October 1784. The 9ᵉ was formed in 1810 from the former Dutch Foot Artillery. In 1799 a company of foot artillery consisted of 93 men:

- 2 captains (one 1st class, and one 2nd class)
- 1 lieutenant *en premier*
- 2 lieutenants *en second*
- 1 sergeant major
- 1 *fourrier*
- 1 *tambour*
- 5 sergeants
- 5 corporals
- 35 gunners, 1st class
- 40 gunners, 2nd class

The gunners were clothed in the same manner as the line infantry – the uniform being blue with scarlet piping and cuff facings. The 1806 clothing tariff allowed the following materials:[1]

Item	Cloth	1806 to 1809	1810 to 1811	Bardin
Habits	Blue broadcloth	1m 88	1m 65	1m 60
	Scarlet broadcloth	0m 11		
	Red *garance* broadcloth		0m11	0m 10
	Scarlet serge	4m 16		
	Red *garance* serge		2m 12	1m 02
	Linen for lining	0m 59	1m 09	1m 40
	Large buttons	11	11	8
	Small buttons	22	22	22

Item	Cloth	1806 to 1809	1810 to 1811	Bardin
Vestes	Blue broadcloth	1m 19	1m 15	0m 98
	Scarlet broadcloth for piping	0m 2		
	White serge	2m 97		
	Linen for lining	0m 30	1m 40	1m 20
	Small buttons	12	12	12
Culottes	Blue tricot	1m 41	1m 50	1m 99
	Linen for lining	1m 09	1m 18	0m 32
Pantalons a Toile	Toile Blondine			1m 55
	Linen for pockets and lining			0m 32
Capotes	Blue broadcloth		2m 40	2m 43
	Linen for lining			

Of interest, the 1806 *habits* had costly scarlet facing and piping, switched in 1810 to the much cheaper madder red. Under Bardin the artillery adopted the same uniform as the line infantry but with the traditional blue and red uniform. Drummers since December 1811 in theory had green *habits* with Imperial Livery. We also see that already by 1810 the gunners' *habits* had short tails!

Bardin

As part of the review of the clothing of the French Army during the Bardin regulation, the dress of the artillery and train came in for sharp criticism:

> Engineers: The new *habit* tested for the sappers and miners doesn't have the necessary ampleness needed for ease of movement of these soldiers, who are larger men than the infantry. Therefore, the quantity of fabric indicated in the specifications is insufficient. The lapels of the miner's jacket should be in black velvet like the sappers. Shoulder straps have been used instead of the woollen epaulette. The *culotte* have been found to be too short and we'd be hard pressed to find two men in each company that could wear them.
>
> The Imperial Corps of Artillery (Foot Artillery): The height of the men, being larger than those of the infantry, coupled with the bad quality of the fabrics used, which frequently shrink when exposed to the rain, make it impossible to construct suitable *habits* with the quantities of cloth allocated under the existing tariff. We have omitted the fabric needed to make the cuff flaps. The cuff piping should be blue and not red. It is necessary that quantities of serge be increased if it is intended to completely line the body and add linen to the front where the hooks and eyes are located […] In order to have *capotes* that are long enough and ample enough

Foot Artillery 197

Officer of foot artillery in full dress c.1805.    Officer of foot artillery in full dress c.1812.

Gunner of foot artillery in full dress during the 100 Days. (*Collection KM*)

to protect the gunners from the cold, and so as not to hinder their movements, additional material is necessary.

Based upon what we have reported above, the uniforms of the army have three drawbacks:

1° There is a shortfall in the amounts of cloth and materials allowed to make the uniforms of all units;

2° The switch from wool to black velvet for certain parts of the proposed uniform, as well as the change from a woollen epaulette to a shoulder strap, for the engineer corps; the change from madder red to scarlet red on the cuffs of the uniform of the line infantry; switch from *bleu-celeste* to *gris-de-fer* for the artillery train and the use of serge instead of bay for the tails of tails of the light infantry;

3° The expected lifespan of most of the articles of the artillery train, as well as the abolition of the annual issue of stable trousers, leads us to the conclusion that it is crucial to adopt a new model of uniform that will give the soldier greater freedom in his movements and dress him well. *Habits* of a larger size, cut longer and with squared *revers* descending over the waistband of the *pantalons* will satisfy these criteria and will better protect the soldier's health. With regards to certain proposed changes, it will not be permissible to allow them without the inconvenience of touching upon the uniform distinctions that certain units have benefitted from for a long time now.[2]

Clearly, all was not well with the uniforms then in use. We also see that the gunners were more robust than their colleagues in the infantry: they had to be. Artillery pieces and munitions are heavy, and humping them about all day needs men with well-developed muscles and a more robust physique.

About artillery uniforms, Bardin states:

Art 1 Clothing
542. Composition of the Clothing
The clothing of the *sous-officiers*, gunners will comprise and be made according to the general dispositions Viz. No. 1 & 2. The clothing of the artillery workers, the companies of armourers and also the *pontoniers* will be the same as the artillery.

543. *Habits-veste*
The *Habits-veste* will conform to the general model viz. No. 4 and will be coloured as indicated in table No. 99 [four lines of text redacted and totally illegible]

544 *Gilet a Manches*
The gilet will conform to the general model Viz. No. 12 and will be cut from blue broadcloth for the artillery and from white broadcloth for the workmen, armourers and *pontoniers*: it will have a collar made from blue broadcloth for the artillery and *pontoniers* and in white broadcloth for the workmen, and in red broadcloth for the armourers. The cuffs will be blue and will fasten in the same manner as the line infantry.

Gunner of foot artillery *c.*1808 by Martinet.

545 Buttons
The buttons are stamped from copper. They will carry two crossed cannon '*en sauter*'.

546 *Pantalons*
The *Pantalons* are made from blue tricot and will conform to the general dispositions No. 18.

547 Underwear
The underwear is of the general model Viz. No. 21.

548 Capote
The capote is made from imperial blue broadcloth and will conform to the general model of the Infantry, Viz. No. 23.

Art 2 Headdress
549
The headdress of the *sous-officiers* and gunners of artillery will be the same as the infantry Viz. no. 30 & 32 and the pompoms will distinguish the companies. The schakos will not differ except for the plate will be of a particular design and conform to the general engraving Viz. No. 549.

Art 3. Distinctive Markings
550
The distinctive marks of the *sous-officiers* will be parallel to those of the infantry.

551 Drummers.
The uniform of the drummers will be the same as conform to the model general of the infantry of the line. Their *gilets* as well their *pantalons* and their *bonnets de police* will be in green broadcloth pantalons and bonnet de police are to be green and will be equipped in the same manner as the infantry. [Line of text illegible]

Art 4 Weapons and Equipment
552 The weapons of the *sous-officiers* and gunners and pontoniers will be a dragoon musket, armourers, pontoniers and artillery workers will comprise a dragoon musket with bayonet as well as a *sabre briquet*. Their equipment is the same as the infantry Viz. No 107 and later.

Art 5 *Petit Equipment*
553 The Petit-Equipment as well as the linen and foot wear of the The first issue for the *sous-officiers* and gunners will be the same as the infantry Viz. No. 169.[3]

In essence, the foot artillery was dressed the same as the line infantry. No mention is made at all about *aigrettes*, fringed epaulettes or grenadier *schakos*. Presumably therefore the artillery lost their symbols of being elite troops.

What follows is a resume of the little that is available in the archives about the dress of the foot artillery.

1ᵉ *Artillerie à Pied*

Disbanded in summer 1814, the men were dressed in *habits*, had both blue tricot *pantalons* and 488 pairs of linen *pantalons*, 1,318 black stocks, 2,279 white stocks, 265 pairs of linen

Officer of foot artillery observed around Dresden in summer 1813. (*Collection KM*)

stockings, 35 pairs of woollen stockings, 2,101 pairs of shoes – two pairs per man – two pairs of black gaiters per man and a pair in linen. We also note 349 water bottles were issued. Stores held 77m 98 of green broadcloth and 7m 92 green tricot: proof positive the drummers had Imperial Livery. In stores were 81 grenadier *schakos*, although none were in use, and 244 pompoms.[4] This is the sum total of our knowledge.

2ᵉ *Artillerie à Pied*

We know nothing of the dress of the regiment until it was disbanded in November 1815, when the men were allowed to take away with themselves the following items:[5] 146 *habits-vestes*, 108 *vestes*, 140 pairs of *pantalons du tricot*, 121 pairs of *caleçons*, 135 *capotes*, 170 *schakos*, 79 *bonnets de police*, 29 *gibernes*, 29 *porte-gibernes*, 37 *baudriers*, 5 drum carriages, 5 drums, 16 muskets with slings, and 36 sabres.

In stores were 0m 53 green broadcloth accompanied by 164m 50 of drummers' lace, hints that the drummers wore green *habits* in 1815. Clothing and equipment in the *dépôt* comprised 495 *houpettes*, 1,068 *schako* covers, 301 pairs of *pantalons de tricot*, 349 pairs of braces, 326 *schakos*, 64 *bonnets de police*, 291 *gibernes* and 1 drum. The gunners had no epaulettes or other indicators of elite troops, which is as we would suppose from the text of the Bardin regulation.[6]

3ᵉ *Artillerie à Pied*

Inspected in September 1814, the regiment had the following items of clothing and equipment in use:[7]

Item	In Good Repair	In Need of Repair	Need Replacing	Items due to be replaced	Items missing
Habits	192	319	476	267	16
Gilets manches	179	284	496	292	19
Pantalons du tricot	175		792	243	60
Caleçons	175		792	243	60
Capotes	516		387	294	73
Bonnets de police	485		499	247	39
Schakos	534		375	332	29
Houpettes					1,270
Schako covers					1,270
Gibernes					1,234
Porte-gibernes					1,234
Baudriers	992	46	38	49	145
Drums	21				
Drum carriages	21				
Musket slings					1,234
Muskets			Nil		
Sabres	954	104	45		
Bayonets			Nil		

Group of engineers and artillerymen noted around Dresden in summer 1813. (*Collection KM*)

The total absence of muskets, *gibernes* and belts comes as a surprise! The *habits* are all described as 'old model', i.e., they are *habits a revers*. In addition, the men were issued 2,867 brand-new shirts, accompanied by 818 pairs of linen *pantalons*, 1,249 black stocks, 1,277 white stocks, 433 pairs of linen socks, 148 pairs woollen stockings, 1,845 pairs of shoes, 1,233 pairs of black worsted gaiters, 895 pairs of grey linen gaiters and 1,252 *havresacs*. Cloth in the *dépôt* included 2,314m 59 blue broadcloth, 128m scarlet broadcloth, 352m 26 white serge, 664m 69 blue tricot, 109m 69 yellow worsted lace and 42m 21 red worsted lace. Clothing in store comprised 8 *gilets* and 210 brand-new *capotes*, 920 *schako* covers and 360 pairs of *pantalons de tricot*. No epaulettes or grenadier *schakos* are mentioned, nor scarlet *aigrettes*: it seems therefore the regiment did not have these items, and used *houpettes de fusilier*, of which stores held 1,077 new examples. We also note in stores 424 dragoon muskets, 805 shirts, 1,314 black stocks, and 624 pairs of *pantalons de route*.[8]

The drummers do not seem to have had green *habits* and Imperial Livery, yet the inspector noted the regiment had not adopted the provisions of 1812, nor those of May 1814, to remove Imperial iconography: does this relate to *schako* plates with eagles rather than Imperial Livery? We guess so. When we look at the regiment in 1815, we find again no grenadier distinctions whatsoever, and not an inch of green broadcloth for drummers' clothing.[9]

4ᵉ *Artillerie à Pied*

At the time of writing very few archive sources can be found for the dress of the regiment. Stores in summer 1814 held 22m of green broadcloth and 44m 85 of Imperial Livery, which was to be burned. Also in stores were 2 grenadier *schakos* and very little else.[10]

5ᵉ *Artillerie à Pied*

At the time of writing the only document we can find that gives us some information on the regiment's clothing is dated 1 September 1814. Stores held 7m 65 green broadcloth, 55m 25 green tricot and 514m 85 of Imperial Livery, which was to burned.[11]

6ᵉ *Artillerie à Pied*

At the time of writing no archive sources concerning the dress of the regiment can be found.

7ᵉ *Artillerie à Pied*

At the time of writing no archive sources concerning the dress of the regiment can be found.

8ᵉ *Artillerie à Pied*

Inspected in September 1814, the regiment had the following items of clothing and equipment in use:[12]

Item	In Good Repair	In Need of Repair	Need Replacing	Items due to be replaced	Items missing
Habits	216	119	172	104	150
Gilets manches	170	53	179	67	302
Pantalons du tricot	259		264	36	271
Caleçons	258		205	26	271
Capotes	204	105	39	96	176
Bonnets de police	192		163	122	289
Schakos	301	152	105	39	173
Houpettes	225		102	19	474
Schako covers	168		11		596
Gibernes	373	240	22	11	50
Porte-gibernes	309	236		11	59
Baudriers	479	134	16	11	107
Drums	20	7	1		1
Drum carriages	23	4	1		1
Musket slings	398	171	1	16	129
Pairs of drumsticks	24	4			1
Muskets		524	70		
Sabres	411	86	173		
Bayonets			Nil		

The *habits* are all described as 'old model', i.e., they are *habits a revers*. In addition, the men were issued 1,920 brand-new shirts, accompanied by 500 pairs of linen *pantalons*, 753 black stocks, 1,401 white stocks, 494 pairs of linen socks, 224 pairs woollen stockings, 1,292 pairs of shoes, 553 pairs of black worsted gaiters, 427 pairs of grey linen gaiters and only 326 *havresacs*: many men lacked this most essential item of equipment.

The *dépôt* held little in the way of materials: 752m 18 red serge to line *habits*, 68m tricot, 30m 22mm wide gold lace, 2m 80 yellow worsted lace 22mm wide for corporals, 45m 04 worsted lace for gunners 1st class and artificers, 47m 64 22mm wide red worsted lace for service chevrons, 76m 10 drummers' livery of the old model, i.e., Imperial Livery, 150 *schako* plates and 215 sets of chinscales. *Dépôt* held 11 *habits* of the new model, i.e., *habits-vestes*.[13]

Moving on to post Waterloo, at the time of disbandment, we know the drummers had green *habits* adorned with Imperial Livery and the regulation green *pantalons de tricot* as stores held 5m 03 green broadcloth, 232m 70 drummers' lace and 27m 86 green tricot. We also note 2m 44 of silver lace for the band's uniforms was in stores. Also in stores were 1 *habit de tambour de modèle*, accompanied by 4 *gilets manches de tambour en drap vert* as well as 4 pairs of drummers' green tricot *pantalons*. No epaulettes, *aigrettes* or grenadier *schakos* existed, which is as one would expect from the Bardin regulation.[14]

9ᵉ *Artillerie à Pied*

Disbanded in September 1814, the contents of the *dépôt* tell us a great deal about the clothing of the regiment. Cloth held comprised 11m 68 blue broadcloth, 25m scarlet broadcloth, 77m 39 green broadcloth, 689m 90 red serge, 338m 50 linen for lining, 4m 80 20mm wide gold lace for *sous-officiers*, 41m 32 22mm wide red lace for service chevrons, 78m 60 drummers' livery marked as old model – here is proof positive of drummers wearing regulation green *habits* with Imperial Livery! The regiment also had 149m 10 black broadcloth for gaiters, which is quite remarkable as in theory broadcloth gaiters were reserved for the *Garde Impériale*! The *dépôt* held 48 old-pattern *habits* that were to be disposed of, 3 brand-new drummers' *habits* and 1 in service, marked as green with Imperial Livery, 3 sleeveless *gilets*, 3 sleeved *gilets* and 1 *gilet* in green broadcloth for drummer. Some 218 brand brand-new pairs of *pantalons de tricot* were also in *dépôt* with 9 *bonnets de police*, 20 *schakos*, 18 *schako covers* and 64 pompoms. The regiment also had 54 pairs of *schako* cords, 215 scarlet sword knots, and 6 pairs of epaulettes for drummers.[15]

With extremely limited archive sources, we cannot draw any firm conclusions about the dress of the foot artillery. More time is needed in the various archives to locate more material, which I am sure exists. Because of the dispersed deployment of the support troops, the inspection returns will be lodged in the relevant army boxes. Perhaps 500 of these boxes await examination by the diligent researcher.

Sapeurs du Genie et Mineur

At the end of 1799 the consular army had only two battalions of *sapeurs due genie* [engineers] and six companies of *mineurs* [miners]. Five battalions of engineers would exist by 1805. From a tariff created in 1806 for the various companies we learn that their *habits* had black velvet collars, *revers* and cuff facings. Piping

Foot artillery or regimental artillery officers' *schako c.* 1813. (*Musée de l'Empéri, Collections du Musée de l'armée, Anciennes collections Jean et Raoul Brunon*)

Engineer noted in summer 1813. (*Collection JM*)   Engineer in full dress *c*.1812.

to the to the collar, *revers* and elsewhere on the *habit* was scarlet, swapped out for madder red in 1810.[16] The elite of all engineer troops were miners, who were largely recruited from civilian life and were created with the decree of 3 October 1801, which formed a single battalion of six companies. A second battalion was created in 21 December 1808. They wore the same uniform, except scarlet epaulettes were used by engineers and yellow by the miners. The bridge builders – *pontoniers* – had scarlet *revers* and collars to their *habits* rather than black velvet.[17]

For the engineer troops Bardin stated that the *habits-vestes* were to have black velvet collar, cuffs and facings, while the tails were lined in red serge. Scarlet epaulettes were officially abolished along with sabres.[18]

The loss of sabres and also red epaulettes for colonels of foot artillery and engineer units was seen as a personal affront. On 17 June 1812, when news reached the artillery

Engineers drawn from life in the first half of 1808. (*Collection KM*)

that they were no longer considered elite troops, the Inspector General of Artillery wrote a furious letter to the Comte de Cessac at the War Ministry demanding their reinstatement.[19] No reply was forthcoming, thus the foot artillery and engineers lost their coveted sabres and epaulettes!

We have been unable to locate any records for the clothing of the engineers: the various boxes for battalions of *genie* make no mention of their clothing.

Foot artillery gunner observed from life in 1808. (*Collection KM*)

Chapter 9

Horse Artillery

In France, the National Assembly recommended the formation of horse artillery on 28 September 1791. Minister of War Narbonne was enthusiastic, and in January 1792 allowed the formation of two companies in Metz. On 17 April, nine more companies were ordered to be created, the remaining seven being formed in May. Each of these companies was armed with six 4-pdr guns and a 6in howitzer. Beside cannon, nearly all horse artilleries in Europe were also equipped with light howitzers. The new horse artillery became an important part of the Revolutionary *levée en masse* armies, and every general in the field clamoured for it, greatly increasing the number of companies. The new artillery arm became operational on 7 February 1794, the existing companies being organised into eight regiments, each having six companies and a *dépôt*. The new regiments were numbered 1 to 8, and were organised during the summer of 1794. The gunners were dressed in fashionable hussar dress, and they rapidly developed a style and panache of their own.

By 1798, the French had two kinds of light artillery: the first was called *Artillerie Légère*, and was armed with 8-pdr field guns. Its crew of eight was seated on the ammunition caisson belonging to the cannon, which was always following the gun. The name of this wagon, *wurst*, is of German origin. The gunners wore dragoon helmets and *chasseur*-style uniforms. The concept was copied directly from contemporary Austrian practice of gunners riding into battle on the *wurst* wagon rather than being taught to ride. It was far cheaper as each company needed fewer horses.

The other kind was called *Artillerie Volante*, armed with 4-pdr field guns. The crew was mounted as in the Prussian system, i.e., every man rode, and each company had designated horse holders. They were dressed as hussars. Tactically the *Artillerie Légère* was used to occupy positions with speed, while the *Artillerie Volante* had to follow the cavalry at all times. In 1801 six regiments of *Artillerie à Cheval* were formed in the Prussian manner; all were dressed now as hussars. In 1814 the number of regiments was reduced to four.

The uniform specifications of 1806 and 1810 were as follows:[1]

Item	Cloth	1806	1810
Dolmans	Blue broadcloth	1m 26	1m 12
	Scarlet broadcloth	0m 03	0m 03
	White serge	2m 67	
	Linen	0m 60	1m 34
	Red leather	1m 16	1m 16
	Round buttons	18	18
	Half round buttons	38	38
	Scarlet worsted square braid	11m	11m
	Scarlet flat worsted braid	9m 52	9m 52

Item	Cloth	1806	1810
Surtouts	Blue broadcloth	1m 68	
	Scarlet broadcloth	0m 12	
	Linen	1m 58	
	Small buttons	10	
Vestes	Blue broadcloth	1m 09	1m 09
	White serge	1m 56	
	Linen for lining	0m 06	1m 30
	Buttons	24	24
Bonnets de police	Blue broadcloth	Made from materials recovered from old clothing	0m 25
	Red		0m 02
	Linen		0m 12
Manteaux	Blue broadcloth	3m 86	
	Green broadcloth		3m 77
Stable coats	Blue broadcloth	Made from the old *surtouts*	1m 19
	Linen		1m 34
	Buttons		24
Portmanteaux	Blue tricot	1m 34	
	Green tricot		0m 89
	Treillis	1m 78	0m 69
	Scarlet lace 0m 22 wide	2m 97	1m 34
	Strong leather	0m 2	0m 2

We remark that green *manteaux* and *portmanteaux* are a total surprise! For undress a sleeved *veste* was issued, and was clearly double-breasted with 24 small buttons. We note from the tariff that the *dolman* had blue cuffs and collar as scarlet broadcloth was provided solely for piping to collar and cuffs. The gunners wore *culottes hongroise* made from blue broadcloth, needing 0m 89 in 1806 and 1m 10 from 1810. They required 0m 40 of linen for linings and 4m 17 of 13mm wide scarlet flat worsted braid, and a small amount of fine leather to make the foot strap.

Bardin

Under Bardin the *dolman* was replaced with a *habit-veste*, and the double-breasted *veste* was replaced by a single-breasted *gilet* with no sleeves. The *manteau* gained sleeves, and reverted back to blue.

Officer and (overleaf) gunner of horse artillery wearing full dress c.1804.

Gunner (and overleaf) of horse artillery wearing full dress *c*.1800. (*Collection KM*)

For the dress of the 'light artillery', the Bardin regulations state the following:[2]

Art 1. Clothing
1215.
The clothing of the *sous-officiers* and gunners will comprise ~~a *habit-veste* made from blue broadcloth, a *gilet* made from blue broadcloth, a *gilet d'ecurie* from blue tricot, blue *culotte hongroise*, a pair of linen underwear, a pair of *pantalons à cheval*~~ will confirm to general dispositions No. 297.

1216
The *habit-veste* will be cut from blue broadcloth and lined in the same, it will be of the same dispositions as the infantry but will not include the piping to the *revers*, to the back and to the pockets placed in the pleats which ^(will be cut to resemble those of the chasseurs à cheval viz. No.) It will be garnished with grenadiers' epaulettes. The cuffs ~~will be cut in points and will be 55mm deep at the edges and measure 95mm in the centre. It will be closed by three small buttons, two set on the cuff and one on the sleeve of the habit. The opening of the sleeve will be 110mm~~ will conform to the dispositions of light troops and conform to model No. 647.^(copy the dispositions for the habit of the chasseurs à cheval.)

1217.
The *gilet* will be made from blue broadcloth and have sleeves, the cuffs will be in ~~red~~ broadcloth ~~and will be 13mm smaller than those of the *habit*~~ of the same form ~~as the *habit*~~ except be 15mm shorter and will confirm to the general dispositions of the infantry viz. No 42, except that it will not have the button at the back to attach the *giberne*.

1218.
The *gilet d'ecurie* is made in blue tricot and will conform to the general model, viz. No. 302.

1219.
The buttons are in yellow metal, solid cast and domed, the same model as the hussards.

1220.
The *culottes hongroise* are made from blue broadcloth and conform to the general model viz. no. 306 and they are garnished with red braid.

1221.
The linen *caleçons* are of the same model as the infantry viz. No. 21.

1222.
The *pantalons à cheval* are in blue tricot and conform to the model No. 3 [illegible].

1223.
The stable trousers conform to model No. 311.

1224.
The braces conform to model No. 22.

Trumpeter of 2ᵉ Horse Artillery following the Markholsheim manuscript by Rousselot. We know almost nothing about how the trumpeters were dressed. (*Collection KM*)

1225.
The sleeved *manteau* will conform to the general model No. 320 and is the same colour as the body of the *habit*.

Art 2. Headdress
1226.
The headdress of the *sous-officiers* and gunners will comprise a *schako* and *bonnet de police*.

1227.
The *schako* is identical to that of the grenadiers of infantry, No. 37.

1228.
The *bonnet de police* is of the general model viz No. 45.

Art 3. Distinctive marks
1229.
The sergeants and *fourriers* will wear the same rank marks as the foot artillery, but will be placed as for the light infantry [viz. No. 660]. The corporals will wear their rank stripes in red wool; which will be conserved also for their chevrons.

1230.
The veterinarians' and the farriers' distinctions will conform to general dispositions No. 326 and 340.

1231.
The trumpeters' distinctions of the light artillery will conform to the general dispositions viz. No. 338 & 339. Their *habits* however will be of the general model No. 83 as for the light cavalry.

Art 4. Armament and Equipment
1232.
The armament of the sergeants, *fourriers*, corporals, gunners, trumpeters and farriers will comprise a light cavalry sabre and a pair of pistols. These items will be delivered from the arsenals of the Empire.

1233.
The equipment of the *sous-officiers* and gunners will compose a *giberne*, a *banderole porte giberne*, a sabre belt, a sabre knot, a pair of boots and a *porte-manteau*.

1234.
The *giberne* will comprise a box or coffret, the wooden block for the cartridges and the two straps for the *bonnet de police*.

1235.
The box of the *giberne* is to be made from blackened cowhide on the flesh side only; the external dimensions will be 220mm wide, by 80mm tall and 60mm deep; it will be made from three main pieces: two pieces for each side, and one for the flap.

Gunner of horse artillery in dull dress c.1808 by Martinet.

Horse artillery *schako* for the 3ᵉ Regiment. (*Musee de l'Armée*)

1236.
The piece forming the body of the coffret will measure 2,200mm by 220mm and will envelop the wooden cartridge box, and it will be sewn to the side pieces, which will be made from strong cowhide, 60mm deep and prolonged in their height to cover the D ring of the *giberne*.

1237.
The piece that covers the junction with the coffret, is the same width as the body but is 75mm deep. It is sewn to the interior of the coffret, parallel to the wood with at least 30 stitches made in strong shoemaker's thread.

1238.
The flap is joined to the piece by a seam and gusset and has a bound edging [jonc]. The joint is made with at least 40 stitches in strong shoemakers' thread. The flap measures 100m tall. It is as wide as the body where the two are sewn together and flares out to 240mm at the widest point.

1239.
Placed on the interior of the coffret are two tabs or 'ears' made from oiled cowhide, each one 130mm long and 50mm wide, destined to cover the wooden cartridge box, and to guarantee that the cartridges are kept dry; these two tabs are fixed to each side piece, and sewn below the envelopment of the D ring.

Gunner of 3ᵉ Horse Artillery drawn from life in summer 1808. (*Collection KM*)

Horse Artillery

1240.

The buckles of the *giberne* are known as D rings; they are forged from copper 5mm in diameter. The smallest radius of the curve is 25mm in height and 40mm at the largest point; the bottom edge is totally encased by the side pieces with a horizontal line of stitching in strong shoemaker's thread.

1241.

The edges of the piece that covers the wood cartridge box are bound over in blackened calf skin that has been oiled; this edging is 15mm wide and it will be sewn with 10 stitches for every 30mm.

1242.

Under the flap, in the centre, 30m from the seam, and placed perpendicular to the seam is the tab, sewn in place with 5 stitches, and will measure 160mm long and 25mm wide, is the piece destined to fasten the *giberne* in the middle to the copper buckle and slide. This buckle is 25mm on each side and is held in place with tab with 15 stitches. It also has a loop made from cow leather, that tab is 25mm wide and 100mm long and folded back on itself and sewn in the middle of the piece that covers the coffret.

1243.

The wooden cartridge box is pierced with 18 holes in proportion to the depth of the wooden box. It is stitched to the part that envelops it with stitches made in strong shoemaker's thread, both front and back.

1244.

The two straps for the *bonnet de police* are the same as for the *giberne* of the infantry and placed the same.

1245.

The *banderolle dit porte-giberne* is composed of two belts of leather 45mm wide.

1246.

The belts forming the large and small part of the *porte-giberne* are the same length as indicated for the dragoons, viz. No. 1048, and are pierced at the extremities in the same way to take the four copper buttons to fix the *porte-giberne* to the *giberne*.

1247.

The large part has the same extremities and form as No. 1049; however, it is 40mm in diameter and 20mm tall.

1248.

The small part is the same as for the dragoons (viz. No. 4050), enveloping at one end the copper buckle garnished with two tongues in iron. The buckle is 55mm by 40mm on the extremity, and 40mm by 30mm inside the copper.

Officer of horse artillery c.1812 wearing undress.

Horse artillery gunner in campaign dress somewhere near Dresden in summer 1813. (*Collection KM*)

1249.
The slide is placed the same distance as in No. 1052 but is 45mm by 10wide with an aperture of 6mm.

1250.
The sabre belt is made in white buff leather; the waistbelt is made from three pieces, a frog for the bayonet, two sword slings with buckles and garnitures in copper.

1251.
The pieces making the waistbelt are 40mm wide, there are three of them: the large side, the central piece and small side.

1252.
The large side is 650mm long. It is garnished with a sliding hook in copper to an S clasp in the same metal, and at one end is a buckle and tongues made from copper

and a loop in buff: this buckle is sewn in place with natural linen thread in two parallel rows of stitching, of at least 8 stitches which comprises the point turned back. The other end of the large side is fixed to a copper ring, stitched in the middle with a double row of stitching from strong natural linen thread, at least 20 stitches per row.

1253.
The middle piece is sewn at one end to the same ring in the same manner; it measures from the ring 180mm until it is joined to the ring at the small side with the same manner of stitching.

1254.
The small side is sewn to the ring, with the same stitching as before. It measures 150mm till it is sewn with a double line of stitches and at least 20 stitches per row, to the slide and ring for the hook on the large side. The slide with the hook destined to receive the S and thus close the waistbelt.

1255.
The bayonet frog is formed from a piece of buff that is folded perpendicularly and one side is stitched down with strong ecru linen thread, with at least 20 stitches. The dimensions of this piece are 155mm tall and 150mm wide. The top edge is joined to the middle part between the two rings with two rows of horizontal stitching of at least 20 stitches in each. ~~The bayonet frog is pierced in the middle of the prolongation~~ in the middle of the side that is folded is sewn a copper buckle 20mm square, with slide, to take the buff slide [of the bayonet scabbard].

1256.
The slings are 35mm wide; the first is 325mm long, one end is fixed to the ring at the front with a double row of stitching, at least 20 stitches in each the end turned back; the other is 700mm long and is sewn to the second ring in the same manner. At the end of the slings are the buckle pieces, they are 160mm long and 35mm wide. At one end of each buckle piece is a sewn a buckle by at least 10 stitches, ends turned back.

1257.
The buckles, hooks, rings and other items are made from copper, and will conform in all regards to those of the waistbelt and sabretache of the hussars viz No. 1363, except on the first ring there will be a hook to hang the sabre from.

1258.
The sword knot is of the general model, viz. No. 366.

1259.
The boots and spurs will conform to the prescribed model for the light cavalry viz. Nos 1372 and 1059.

1260.
The *porte-manteaux* are made from imperial blue broadcloth and will conform to model No. 350.

Art 5. Small equipment, linen and socks
1261.
The small equipment for the *sous-officiers* and gunners will conform to general dispositions No, 372 one [illegible], a pair of black gaiters, three shirts, two stocks, three rabats, two handkerchiefs, two serviettes, two pairs of *manchette du botte*, to conform to the general model 378.

Art 6. Harness
The harness will comprise one saddle, one bridle and its accessories, one head collar, one *schabraque* and surcingle.

1297
The *schabraque* is made from white sheep fleece lined in linen with a festoon on the edge made from imperial blue broadcloth, which when measured around the external edge of *schabraque*, not including the festoon, is 1m 36. The festoon is 1m 450mm on the outside edge and projects from the exterior edge of the *schabraque* by 25mm …

Officers

The most recent regulations for artillery officers prior to Bardin had been issued in 1811 and was to be implemented by 1 February 1813. Less than six months after the 1811 decree, Bardin stated:[3]

Section 2. Light Artillery.
Art 7. Clothing, headdress & C of the officers
1301. The clothing of the officers of light artillery will comprise that as outlined in the general dispositions (Viz. No. 426 to 438). The *manteau, frac,* and redingote are in Imperial Blue superfine broadcloth and will conform to details No. 430 to 435 except the *retroussis* which will carry as small patch in the distinctive colour and a regimental button and will conform to design No. 434.

1302. The headdress will comprise as outlined in the general dispositions (Viz. No. 439 a). The *schako* will conform to that detailed at No. 441 and its fittings will be gilded. The *chapeau* and *bonnet de police* will conform to the decree No. 445 and 448.

1303. The distinctive marks of the officers will conform to the general disposition No. 449; the epaulettes, sabre knot and sword knot will be in gold wire and conform to the details No. 451 to 453.

1304. The footwear of the officers of the light artillery will conform to the general dispositions No. 452 to 458.

1305. The officers are armed according to the general dispositions No. 459, except the sabre which is detailed as follows.

1306. The hilt is gilded and will conform to the engraved design No. 1306. It will be covered by two branches which will support a shield which will be the same as detailed in No. 951.

1307. The blade is 840mm long and is curved, and has one gutter; the talon is 35mm. The gutter is 25mm from the top edge and is 130mm from the point. The blade terminates in *'false tranchent'* 215mm long. The curve of the blade is 50mm. The thickness of the blade at its origin is 6mm in the centre and 10mm at the edge. The length of blade that is blue is 250mm and there is written in gold letters on each side *'Vive L'Empereur'*, see engraved design No. 1307.

1308. The scabbard is polished, garnished with two rings and button in gilded copper. The two rings are placed 250mm apart. The chape is in gilded copper, it measures 270mm in height, see engraved design No. 1308.

1309. The equipment of the officers of light artillery will be as described in the general dispositions Viz. No. 465. The *portmanteau* is in Imperial Blue broadcloth and laced in gold. The waistbelt will be as follows later.

1310. The waistbelt is made in red Moroccan leather, reinforced on the inner face with yellow leather; it is 40mm wide. It has a gold embroidered line on each edge all along its length as well as the slings…the fittings are likewise gilded. The bosettes will conform to engraved design No. 1310.

1311 … the sword sling buckles are gilded with iron tongues and conform to engraved design No. 1311.

1312. The harness of the officers of Light Artillery is composed of a saddle, the curb bridle and accessories, the head collars and *schabraque*. The saddle and all its fitting conform to those of the others ranks.

1321. The *schabraque* is cut from Imperial Blue broadcloth, lined in white and blue stripped ticking. It is garnished around the outside edge, Moroccan leather rubbing patches except by one or two rows of gold lace, their width depending on the rank as defined for the *housses* and *chaperons* of the officers of cavalry Viz No. 977. The length of the *schabraque* from one edge to the end of the point is 1metre 400mm and is 1metre 250mm wide …

1322. The outside edge of the *schabraque* is piped in the distinctive colour and is placed between the body cloth and the lining. The number of the regiment is placed in the angle at the back of the *schabraque*; the letters of the numbers are embroidered in gold and are to be [illegible]mm tall and 10mm wide.

1323. There is placed on each side of the *schabraque* two pieces of green Moroccan leather, cut into the shape of a semi-circle, and will measure along their base 225mm and be 145mm tall.

What follows is a study of the archive documents as they can be located in 2024.

1ᵉ *Artillerie à Cheval*

We have been unable to find earlier inspection returns for the regiment before 1814. The unit was inspected on 16 September 1814:[4]

Item	In service, but due to expire in the next year.	In need of repair	To be replaced in the next year	To be replaced	Items Missing
Habits–vestes	66	30	45	23	14
Culottes hongroise	45		40	45	48
Gilets	37	15	30	58	38
Gilets d'ecurie	60	30	45	29	14
Pantalons à cheval	45		44	34	55
Stable trousers	50		36	40	52
Manteaux	56	36	18	38	20
Bonnets de police	55		40	35	48
Braces	45		40	45	48
Schakos	60	45	20	14	29
Pairs of gloves	50		34	45	49
Pompoms	75		30	45	28
Pairs of epaulettes	60		26	52	40
Schako covers	66		55	33	24

The *dépôt* was sparsely furnished with materials, holding 20m 39 scarlet broadcloth, 25m 72 red serge, 1m 18 blue tricot, 47m 45 22mm wide yellow worsted lace, 7m 70 22mm wide scarlet worsted lace, 62m 50 13mm wide scarlet worsted braid, and 1m 49 *treillis*. The *dépôt* held 6 *habits-vestes* and 8 pairs of *culottes hongroise, hors de service*, along with 7 *schakos* and very little else. Trumpeters clearly wore blue *habits*.

The *dépôt* held the following items on 26 October 1815:[5]

835m 76 blue broadcloth
52m 54 scarlet broadcloth
57m 07 green broadcloth
886m 42 blue tricot
11m 63 green tricot
248m 23 linen for linings

64m 68 linen for *caleçons*
102m 38 *treillis* for *portmanteaux* and stable trousers
414m 44 scarlet serge
24 leather hides
19m 75 gold lace
68m yellow wool lace
588m 70 scarlet soutache
776m 59 scarlet flat lace
80m 57 red leather for lining *dolmans*
40¾ hides of black basane
1 *habits-veste de modèle*
1 *gilet sans manches de modèle*
1 *gilet d'ecurie de modèle*
1 *bonnet de police de modèle*
162 pairs of braces
1 *schakos de modèle*
1 *pompom de modèle*
38 waistbelts
116 sword knots
2 saddles
1 saddle blanket
2 *schabraques*

The big stockpile of green cloth strongly indicates that trumpeters had green clothing at Waterloo. Only 5m 95 of green broadcloth and 23m 18 of green tricot was held in the *dépôt* in August 1814. No trumpeters' livery existed in 1814 or 1815, so we ask were the *habits* devoid of lace? Arguably no, as we assume that whatever stocks that existed it had entirely been used to make trumpeters' clothing.

The clothing worn by the men on 26 October 1815 was as follows:[6]

Item	Good conduction	In need of repair	To be replaced
Habits-vestes	24	33	83
Gilets sans manches	49	8	45
Culottes hongroise	38		56
Gilets d'ecurie	41	18	47
Pantalons a cheval	38	31	53
Stable trousers	1		38
Caleçons	45		40
Manteaux a manches	112	12	8
Bonnets de police	84		38
Schakos	106		67

Item	Good conduction	In need of repair	To be replaced
Gibernes	136	2	4
Waistbelts	134	4	5
Sword knots	115		4
Portmanteaux	92	34	10
Pairs of gloves	44		33
Pairs of boots	39		76
Sabres	127	4	2
Item	Good conduction	In need of repair	To be replaced
Pistols	9		
Saddles complete, bridle complete	87	57	8
Saddle blankets	123	16	13
Schabraques	86	45	24

It is clear that the regiment had adopted Bardin regulation in 1813, and wore it until the regiment was passed into Royalist service after Waterloo. No mention is made of *aigrettes* or epaulettes: were they counted with the *habits* and *schakos*? Possibly as the regulation *schako* was the grenadier type.

2ᵉ *Artillerie à Cheval*

At the time of writing, minimal archive documents can be found for the regiment's clothing. At the time of the summer 1814 review:[7]

Item	In service, but due to expire in the next year	In need of repair	To be replaced in the next year	To be replaced	Items Missing	Observations
Dolmans	77	24	40	5		The *dolmans* are to be suppressed as soon as replacement clothing is provided.
Habits-vestes	84	49	8	51	202	
Vestes	47	40	64	21	232	
Pantalons à cheval	69	51	89	31	154	
Culottes hongroise	28	41	69	35	226	
Caleçons	34	15	32	1	292	
Stable trousers	58	29	53	1	253	
Capote manteaux	137	63	2	15	177	
Schakos	157	56	14		87	
Schako covers						
Bonnets de police	49	56	90	23	176	
Gilets d'ecurie	25	76	77	33	183	

Also in use were 44 pairs of epaulettes, with 337 pairs needed. In stores was 1 *habit de trompette de modèle*, which it seems was never copied, and 40 *surtouts*, which we assume were *kinski*-style garments.

3ᵉ *Artillerie à Cheval*

In August 1814, the regiment possessed the following items of clothing:⁸

Item	In service, but due to expire in the next year	In need of repair	To be replaced in the next year	To be replaced	Items Missing	Observations
Habits-vestes	92	12	14	15	107	This does not include the items carried away by the men who have been discharged, namely 213 *habits, gilets, pantalons*, pairs of underwear, *schakos*, and *bonnets de police*
Vestes	61	5	14	18	142	
Pantalons à cheval	38	17	6	46	143	
Culottes hongroise	45	3	52	8	132	
Caleçons	34	7	11	7	191	
Stable trousers	40	2	23	8	167	
Capote manteaux	100	3	13	7	117	
Schakos	182	13	32	13		
Schako covers	69	10	32	13	116	
Bonnets de police	56	3	6	13	162	
Gilets d'ecurie	35	16	1	1	187	

The clothing was in terrible condition, and not enough of any one item existed to give each man his regulation issue! Interestingly, no epaulettes are listed. The following items of equipment were in use:⁹

Item	In service, but due to expire in the next year	In need of repair	To be replaced in the next year	To be replaced	Items short
Gibernes	185	16			39
Porte-gibernes	192	9			39
Waistbelts	175	25			40
Sword knots	47	27			166
Pairs of boots	42	12	46	26	114
Pairs of gloves					240
Pairs of epaulettes					240
pompoms					240
trumpets		6			7

In the regiment's magazine were the following items:[10]

Item	New	To be Repaired	To be replaced	Total	Observations
Pantalons à cheval	241				
Culottes hongroise	131				
Caleçons	305				
Braces	337				
Gibernes		80			
Porte-gibernes		80			
Waistbelts		80			
Gilets d'ecurie	1				*effect de modèle*

Cloth in the *dépôt* was as follows:[11]

0m beige broadcloth for *manteaux*
706m 90 blue broadcloth
34m 20 white broadcloth
0m scarlet broadcloth
0m green broadcloth

The beige cloth was likely used to make *manteaux capote*. The white broadcloth is problematical – was it used to make white sleeveless *vestes* to be worn under the *habit*? In theory these were blue, but in this case they were white. At disbandment in September 1815 in the regiment's magazine were the following items:[12]

Item	New	To be Repaired	To be replaced	Total
Habits	102	21	12	145
Gilets	60	24	3	87
Gilets d'ecurie	26	45	33	104
Culottes hongroise	96	12	4	112
Pantalons à cheval	34	67	41	142
Caleçons		25	65	90
Stable trousers		26	58	84
Bonnets de police	84	31	3	118
Manteaux	50	44	28	122
Schakos	96	41	8	145
Schako covers	81		17	98
Braces	77		62	139
Porte-Manteaux	104	27	12	143
Pairs of boots	83	26	27	136
Gibernes	130	15		145

Item	New	To be Repaired	To be replaced	Total
Waistbelts	145			145
Sword knots	101	14	10	125
Pairs of gloves	44		52	96
Pairs of epaulettes	92	23	16	136
Pompoms	131		3	134
Trumpets	4			6
Sabres	134	11		145
Pistols	NIL			

When the regiment was wound up on 31 August 1815, the *dépôt* contained the following amount of materials:[13]

37m 31 blue wool cloth
77m 10 blue tricot
0m 23 linen lining
0m 60 lace 22mm wide
1m 10 lace for *culottes hongroise*
5 dozen large buttons

Compared to the stock of cloth that existed in 1814, clearly, the blue cloth in the *dépôt* had been almost entirely used, along with the limited stock of scarlet, to make new *habits* and other items of clothing. As no green cloth existed in 1814 and none in 1815, and not an inch of Imperial Livery, it is clear that neither the 3e or 6e Horse Artillery never had green trumpeters' *habits* with Imperial Livery. They were dressed in blue *habits-vestes* like the gunners. We can only assume the regiment gained epaulettes during the 1st Restoration and they were counted with the *habits* as none are mentioned in use or in stores. But, of course, their absence may well be because the regiment never received any in 1814 or the 100 Days.

4e *Artillerie à Cheval*

At the time of writing, almost no archive material can be located relating to the dress of the regiment. Sent to the regiment's companies serving in Spain, among other items despatched in June 1812 were 20 *dolmans*, 40 *habits-kinski*, 12 *schakos* and 19 sabre knots.[14] At the time of the summer 1814 review the trumpeters had Imperial Livery, while stores held 1m 27 green broadcloth and 11m 14 green tricot, all that was left from making their clothing. Stores held 24 pairs of grenadier epaulettes and 85 sword knots.[15]

5e *Artillerie à Cheval*

We have been unable to find earlier inspection returns for the regiment before 1814. The unit was inspected on 16 September 1814:[16]

Item	In service, but due to expire in the next year	In need of repair	To be replaced in the next year	To be replaced	Items Missing
Habits-vestes	71	21	30	16	20
Culottes hongroise	35		39	45	39
Gilets sans manches	38	29	39	27	25
Gilets d'ecurie	70	15	32	20	21
Pantalons à cheval	31		49	38	40
Stable trousers	86		17	20	35
Manteaux	102				56
Bonnets de police	70		38		50
Braces	35		39	48	36
Schakos	100			30	28
Pairs of gloves	110				48
Pompoms	100			30	28
Pairs of epaulettes	71		51	16	20

The *dépôt* was sparsely furnished with materials, 5m 95 green broadcloth for trumpeters' *habits*, 0m 33 blue tricot, 23m 18 green tricot for trumpeter's *culottes hongroise*, 62m 97 linen for lining, 22m 57 22mm wide scarlet worsted lace, 719m 20 of 13mm wide scarlet worsted braid, 1m 40 gold lace, 776m 59 scarlet square worsted braid, 80m 57 scarlet leather, 40 hides of black leather, and 19m 15 *treillis*. The square worsted braid we suppose had been used to make *dolmans* and or braided waistcoats prior to 1813. *Dépôt* held 48 brand-new pairs of stable trousers and 214 pairs of *caleçons*, 25 *manteaux* needing repairs and 9 life-expired *manteaux*, a single *schako* cover and very little else. We assume the trumpeters wore green *habits*, but no Imperial Livery existed, which we supposed was entirely used to make trumpeters' *habits*.[17]

6ᵉ *Artillerie à Cheval*

In August 1814, the regiment possessed the following items of clothing:[18]

Item	In service, but due to expire in the next year	In need of repair	To be replaced in the next year	To be replaced	Items Missing
Habits-vestes	104	22	7	8	29
Gilets en drap	98	17	4		51
Pantalons à cheval	62	5	25	5	73
Culottes hongroise	84	3	41	1	41
Caleçons	84	3	41	1	41
Stable trousers	23		41	2	104
Capote manteaux	138	9			23
Schakos	119	5	8	4	34

Item	In service, but due to expire in the next year	In need of repair	To be replaced in the next year	To be replaced	Items Missing
Schako covers	43			40	87
Bonnets de police	99		7	2	62
Gilets d'ecurie	91	3	7	4	65

The clothing was in terrible condition, not enough of any one item existed to give each man his regulation issue! Interestingly no epaulettes are listed. The following items of equipment were in use:[19]

Item	In service, but due to expire in the next year.	In need of repair	To be replaced in the next year	To be replaced	Items short
Gibernes	161	2			7
Porte-gibernes	161	2			7
Waistbelts	144	6			20
Sword knots	108				62
Pairs of boots	91	9	9	21	40
Pairs of gloves	70		1	21	78
Pairs of epaulettes	134				36
Pompoms	132			4	34
trumpets	Nil				

For the 171 men on parade just 93 saddles in good condition existed, accompanied by 75 sheepskin *schabraques*. The men were also issued 534 shirts, 217 black stocks, 364 white stocks, 202 pairs of woollen stockings, and 147 pairs of shoes. In the regiment's magazine were the following items:[20]

Item	New	To be Repaired	To be replaced	Total
Manteaux capote	10	78		88
Habits	29			29
Gilets	6			6
Pantalons à cheval	Nil			
Culottes hongroise	59			59
Stable trousers	87			87
Bonnets de police	52			52
Caleçons	236			236
Braces	14			14
Schakos	Nil			
Gibernes	45	29		74
Porte-gibernes	45	29		74

Item	New	To be Repaired	To be replaced	Total
Waistbelts	83	36		119
Yellow wool lace		91m		
Red wool lace 27mm wide		7m 18		
Gold lace		12m		
Linen lace		20m 60		
Pairs of boots	40			40
Vestes d'écurie	17			17
Porte-manteaux	46			46

Also in stores were 1 *habit de cannonier de modèle*, 1 *habit de trompette de modèle*, 1 *capote-manteau de modèle*, 1 pair *pantalon a cheval de modèle*, 1 *gilet de modèle*, 1 *veste d'écurie de modèle*, 1 pair of boots de *modèle* and 1 *porte-manteau de modèle*. Clearly the regiment had received its 'Bardin start-up kit'.

Also lodged in *dépôt* were two *dolmans* for trumpeters: were these green with Imperial Livery or were they in reversed colours? Here is proof that at the least the 6e had green trumpeters' *habits*, but also it seems *dolmans* in use side by side! The 1815 inspection returns make no mention of these three garments: they were presumably burned or sold to rag merchants. The regiment's *manteaux-capotes* were made from beige broadcloth. *Dépôt* held no cloth bar 7m 78 of blue broadcloth and 698m 80 of linen.

Chapter 10
Artillery Train

The second great innovation of the Consular years, after the introduction of *cuirassiers*, was the militarisation of the artillery train.

The desire to maximise returns led the contractors to neglect the drivers, their animals and equipment. To preserve their investment in material and horses, the contractors frequently un-hitched their guns and abandoned them at the first shot, leaving the gunners to manhandle the guns about the battlefield as best they could. At the Battle of Novi (15 August 1799) the contractors abandoned their guns and caissons in a defile during a retreat, which led to the rearguard being cut off from its line of retreat. Upon becoming First Consul, Napoléon militarised the artillery train with the decree of 3 January 1800. Under the terms of the decree each battalion had an elite company, usually attached to the mounted, or horse, artillery, the remaining three companies being attached to foot artillery, *dépôt* and parks.

Each battalion was a self-contained, cohesive organisation permanently attached to an artillery regiment. The decree of 20 September 1804 increased the number of battalions to 10. An 11e battalion was formed on 3 October 1805, two more were formed on 22 August 1808 for service in Spain, two more were formed for the Army of Germany and a 14[e] battalion was formed from former Dutch troops on 18 April 1810. Each battalion was doubled in wartime, with 28 battalions at such times, 14 of which carried the original battalion number and were classed as 'principal' battalion. The doubled battalions were named '*bis*'. At the time of the Restoration, the artillery train was reduced to eight squadrons.

An idea of how the men were dressed can be gleaned from archive sources, albeit exceptionally rare. The 1[e] bataillon was reviewed at Lille on 4 November 1804. The men were dressed in 476 *habits* worn with a sleeveless *gilet*, 570 *capotes*, 408 stable coats, 234 pairs of *culottes de peau* and 230 pairs of stable trousers. Headdress was a *chapeau*, 504 being in use, the men wore dragoon boots, carried a *sabre briquet* from a cowhide waistbelt

Portrait of an officer of an artillery train *c*.1810. (*Photograph and Collection of Bertrand Malvaux*)

and were issued a *giberne* and *banderole*. Clothing was made from *gris de fer* and *bleu nationales* broadcloth. For stable duties, 500 pairs of shoes were issued.[1] A document from *1 Vendémiaire An 14* (23 September 1805) tells us a *habit* required 1m 22 of gris de fer broadcloth, and they had *bleu impériale revers*, collars and cuffs, and the *veste* was also *gris de fer*. The *habit* needed 9 large buttons and 14 small, the *veste* needed 20 and was clearly double-breasted.[2]

In March 1810, the artillery train was ordered to abandon *gris de fer*, and adopt *bleu celeste*, the new model of *habit* requiring 1m 34 of broadcloth. The *revers*, cuffs and collar were still *bleu impériale*, but now needed 0m 17 of broadcloth rather than 0m 20. The *revers* were now piped white. Each *habit* needed 17 large buttons and six small. Legwear in both cases were *culottes de peau*, with *schakos* adopted from 1810 in lieu of the *chapeau*.[3]

Reviewed on 1 May 1811, the inspector noted the 1^e, 2^e, 3^e, 4e and 5^e companies of the 8^e battalion had 5 officers, 500 men and 791 horses. He notes the men were issued *capotes*, *habits-vestes*, stable coats, white sleeveless *vestes*, *culottes de peau*, stable trousers, *bonnets de police*, and dragoon boots with spurs. Headdress was a *schako*. Trumpeters wore reverse colour *frac* – a single-breasted garment with short tails. The companies were missing *petit-bidons*, *marmites*, shovels and pickaxes. The inspector also noted that many old soldiers had bought from their pay grey broadcloth *surculottes* with leather reinforcement to the inner leg. As most men lacked *culottes de peau*, these items were in constant use for both parade, stable duties and training. Many men were also missing a stable coat, and nearly all the driving harnesses were irreparable or missing. The 9^e battalion was also in a similar poor condition: for 608 other-ranks, 420 *habits*, *vestes* and stable coats needed immediate replacement, 25 men had no *giberne* and belt, 82 had no sabre belt, 117 sabres were missing, and no man had a pistol. The harness was also in deplorable condition, with 217 saddles needing to be replaced, 84 bridles and 200 collars. The 8^e battalion (bis) with some 11 officers, 395 men and 498 horses, was also in very poor shape: 72 men had no boots, while 16 were lacking a *giberne* and belt. We note the men carried *sabre briquets* and not An XI light cavalry sabres.[4]

Equipment Train

Another innovation came on 26 March 1807, when eight battalions of equipment train were formed, each having 9 officers' mounts, 37 riding horses, 576 draught horses, 32 pack horses to move 144 wagons (136 caissons, 4 wagons, 4 field forges), a total of 72 officers' mounts, 296 riding horses, 4,608 draught horses and 256 pack horses. All were to be purchased by the *Department Remonte* under the guidance of General Bourcier. The uniform finally adopted on 6 April 1807 had been published in the *Journal Militaire* of 28 May, in the collection of instructions addressed to Inspectors of Reviews, for the administration and accountability of the battalions. This very succinct description restricts itself to indicating the differences in colour that should exist between the equipment train and the artillery train:

Officer and driver of an artillery train drawn from life in summer 1808. (*Collection KM*)

The uniforms of the equipment train battalions will be the same as those of the artillery train with the exception that their lapels, cuffs, collar, piping and lining will be chestnut brown. That portion of the plume which is dark blue shall be chestnut brown. Buttons to be white with the battalion number. The coat turnbacks will be fastened back by a star of the same material as the coat for the men and silver for the officers.[5]

In 1808 the price for an equipment train draught horse was fixed at 360 to 380fr, mules for use in place of pack horses at 450–600fr a piece. The men wore the same basic uniform as the artillery train but with chestnut brown replacing the dark blue facings. In a letter of 26 March 1808, the Emperor wished the equipment train to be:

> armed with a carbine or a musketoon, with a pair of pistols in the holsters, and a sabre; that the *maréchaux-des-logis* and brigadiers will have the same weapons. The soldiers will have a carbine, a shoulder-belt and a sabre. Consult General Bourcier as to the most convenient manner of carrying the carbines, perhaps like the *chasseurs*? I suppose that they have been given a general uniform with distinctions on the buttons.[6]

A letter from Count Daru, addressed on 10 April, 1808 to the Director-in-Chief, adds:

> This armament necessitates hussar-type *gibernes*, *giberne* belts and *banderole porte mousquetons* […][7]

Archive documentation for the clothing and equipment of the equipment train has so far proved highly elusive.

In a convoy destined for the troops stationed in Spain that left Bayonne on 15 March 1812, a number of packages destined for the 13ᵉ battalion contained 33 saddle cloths and as many pairs of *chaperons* (holster covers certainly intended for the *sous-officiers* and corporals), *schako* linings, wool covers, shirts, buttons, pairs of linen gaiters, shoes, 7 shoulder belts, 13 *giberne* belts, 10 *gibernes* and 5 colpacks (presumably for the battalion's trumpeters). The equipment train was reclothed in Bardin-regulation items from 1813.[8]

On 14 March 1809 auxiliary battalions of equipment train were created; dressed in brown *habits* with *bleu de ciel* facings. The *habit* was of the dragoon pattern but brown with *bleu de ciel* revers, collars, cuffs, and lined in brown serge. The stable coat was also brown, worn with a *bleu de ciel veste*. Legwear was a pair of *culottes de peau*, dragoon boots and dragoon harness. They were armed with a *chasseur*-pattern sabre and had the *chapeaux* as headdress.[9]

On 23 March 1809, the equipment train organisation was changed with the addition of a train for the engineers, which was to be administered by the artillery train. It was to consist of two battalions. The first battalion was based at Metz, and the second at Alexandria in Italy. On the 25th of the same month, six companies were formed to transport siege artillery and equipment in Spain. They were dressed in the same manner as the equipment train but with black facings.

Bardin

A major change with the artillery and equipment change was the 'switch from *bleu-celeste* to *gris-de-fer*' for the base colour of the uniform.[10] For the dress of the artillery and equipment train, Bardin states:

Artillery Train

Equipment train officers, drivers and trumpeter observed by Suhr in Hamburg sometime in 1808.

242 Napoleon's Light Infantry and Artillery

Artillery Train

Article 1. Clothing
1085. Composition of the clothing.
The clothing of the *sous-officiers* and soldiers of the artillery train, equipment train and engineer train, as well as of regimental drivers, will comprise those laid out in section No. 297.

1086.
The *habit-veste* will be made from iron grey broadcloth of the general model used by the infantry No. 4, but the sleeves will be cut larger. The collar, the revers and cuffs will be the colour indicated in item No. 1018 [blue for artillery train, chestnut brown for equipment train, black velvet for engineer train – ed]. There will be placed on the tails a crowned N cut from cloth the same colour as the *habit*.

1087.
The sleeved *gilet* will be in iron grey broadcloth and conform to the general model, vis. No. 2. The collar, the cuffs and shoulder straps will be in the distinctive colour viz. No. 1018.

1088.
The *gilet d'ecurie* will be cut from iron grey tricot and will conform to the general model No. 302.

1089.
The buttons will conform as prescribed to the table No. 1018.

1090.
The *culottes de peau* will conform to the general model No. 303.

1091.
The *manteau* will be cut from iron grey broadcloth and conform to the general model No. 315.

Article 2. Headdress
1092.
The headdress of the *sous-officiers* and soldiers of the artillery train, engineer train and equipment train will comprise a *schako* and a *bonnet de police*.

1093
The *schako* ~~will be the same as that of the light infantry, garnished with a white metal plate and chinscales also in white metal~~ will conform to the general model. Viz. No. 2.

1094
The *bonnet de police* is made from iron grey broadcloth and will conform to the general model viz. No. 45.

Art 3. Distinctive Marks
1095
The distinctive marks of the *sous-officiers*, corporals will be in silver and white and will be identical to the general dispositions viz. No. 336 & 337. The distinctions of the veterinarians and farriers will conform to No. 326 and No. 340.

1096
The distinctions of trumpeters will conform to the prescribed general dispositions viz. No. 338 & 339. Their *habit* will conform to description No. 83 [line infantry].

Art 4. Armament and Equipment
1097.
The armament of corporals and soldiers will comprise a *mousqueton* ~~with bayonet~~, a *sabre briquet*. The *sous-officiers*, *fourriers* will be armed with a pair of cavalry pistols and a dragoon sabre. The sergeants, *fourriers*, trumpeters and farriers will not carry a *mousqueton*.

Artillery Train

1098.
The equipment will be the same as for dragoons, except that the waistbelt will be replaced by a *baudrier* and also a *porte-mousqueton*.

1099.
The ^{banderole}-*porte-mousqueton* will conform ~~to the general dispositions viz. No. 367~~ to general dispositions viz. No. 365.

1100.
The *ceinturon-baudrier* will be used to carry the *sabre briquet*. The *sous-officiers* will carry a dragoon sabre from the waistbelt of that arm. The *ceinturon-baudrier* will comprise one waistbelt and a sabre frog.

1101.
The waistbelt comprises three pieces, two rings and a button in copper and will conform to the waistbelt of the *carabiniers* viz. No. 807.

1102.
In lieu of the slings, the waistbelt is adapted to have a sabre frog. The frog will be of the same dimensions as the infantry *baudrier*, and garnished with the same buckle to receive the leather tab on the sabre scabbard. It will be attached to the waistbelt by two pieces in buff leather 65mm wide; one 110mm long and will be placed perpendicular and will be fixed to the first of the two rings, and will be folded back on its self 30mm … the other will be placed diagonally, and will be 240mm long and fixed to the rearmost ring of the waistbelt and will measure on the inside from the frog to the ring 130mm …

Art 5. Small Equipment
1103.
The items of small equipment, linen and footwear will conform to that prescribed in general disposition No. 372.

Art 6. Harness
1105.
The horse harness for the *sous-officiers* will be the same as for the dragoons, except that the *housse* will be the same colour as the cloth of the *habit* ~~and bordered with white lace~~, and a *schabraque* bordered with a festoon in the same colour as the habit.[11]

The campaign dress *surculottes* were made from grey broadcloth. Judging by the published tariff, the men recruited into each arm of the train were graded on height and physical build: the tallest and most robust men went to the *train d'artillerie*, whose *habit* needed 1m 47 of *gris de fer* broadcloth. The smallest men went to the *train d'genie*, whose *habit* needed 1m 43 of *gris de fer* broadcloth, with those of medium build and height being sent to the equipment train.[12] At the time of writing, no archive sources for the dress of the artillery or equipment train can be located.

Chapter 11

Guides and Other Troops

As well as relying on regular troops, the French relied on specialists to carry out essential courier and route-marking duties. We list these units in date of formation. Two companies of the 21ᵉ *Dragons* were attached to headquarters during the 1805 campaign: 36 men including 2 officers were with headquarters, and 34 men, including 2 officers, were detached at Augsburg to escort prisoners and guard hospitals. In addition, four troopers were orderlies for Marshal Berthier, in his capacity as Minister for War – a post he held from 18 May 1804 through to 9 August 1807 – and five more dragoons acted as camp guards to his headquarters. Another four dragoons were attached to the staff.[1] This unit was replaced by the Guides du Berthier.

Compagnie des Guides Interprètes du Premier Consul

The Guide Interpreters of the Army of England, as the unit became known, was formed from Irish, Scottish and English radicals exiled in Paris and Hamburg to act as interpreters – and what else we ask? – on 5 October 1803. A well-known secret agent, and former British soldier, Colonel Robert Dupont d'Erval was named Inspector General of the *Compagnie des Guides Interprètes du Premier Consul*. Created from among the men who were under d'Erval's orders, we find Henry Jones. He arrived in France from Hamburg in July 1791. He joined the National Guard of Nantes in June 1793, and served in the Vendée in the rank of sergeant major. He participated in the massacres that took place during winter 1793 into 1794 during the 'pacification' of the Vendée in 1794 and fought at Quiberon in 1795. As a member of the Legion Nantaise, he fought 'for the republic and to maintain equality'.[2] By summer 1803 he had been convalescing in Belgium and was lodging in the home of M. Fould, a banker of 1004 rue Bergere Paris.[3] Judging by the episodes of the war he participated in, one could say he was a war criminal by the time his service in that theatre ended in 1796. A comrade of Jones was the future General Cambronne. Both had happily drowned babies in wells, raped women and committed all manner of atrocities, with apparent, relish. Serving alongside Jones were Peter MaCarthy, Charles Max, Peter Bovay and Jack Descourtes: all former British soldiers. Others included Charles Weber, a former soldier of the Austrian Army; Adrian Paridaans, a former officer in the Batavian army during the revolution of 1786; Francis Moffatt a United Irishman from County Wicklow;[4] Peter Murray, a United Irishman exile from Dublin;[5] and Joseph Murray, a student from Edinburgh.[6] John Deal, born in Bingley, West Yorkshire, in August 1773, having previously served in the 11ᵉ *Chasseurs*, transferred to the new unit. We also find Pierre Brennan, an escaped slave, from Saint Domingo, who had lived in Philadelphia for 12 years before enlisting on 29 March

Guides and Other Troops 247

The guide interpreters of the Army of England were dressed in a hybrid dragoon and hussar manner.

Guide of Berthier drawn from life in summer 1808. (*A.S.K. Brown Library*)

1804.⁷ Louis Welling asked to join up on 12 October 1803, and stated to Marshal Brune and Dupont d'Erval that despite being a subject of the British Crown, he loved France and had a hatred of England. He was well known to the French secret police for his outspoken political views in support of Jacobinism.⁸ Another man was M. Jachonon of 17 rue Bertin Poiree, Paris, who informed d'Erval that he was aged 42 and had lived for 35 years in England, had English customs and habits, and could be of use as a translator, and 'to gather intelligence about enemies of the government'.⁹ Every man in the unit had military experience, perfect English and could pass as 'English'. How far d'Erval utilised his men in his clandestine operations in England and Ireland we cannot say, as he was a spy master par excellence for Napoléon. For more on Dupont see the author's *French Invasions of Britain and Ireland 1792–1815*, also published by Frontline.

On 22 October 1803, the dress of the unit was to be a green dragoon *habit* with white metal buttons, the headdress to be a *chapeau*.¹⁰ On 19 February 1804, the unit's colonel, Robert Dupont d'Erval, reported that its uniform was to be a dragoon *habit*, a white *veste*, *culottes de peau* and *bottes a l'americaine*. Armament was to be a dragoon sabre and waistbelt. Officers and *sous-officiers* had a hussar saddle and green broadcloth *schabraque*, while troopers rode on a dragoon saddle with *housse* and *chaperons*.¹¹

Inspected on 19 September 1805, the unit mustered just 40 men, commanded by two sergeants. Dupont d'Erval reported that many men had been reluctantly taken into the *Guides* that could not speak fluent English, in favour of Dutch or German, and that the unit had been attached to the staff of Marshal Brun. Dupont d'Erval furthermore informed the Minister of War that because many of the men were short, the regulation-issue dragoon boots and *culottes de peau* were unsuitable, and proposed changing the dress to hussar uniforms.¹² We do not know if this was carried out.

Still based in Boulogne in new year 1806, on 4 February, Dupont d'Erval wrote to Marshal Berthier in his capacity as Minister of War, asking for clothing and equipment to be provided, particularly sabres, adding he had discharged three men for being troublemakers and the unit needed horses.¹³ Just over a week later, Marshal Brune was asked to recruit new men into the unit from among Irish émigrés in France who were at least 35 years old, knew English habits and customs, could speak fluent English, translate, and provide topographical information on Ireland and England.¹⁴ The lack of horses was still a major point of issue, and on 7 June Brune requested 35 mounts be sent.¹⁵

The unit was dressed in a green dragoon *habit* with scarlet collar, *revers*, cuffs and lining with white metal buttons, white veste, *culottes de peau*, cavalry boots and dragoon helmet.

Under the decree of 15 January 1807, the unit was increased to squadron strength, with many men coming into the unit who could speak Dutch, Polish or German, with many of the English speakers taking their ticket of leave. At the same time, the opportunity was taken for the unit to be totally reclothed, being issued: 162 *habits*, 81 *vestes manches*, 100 pairs of *culottes de peau*, 5 *capotes*, 191 pairs of shoes, 54 shirts, 231 pairs of boots and 241 *manteaux*.¹⁶ It was brought up to strength of a full squadron of two companies with an intake of 48 troopers from 16 dragoon *dépôts* in Germany on 16 May 1807.¹⁷ The unit was stood down on 17 October 1808, and the remaining men passed to the *Compagnie d'Elite du Grand Quartier General*.¹⁸

Officer of *Compagnie d'Elite du Grande Quartier General* drawn from life in August 1813. (*Collection and Photograph of Bertrand Malvaux*)

Potentially a 2nd company trooper of *Compagnie d'Elite du Grande Quartier General* drawn from life in August 1813. (*Collection KM*)

Potentially an elite company trooper of *Compagnie d'Elite du Grande Quartier General* drawn from life in August 1813. (*Collection KM*)

Guides du Berthier

In May 1807 Marshal Kellerman was charged with the formation of the unit. He was ordered to instruct each of the 24 dragoon regiments to send two men, to be armed and equipped as guides.[19] The new unit was to be dressed in an all-green *surtout*, with white cuffs in undress with white epaulettes and *aiguilette*, and a colpack. In full dress a dragoon *habit* was worn: it had green collar piped green, green *revers* piped green, white cuff facings and flaps, and was lined in green serge. In addition, the men were issued with *culottes de peau* and dragoon pattern boots.[20] A document from August 1807 concerning the death of Gabriel Grumet gives us a snapshot about the unit's uniform. MAT No. 169 Gabriel Grumet was admitted to the Guides du Berthier on 4 June 1807 with the rank of sergeant major. He was born on 25 December 1784, son of Francis Grumet and Marie Bourgmarie, at Saint Rembert in the department of the l'Oise. He died of fever at Bullestadt, Saxony, on 12 August 1807.[21] The following effects were found in his room when he died:[22]

- 1 redingote in green broadcloth
- 1 uniform *surtout* in green broadcloth
- 1 pair of *pantalons* in green broadcloth
- 1 pair of *pantalons à cheval* in green broadcloth
- 1 pair of *pantalons* in nankeen
- 1 pair of *culottes* made from white casimire
- 2 white waistcoats
- 3 shirts
- 5 neck cloths
- 3 pairs of white stockings
- 1 white cotton night cap
- 1 white silk taffeta neck cloth
- 1 green broadcloth *portmanteaux*
- 1 *chapeau*
- 1 pair of boots
- 1 sabre
- 1 pair of spurs and straps
- 1 leather portfolio

The letter detailing his death is dated eight o'clock on the night of 12 August 1808, yet his regimental record states his death to have occurred on 12 August 1807. Which is correct? We assume he was also issued a colpack, *aiguilettes* and had dragoon-pattern harness. We are not seeing of course what he was wearing when he died, or was buried in.

Guides du General en Chef

Created in January 1804 in Hanover, the unit had 58 other ranks and 3 officers. It was dressed in scarlet *habits-long*, with scarlet collar, and *bleu de ciel* collar, cuffs and piping as well as lining. The *vestes* and *culottes* were also *bleu de ciel*. Headdress was to be a colpack.[23]

Guides à Cheval du Marechal Massena

Formed on 26 October 1805 to act as couriers and headquarters guards to the Army of Italy, it drew its manpower from the 3ᵉ, 5ᵉ, 14ᵉ, 23ᵉ and 29ᵉ *Chasseurs à Cheval* and 23ᵉ, 24ᵉ, 29ᵉ *Dragons*. It totalled 5 officers, and 67 other ranks; 88 men when we include the *sous-*

officiers, corporals and trumpeters.[24] A document dated 1 March 1806 from the colonels of the 23ᵉ and 24ᵉ *Dragons* agrees that for the *Guides* they would purchase:[25]

1,004m green broadcloth
1,309m white broadcloth
38m scarlet broadcloth
1,226m linen
336m *treillis*
206m white serge
903m scarlet serge
84 *houpettes de bonnet*
100 pairs of epaulettes
84 pairs of *culottes de peau*
84 bearskins
84 pairs of boots
84 complete saddles

The production cost of the clothing was 206fr and the materials came to 10,627fr. Ostensibly, this list of items describes a green dragoon *habit* with scarlet facings, lined in scarlet, a white *veste*, a white *manteau*, a pair of *culottes de peau*, and we also assume green stable coat and *bonnet de police*. The *housse* and *portmanteaux* were no doubt green. Given the 23ᵉ and 24ᵉ *Dragons* used cloth *chaperons*, we assume these were used, as the saddlery was provided by the parent dragoon regiments. The *houpette de bonnet* we assume to be feather plumes, the colour of which we are ignorant. Likewise, we are ignorant of the colour of the bearskin cords and epaulette, which notably does not include an *aiguilette*. Some artists have reconstructed this uniform to have white epaulettes, bearskin cord, white *aiguilette* and white *revers* to the *habit* based on the Otto MS depicting this unit. However, given that the *Guides du Massena* did not leave Italy, it was impossible for these men to be observed in the Paris region in winter 1807. We cannot provide a definite answer that provides an accurate depiction of this ephemeral unit.

Guides de la Grande Armée

Created on 19 October 1805 to escort couriers and to guard headquarters, Marshal Kellerman was to form the unit in Strasbourg to muster 482 officers and men from 16 dragoon *dépôts*. General Bourcier, the senior inspector general of dragoons, was named as titular commander. It became the Guide Interpreters of the Army of Germany: the men had to be fluent German speakers, and were to act as way markers, collect intelligence, organise lodgings and billets, and escort army couriers. They wore dragoon *habits* with red collars, with white *revers*, red cuffs and lining, while white *aiguilettes* and epaulettes were worn at the shoulder. The headdress was a *chapeau*.[26]

Compagnie d'Elite du Grand Quartier General

The *Guides du Berthier* were assembled at Versailles, with the remaining Guide Interpreters of the Army of England and Guide Interpreters of the Army of Germany, on 1 October 1808, and these units were amalgamated to become the *Compagnie d'Elite du Grand Quartier General*. Its function was for its men to act as orderlies, couriers and camp guards. It headed to Spain with the Emperor to take part in his short campaign. It remained in Spain when Berthier and the Emperor left in new year 1809. On 26 May 1809 the unit was expanded, with 7 men being sent from the 1^e to 26^e *Dragons*, and men from the 1^e, 5^e and 7^e *Chasseurs* as well as the 3^e, 5^e, 7^e, and 8^e *Hussards*.[27] The unit remained in Spain until the end of 1811.

From its formation the regiment was dressed and equipped as dragoons. A report of 30 November 1811 comments that the company, which had been on continuous service in Spain since 1808, was ordered to Bayonne to be re-equipped before heading back to France. The letter concludes that the regiment was dressed in a green *habit*, with white *revers* and cuff flaps, red cuff facings, collar, piping and tail lining, while white epaulettes and *aiguilettes* appeared at the shoulder. Headdress was a bearskin. In order to harmonise with Berthier's Neuchâtel Battalion, the *habits* of the regiment were to be replaced and have chamois facings, and the bearskins were to be replaced by dragoon helmets.[28] On 4 February 1812 the minister of war ordered that lancer helmets were to be adopted and grey broadcloth *surculottes* were to be worn on campaign in lieu of costly *culottes de peau*.[29] Reviewed on 8 February 1812, 'the major part of the clothing is very bad, the equipment is in need of repairing, the weapons are in acceptable condition except the bayonet scabbards […] the men's boots are good enough …'[30] The company was lost in Russia and we do not know if it received new clothing.

The unit was recreated in time for the Dresden campaign of 1813; based on a painting dated August 1813, the company took back its old uniform. Recruited back to strength in February 1814, the unit was disbanded in June 1814, by which time it had adopted Bardin-regulation clothing:[31]

Item		In good condition	In need of repair	To be Written off	Total	Observations
Habits		6		28	34	Twenty-eight of these were furnished directly by the guides themselves, 34 pairs of *pantalons* were purchased by the guides
Vestes en drap blanc						
Culottes de peau						
Stable trousers						
Epaulettes	*Sous-officier*	1		4	5	
	Guide	6		20	26	
Aiguilettes	*Sous-officier*	1		4	5	
	Guide	6		20	6	
Manteaux		5		23	28	
Grey broadcloth *pantalons*				34	34	
Gilets d'ecurie				34	34	

Item						Notes
Bonnets de police				34	34	Twenty-eight of these were furnished directly by the guides themselves, 34 pairs of pantalons were purchased by the guides
Helmets	10			20	30	
Gauntlets						
Gibernes and belts	12		12		24	
Banderole-porte carabines	24				24	
Waistbelts	29				29	
Sabre knots				29	29	
Portmanteaux	2		2	26	30	
Pairs of boots					30	
Pairs of spurs						
Trumpets and cords				3	3	

Clearly the men who joined the outfit provided their own clothing! The distinctions for *the sous-officiers* were, we assume, in white and silver or indeed crimson and silver like the *sous-officiers* of the Polish Lancers of the Imperial Guard. The horses were equipped with dragoon saddles, 30 green *housses* with white lace, and 30 sheepskin *schabraques* with a red festoon. The company was armed with 24 carbines, 24 bayonets, 30 sabres and 24 pistols. In the action at Fere Champenoise on 25 March 1814, the unit lost 40 out of the 71 men, 28 horses, 38 *housses*, 19 saddle blankets, 9 bridles, 12 *schabraques*, 19 headcollars and 10 surcingles.[32] The unit was finally disbanded on 14 July 1814 when the detachments from the garrison of Magdeburg were admitted into the new *Dragons du Roi*.[33]

Infirmiers

As well as soldiers, the army needed surgeons, doctors and medics. On 13 April 1809, 10 companies of *infirmiers* to man military hospitals were created. The decree of 22 April 1812 noted the *infirmiers* were issued a single-breasted brown *capote*, a sleeve *veste*, *pantalons*, shoes and a *chapeau*.[34]

Of the 10 companies, five served in Vienna, two in Italy and three were sent to Spain. An 11ᵉ Compagnie was formed on 29 November 1811 and took part in the Russian campaign. Each company was increased in April 1810 to comprise one *centenier*, 1 *sous-centenier*, 1 sergeant major, 5 sergeants, 1 fourrier, 10 first-class infirmiers, 96 infirmiers, and 8 workmen, which included a tailor, shoemaker, a cutler and a cook.

When we look at the various companies serving in Spain in 1811, the infirmier companies were brigaded with the equipment train – a company of wagon drivers and a company of workmen – and *gendarmes*. The 6ᵉ Compagnie was with the Army of the Centre – 2 officers, 46 men, 48 horses; and the 5ᵉ Compagnie was with the Army of Aragón – 2 officers, 163 men, 170 horses. The 6ᵉ Compagnie was also attached to a company of muleteers, whose task it was to transport food and munitions to places where carts and waggons could not travel.[35] The 4ᵉ Compagnie – 3 officers, 186 men and 199 horses – was with the Army of Portugal.[36] We do not have a record of these companies being allocated vehicles, but it seems every man was mounted.

Infirmier and surgeon wearing hypothetical Bardin-regulation clothing. *Infirmiers* were attached to hospitals and never part of regimental establishment.

About clothing we record:[37]

Item	Colour	Designation	Cloth amount
Broadcloth 119/100	Red brown	For body of the *habit*	1m 20
		For *bonnet de police*	0m 26
	Madder red	For collar, cuffs and revers of the *habit*	0m 18
	White	For piping the collar, *revers*, and shoulder straps	0m 7
		For the front of the *veste manches*	1m 22
	Beige	For the greatcoat	2m 50

Tricot	Red Brown	For *pantalons*	2m 09
Item	Colour	Designation	Cloth amount
Serge	White	For lining skirts of the *habit*	1m 70
Linen 104/100	For lining the sleeves, pockets and back of the *habit*		1m 09
	For lining the *veste manches*		1m 40
	For lining the knee, pockets, front fall and button stands of the *pantalons*		1m 18
	For lining the sleeves, pockets and button stands of the *capote*		1m 15
	For lining the head band of the *bonnet de police*		0m 12
Buttons	Large for *habit*		2
	Small for *revers* and cuffs of *habit*		16
	Small for *veste manches*		8

We see the men's *habit* had no pockets to the rear, we assume the *revers* had just 12 buttons not the expected 14, the cuffs had no flaps and fastened with a single button, and a single button appeared at the shoulder. Legwear were tricot *pantalons*, worn we assume with gaiters and shoes.

This rather conflicts with the evidence of the men actually being mounted: therefore, was this uniform worn in Spain? Was it ever adopted?

What we must stress is that these men – ostensibly all mounted, which makes us ask how they evacuated wounded or if they ever did – were never part of a regimental organisation, contrary to the prevailing mythos about them. No detailed records for these units can be found at the time of writing in the French Army Archives.

It is also worth noting that the overwhelming evidence from archive documents is that ambulances were incredibly rare. They were attached to regiments with battalion artillery from 1811. They were driven not by the fictitious brown-clad *infirmiers*, but by members of the regimental artillery who, overwhelmingly, were dressed as infantrymen. The ambulances themselves are described as caissons, i.e., it is highly unlikely that they actually carried wounded.

When we look at the 100 Days' campaign we find that ambulances were driven by the men from the *train des equipage*.[38]

Vivandières

Every battalion of *ligne* and *légère*, or squadron of cavalry, had two *vivandières* (canteen keepers) and two washerwomen. What they wore is the subject of much debate. For the 21ᵉ *Ligne* that debate is easily answered by regimental documents that detail the dress of these women. Catherine Maygnet died in May 1811 and her effects were valued and sold off by the regiment. In ready cash she had the substantial sum of over 3,500fr! She possessed a four-wheeled cart valued at 45fr drawn by two horses valued together at 317fr.

Inside the cart was a bed with blankets valued at 13fr 75. Her personal possessions included:

> A top hat with plume, 4 'shirts', two dresses made from printed Indian cotton, a set of clothes *déshabillé*[39] two corsets, two *jupon*,[40] a double-breasted redingote made in blue broadcloth valued at 14fr 45, a black taffeta apron, a shawl, five handkerchiefs, a pair of stockings, a pair of cotton stockings and four pieces of spun cotton, a yard and a half of lace, two pairs of ladies' shoes, two embroidered pockets, a leather belt, hip pad (?),[41] a man's blue broadcloth greatcoat, a gold hunter case watch with key on a necklace worth 110fr, two gold pocket watches, a pair of earrings and ring in gold worth 132fr, a serving spoon, four eating spoons, two forks and three coffee spoons in silver, totalling 44fr 38. Net value 4,294fr 12.

Vivandier of the Imperial Guard by Martiner.

It seems the clothing she was wearing or that was directly associated with her and not packed away in the cart were two dresses, one of which was in printed India cotton, a woman's greatcoat made from heavy broadcloth, a woman's redingote, a petticoat and corset, two shawls, one white one 'colourful', four kerchiefs, two *gilets*,[42] five pairs of stockings, a hurdy-gurdy mounted with silver, two clarinets and two small flutes – it paints a wonderful picture of her part of the camp, which would have been full of music, wine, women and song. We also note a man's shirt and a small *portmanteau* in bad condition containing a copy of her birth certificate, her patent or licence, and an extract of her marriage certificate. The regimental archive reports that these items

> were sold on the 15th of September of the given year for a sum of 38fr and 75 cents. The two shirts as well as the *gilet* (?) and the watch were given to the children on the orders of Mr le colonel, signed Guillaume (rest of name illegible). Signed, members of the council of administration of the 21eme *regiment d'infanterie de Ligne*.

Her stock in trade had been sold for 600fr. In total, the estate was worth 4,572fr 87: her four children, presumably sons, were passed 4,352fr 87 and her daughter 204fr. The cotton

Vivandier mounted on pack saddle wearing fashionable civilian clothing. (*Collection KM*)

Vivandier or washerwoman carrying her young child on campaign, possibly with her unofficial husband. (*Collection KM*)

dresses described as '*indienne*' were not necessarily from India: it was simply printed (or 'painted') with floral designs of Indian origin. *Indiennes* were produced in great quantities in France; among the most famous centres of production were Mulhouse, Jouy-en-Josas near Paris, and several cities in Provence – the famous Provençal prints. (The printing of traditional fabrics in Provence is still known as *indiennage*.) While obviously more expensive than plain or striped/checked fabrics, they were still much cheaper than authentic printed chintzes from India. This archive is a unique and wonderful snapshot of what these women were wearing.[43]

Notes

Chapter 1
1. Etienne Alexandre Bardin (1808) *Manuel d'infanterie, ou Résumé de tous les règlements, décrets, usages, renseignements concernant l'infanterie, dans lequel se trouve renfermé tout ce que doivent savoir les sergents et caporaux.* Chez Magimel Paris, p.335.
2. Bibliothèque Musée de l'Armée, Manuscripts and printed books, Volume 1 du projet de règlement sur l'habillement du major Bardin, pp.27–31.
3. Terry Crowdy (2015) Napoleon's *Infantry Hand Book*, Pen & Sword Barnsley, p.127.
4. Crowdy (2015), pp.121–127.
5. Bardin (1808), p.335.
6. Anon (1779) *Reglement Arête pour le Roi pour l'habillement et l'equipment des ses troupes.* Imprimerie Royale Paris, p.5.
7. Paul Lindsay Dawson (2019) *Napoleon's Imperial Guard Uniforms and Equipment: The Infantry*, Barnsley, Frontline, pp.37–38.
8. Dawson (2019), p.45.
9. Ibid.

Chapter 2
1. Service Historique du Armée de Terre (hereafter SHDDT) Xs 525 PROJET D'ARRÊTÉ Relatif à l'habillement des troupes pour l'an X.
2. SHDDT Xb 349 *4e régiment d'infanterie de la Ligne.* Rapport 28 Messidor An XIII.
3. Bibliothèque Musée de l'Armée. Fonds Rousselot.
4. SHDDT Xs 525 Décret 18 Fevrier 1808.
5. Bibliothèque Musée de l'Armée. Fonds Rousselot. Infanterie de la *Ligne*. Extraits *Journal Militaire*.
6. SHDDT Xs 525 Projet de décret portant création d'une compagnie de voltigeurs dans chaque bataillon des régiments d'infanterie de *Ligne*.
7. SHDDT Xs 525. Circulaire 27 10bre 1807.
8. SHDDT Xb 585 *10e régiment d'infanterie Légère* 1811 a 1815. Dossier 1818. Rapport 29 Octobre 1820.
9. SHDDT Xs 526 Circulaire 27 Xbre 1807.
10. SHDDT Xs 525 Circulaire 7 8bre 1807.
11. SHDDT Xb 477 65e *de Ligne* 1812 à 1815, Dossier 1815. Rapport 13 Avril 1819.
12. SHDDT Xs 525 Décret 18 Fevrier 1808.
13. SHDDT Xs 525 Décret 18 Fevrier 1808.
14. Honoré Hugues Berriat (1812) *Législation militaire* Paris: A Alexandrie Vol. 3, pp.235–236.
15. SHDDT Xs 525 Circulaire 31 Octobre 1809.
16. SHDDT Xs 528.
17. Archives Nationales de France (hereafter AN) AF/IV/1179.
18. Etienne Alexandre Bardin (1813) *Mémorial de l'officier d'infanterie.* Chez Magimel Paris. 2 Volumes. Vol. 2, p.695.
19. SHDDT Xs 528 décret 30 Decembre 1811.
20. Bardin (1813) vol 2, p.703.

Chapter 3

1. Bibliothèque Musée de l'Armée, Manuscripts and printed books, Volume 1 du projet de règlement sur l'habillement du major Bardin, pp.1–20.
2. Ibid., p.44.
3. Ibid., p.9.
4. Ibid., p.48.
5. Crowdy (2015), p.79.
6. Bibliothèque Musée de l'Armée, Manuscripts and printed books, Volume 1 du projet de règlement sur l'habillement du major Bardin, p.29.
7. Ibid., p.22.
8. Ibid., p.25.
9. Planche 22 du volume IV du projet de règlement sur l'habillement du major Bardin.
10. Bibliothèque Musée de l'Armée, Manuscripts and printed books, Volume 1 du projet de règlement sur l'habillement du major Bardin, p.24.
11. Ibid., p.20.
12. Planche 26 du volume IV du projet de règlement sur l'habillement du major Bardin. See Also Planche 32 du volume IV du projet de règlement sur l'habillement du major Bardin p.8; Bibliothèque Musée de l'Armée, Manuscripts and printed books, Volume 1 du projet de règlement sur l'habillement du major Bardin, p.20.
13. Bibliothèque Musée de l'Armée, Manuscripts and printed books, Volume 1 du projet de règlement sur l'habillement du major Bardin, p.20.
14. Ibid.
15. Ibid., p.23.
16. Ibid., p.20.
17. SHDDT Xs 528 'Les forme, coupes, longueurs, largeurs, distance et dimensions sous détermines dans le décret du 19 Janvier 1812.'
18. SHDDT Xs 528 'Devis des quantités d'etoffes, toiles et boutons nécessaires pour confection des différentes parties de l'habillement de l'Infanterie de la *Ligne*, rédige en exécution et conformément aux dispositions du Décret impérial du 19 Janvier 1812,' p.3.
19. Ibid.
20. Bardin (1813) tome 2, p.695.
21. Les Goupil, pp.219–220.
22. Bibliothèque Musée de l'Armée, Manuscripts and printed books, Volume 1 du projet de règlement sur l'habillement du major Bardin, p.23.
23. Bibliothèque Musée de l'Armée, Manuscripts and printed books, Volume 1 du projet de règlement sur l'habillement du major Bardin p.18. 1.
24. Ibid., pp.24–26; see also Ibid., p.41.

Chapter 4

1. SHDDT Xs 525 circulaire, 2 Avril 1812.
2. *Journal Militaire*, 12 Avril 1812.
3. SHDDT Xs 528 Ordre Comte de Cessac 21 Juillet 1812.
4. SHDDT Xs 525 Ordre 24 Juillet 1812.
5. SHDDT Xs 528 Décret 26 Juillet 1812.
6. *Journal Militaire*, 2e tremestre 1812, p.111.
7. SHDDT Xb 477 65e de *Ligne* 1812 a 1815, Dossier 1815. Rapport 13 Avril 1819 citing a War Ministry circular of 11 January 1809 which forbade the use of government money, i.e., the clothing fund and stoppages from the men's pay, to pay for sword knots and epaulettes for *voltigeurs*; ergo if colonels wanted them, the officers' corps had to foot the bill.
8. *Journal Militaire*, 2e tremestre 1812, p.111.

9. SHDDT Xs 528 'Devis des quantitis d'etoffes, toiles et boutons necessaires pour confection des differentes parties de l'habillement de l'Infanterie de la *Ligne*, rédige en execution et conformément aux dispositions du Décret impérial du 19 Janvier 1812,' p.3.
10. AN AF/IN/1179. Lettre a Napoleon 14 8bre 1812.
11. AN AF/IN/1179. Ordre [date illegible]. The order states the reserves made in July 1812 were to be issued and replenished. For the infantry, this reserve would consist of 200 *capotes*, 200 *habits-vestes*, 200 *gilets manches* 200 pairs of *pantalons*, 200 *bonnets de police*, 200 *schakos*, 200 *gibernes* and belts and 200 musket slings. From the sequence of orders to which the paper in question is attached, it must date from between 20 November 1812 and 6 January 1813.
12. SHDDT Xs 525-526. Rapport 21 Avril 1813.
13. SHDDT Xs 525-526. Rapport 10 Mai 1813.
14. SHDDT Xs 525. Décret 22 Juin 1813.
15. SHDDT Xs 525 Décret 19 Aout 1813.
16. SHDDT Xb 449 52e *de Ligne* 1812 à 1815. Dossier 1814. Rapport 14 7bre 1814.
17. SHDDT Xs 525 Décret 17 Novembre 1813.
18. SHDDT Xs 525 Décret 8 Janvier 1814.
19. SHDDT Xs 525 Circulaire 26 Fevrier 1814.
20. SHDDT Xs 528 Décret 22 Avril 1814.
21. SHDDT C15 39 Decrets 1815.
22. SHDDT C15 39 Decrets 1815.
23. Ibid.
24. AN AF/IV/1941, Rapport fait l'Empereur par le ministre de la Guerre, le 26 mars 1815.
25. Ibid, Davout, *Rapport à Sa Majesté l'Empereur*, 5 avril 1815. See also SHDDT C16 Davout à Mollien, 17 avril 1815.
26. SHDDT C15 39 Decrets 1815. Décret 1 Avril 1815.
27. Ibid., Décret 17 Juin 1815.

Chapter 5

1. SHDDT Xb 565 1e *Légère*. Dossier 1814. Rapport 20 août 1814.
2. SHDDT C15 Correspondance Armée du Nord 11 Juin a 20 Juin 1815. Dossier 19 Juin. Rapport du 19 Juin.
3. SHDDT Xb 565 1e *Légère*. Dossier 1815. Rapport 21 7bre 1815.
4. Ibid.
5. SHDDT Xb 567 2e *régiment d'infanterie Légère*. Dossier 1814. Résume d'inspection 3 août 1814.
6. SHDDT Xb 567 2e *régiment d'infanterie Légère*. Dossier 1815. Rapport 21 Juin 1821.
7. SHDDT Xb 567 2e *régiment d'infanterie Légère*. Dossier 1815. Rapport 21 Juin 1821a.
8. SHDDT Xb 567 2e *régiment d'infanterie Légère*. Dossier 1815. Rapport 21 Juin 1821b.
9. SHDDT Xb 567 2e *régiment d'infanterie Légère*. Dossier 1815. Rapport 26 7bre 1815.
10. SHDDT Xb 568 3e *Légère*. Dossier An 13. Rapport 6 Thermidor An 13.
11. SHDDT Xb 568 3e *Légère*. Dossier 1808 Rapport 25 Janvier 1808.
12. SHDDT Xb 570 3e *Légère*. Dossier 1815. Rapport 25 7bre 1815.
13. SHDDT Xb 571 4e *Légère*. Dossier An 13. Rapport 23 Vend An 13.
14. SHDDT Xb 571 4e *Légère*. Dossier An 13. Rapport 24 Messidor An 13.
15. SHDDT Xb 571 4e *Légère*. Dossier An 13. Rapport 24 Messidor An 13.
16. SHDDT C 15 Correspondance Armée du Nord 11 Juin a 20 Juin 1815. Dossier 19 Juin. Rapport du 19 Juin.
17. SHDDT Xb 572 4e *Légère* 1814 a 1815. Dossier 1815. Rapport 16 juillet 1815.
18. Ibid.
19. SHDDT Xb 573 5e *Légère* 1803 a 1814. See also SHDDT Xb 573 bis 5e Légère 1815.
20. SHDDT Xb 575 6e *Légère* 1812 a 1815. Dossier 1815. Rapport 2 May 1816.
21. SHDDT Xb 575 6e *Légère* 1812 a 1815. Dossier 1814. Resume de la Revue 6 Aout 1814.

22. SHDDT Xb 575 6ᵉ *Légère* 1812 a 1815. Dossier 1815. Rapport 2 May 1816.
23. SHDDT Xb 575 6ᵉ *Légère* 1812 a 1815. Dossier 1815. Rapport 22 Septembre 1815.
24. SHDDT Xb 575 6ᵉ *Légère* 1812 a 1815. Dossier 1815. Rapport 3e Bataillon 1815.
25. SHDDT GR 2C 275 Habillement.
26. SHDDT Xb 577 7ᵉ *Légère* 1812 a 1815. Dossier 1815. Rapport 5 décembre 1821.
27. SHDDT Xb 577 7ᵉ *Légère* 1812 a 1815. Dossier 1815. Rapport 5 décembre 1821.
28. SHDDT GR 2C 518 Résume d'revue 1 Mai 1811.
29. SHDDT Xb 577 7ᵉ *Légère* 1812 a 1815. Dossier 1814. Rapport 5 Septembre 1814.
30. SHDDT Xb 577 7ᵉ *Légère* 1812 a 1815. Dossier 1815. Rapport 25 7bre 1815.
31. SHDDT Xb 577 7ᵉ *Légère* 1812 a 1815. Dossier 1815. Rapport 5 décembre 1821.
32. SHDDT Xb 581 9ᵉ *Légère*. Dossier An 13. Rapport 26 Thermidor An 13.
33. SHDDT GR 2C 275 Habillement.
34. SHDDT Xb 581 9ᵉ *Légère*. Dossier 1808. Rapport 1 Janvier 1808.
35. SHDDT Xb 583 9ᵉ *Légère* 1812 a 1815. Dossier 1814. Rapport 1 Aout 1814.
36. SHDDT Xb 583 9ᵉ *Légère* 1812 a 1815. Dossier 1814. Résume de la revue 1 Aout 1814.
37. SHDDT GR 1K61 Correspondence General Gerard. Mai Juin 1815.
38. SHDDT Xb 583 9ᵉ Légère 1812 a 1815. Dossier 1815. Rapport 24 août 1814.
39. SHDDT Xb 584 10ᵉ *Légère*. Dossier An 13. Rapport 25 Vend An 13.
40. SHDDT Xb 584 10ᵉ *Légère*. Dossier An 13. Rapport 25 Thermidor An 13.
41. SHDDT Xb 585 10ᵉ *régiment d'infanterie Légère* 1811 a 1815. Dossier 1818. Rapport 29 Octobre 1820.
42. SHDDT Xb 585 10ᵉ *régiment d'infanterie Légère* 1811 a 1815. Dossier 1814. Rapport 1 août 1814.
43. SHDDT Xb 585 10ᵉ *régiment d'infanterie Légère* 1811 a 1815. Dossier 1814. Rapport 1 août 1814.
44. SHDDT Xb 585 10ᵉ *régiment d'infanterie Légère* 1811 a 1815. Dossier 1814. Résume de la revue 1 août 1814.
45. SHDDT Xb 585 10ᵉ *régiment d'infanterie Légère* 1811 a 1815. Dossier 1815. Rapport 9 7bre 1815.
46. SHDDT Xb 586 11ᵉ *régiment d'infanterie Légère* 1811 a 1815. Dossier 1811. Rapport 10 Novembre 1811.
47. SHDDT Xb 586 11ᵉ *régiment d'infanterie Légère* 1811 a 1815. Dossier 1814. Rapport 4 Aout 1814.
48. SHDDT Xb 586 11ᵉ *régiment d'infanterie Légère* 1811 a 1815. Dossier 1814. Rapport 4 Aout 1814.
49. SHDDT Xb 586 11ᵉ *régiment d'infanterie Légère* 1811 a 1815. Dossier 1814. Résume de la revue 1814.
50. SHDDT Xb 586 11ᵉ *régiment d'infanterie Légère* 1811 a 1815. Dossier 1815. Rapport 3 Aout 1815.
51. SHDDT Xb 587 12ᵉ *Légère* An XII a 1811. Dossier Ab13. Rapport 15 Thermidor An 13.
52. SHDDT Xb 587 12ᵉ *Légère* An XII a 1811. Dossier 1807. Rapport 3Xbre 1807.
53. SHDDT Xb 587 12ᵉ *Légère* An XII a 1811. Dossier 1807. Rapport 3Xbre 1807.
54. SHDDT Xb 588 12ᵉ *régiment d'infanterie Légère* 1811 a 1815. Dossier 1814. Rapport 2 7bre 1814.
55. SHDDT Xb 588 12ᵉ *régiment d'infanterie Légère* 1811 a 1815. Dossier 1815. Rapport 18 7bre 1815.
56. SHDDT Xb 589 13ᵉ *Légère* An XI a 1811. Dossier An XIII. Rapport 11 Vendémiaire An 13.
57. SHDDT Xb 589 13ᵉ *Légère* An XI a 1811. Dossier An XIII. Rapport 9 Thermidor An 13.
58. SHDDT Xb 590 13ᵉ *régiment d'infanterie Légère*. Dossier 1815. Rapport 21 Avril 1800.
59. SHDDT Xb 589 13ᵉ *Légère*. Dossier 1807. Rapport 5 Xbre 1807.
60. SHDDT Xb 590 13ᵉ *régiment d'infanterie Légère*. Dossier 1815. Rapport 21 Avril 1800.
61. SHDDT GR 2C 518 Résume d'revue 1 Mai 1811.
62. SHDDT Xb 590 13ᵉ *régiment d'infanterie Légère*. Dossier 1814. Rapport 1 7bre 1814.
63. Ibid.
64. SHDDT Xb 590 13ᵉ *régiment d'infanterie Légère*. Dossier 1814. Rapport 1 7bre 1814.
65. SHDDT Xb 590 13ᵉ *régiment d'infanterie* Légère. Dossier 1814. Rapport 1 7bre 1814.
66. SHDDT Xb 590 13ᵉ *régiment d'infanterie Légère*. Dossier 1815. Rapport 25 7bre 1815.
67. SHDDT Xb 590 13ᵉ *régiment d'infanterie Légère*. Dossier 1815.
68. SHDDT Xb 590 13ᵉ *régiment d'infanterie Légère*. Dossier 1815.

69. SHDDT GR 2C 518 rapport 9 Janvier 1811.
70. SHDDT Xb 592 14ᵉ *Légère*. Dossier 1812. Rapport 21 Novembre 1812.
71. SHDDT Xb 592 14ᵉ *Légère*. Dossier 1814. Rapport 4 Aout 1814.
72. SHDDT Xb 592 14ᵉ *Légère*. Dossier 1815. Rapport 3 Aout 1815.
73. SHDDT Xb 593 15ᵉ *Légère*. Dossier 1808. Rapport 8 Xbre 1807.
74. SHDDT Xb 593 15ᵉ *Légère*. Dossier An 13. Rapport 14 Thermidor An 13.
75. SHDDTGR 2C 518 Résume d'revue 1 Mai 1811.
76. SHDDT Xb 594 15ᵉ *régiment d'infanterie Légère* 1811 a 1815. Dossier 1813. Rapport 28 Mars 1813.
77. SHDDT Xb 594 15ᵉ *régiment d'infanterie Légère* 1811 a 1815. Dossier 1814. Rapport 1814.
78. SHDDT Xb 594 15ᵉ *régiment d'infanterie Légère* 1811 a 1815. Dossier 1815. Rapport 25 7bre 1815.
79. SHDDT Xb 595 16ᵉ *Légère* An XII a 1811. Dossier AN 13. Rapport 20 Vend An 13.
80. SHDDT Xb 595 16ᵉ *Légère* An XII a 1811. Dossier AN 13. Rapport 8 Thermidor An 13.
81. SHDDT GR 2C 275 Habillement.
82. SHDDT Xb 595 16ᵉ *Légère* An XII a 1811. Dossier 1808. Rapport 27 Janvier 1808.
83. SHDDT Xb 595 16ᵉ *Légère* An XII a 1811. Dossier 1808. État du prix des fournitures 28 janvier 1808.
84. SHDDT Xb 595 16ᵉ *Légère* An XII a 1811. Dossier 1808. Rapport fait au Ministre 23 Mars 1808.
85. SHDDT Xb 595 16ᵉ *Légère* An XII a 1811. Dossier 1808. Rapport 1 8bre 1808.
86. SHDDT Xb 588 12ᵉ *régiment d'infanterie Légère* 1811 a 1815. Dossier 1814. Rapport 2 7bre 1814.
87. SHDDT Xb 597 17ᵉ *Légère*. Dossier An 13. Rapport 15 Vendémiaire An 13.
88. SHDDT Xb 597 17ᵉ *Légère*. Dossier An 13. Rapport 28 Thermidor An 13.
89. SHDDT Xb 597 17ᵉ *Légère*. Dossier 1808 Rapport 1 9bre 1807.
90. SHDDT Xb 460 57ᵉ *de Ligne* 1812 a 1815. Dossier 1814. Rapport 16 Juillet 1814.
91. SHDDT Xb 599 18ᵉ *Légère*. Dossier An 13. Rapport 20 Vend An 13.
92. SHDDT Xb 419 35ᵉ *de Ligne* 1812 a 1815. Dossier 1814. Rapport 16 Juillet 1814.
93. SHDDT Xb 592 14ᵉ *Légère*. Dossier 1814. Rapport 4 Aout 1814.
94. SHDDT Xb 601 21ᵉ *Légère*. Dossier 1807. Rapport 3Xbre 1807.
95. SHDDT Xb 601 21ᵉ *Légère*. Dossier An 13. Rapport 4 Thermidor An 13.
96. SHDDT Xb 438 46ᵉ *de Ligne* 1812 a 1815. Dossier 1814. Rapport 1 Aout 1814.
97. SHDDT Xb 438 46ᵉ *de Ligne* 1812 a 1815. Dossier 1814. Rapport 1 Aout 1814.
98. SHDT Xb 603 22ᵉ *Légère*. Dossier An 13. Rapport 29 Brumaire An 14.
99. SHDT Xb 603 22ᵉ *Légère*. Dossier 1808. Rapport 7 Mars 1808.
100. SHDDT Xb 419 35ᵉ *de Ligne* 1812 a 1815. Dossier 1814. Rapport 16 Juillet 1814.
101. SHDDT Xb 605 23ᵉ *Légère*. Dossier An 13. Rapport 26 Vend An 13.
102. SHDDT Xb 605 23ᵉ *Légère*. Dossier An 13. Rapport 10 Brumaire An 13.
103. SHDDT Xb 605 23ᵉ *Légère*. Dossier An 13. Rapport 27 Fructidor An 13.
104. SHDDT Xb 605 23ᵉ *Légère*. Dossier 1808. Rapport 23 Mars 1808.
105. SHDDT Xb 605 23ᵉ *Légère*. Dossier 1808. Rapport 25 Mai 1808.
106. SHDDT Xb 606 23ᵉ *Légère*. Dossier 1814. Procès-Verbal de la vérification de la compatibilité.
107. SHDDT Xb 572 4ᵉ *Légère* 1814 a 1815. Dossier 1815.
108. SHDDT Xb 607 24ᵉ *Légère*. Dossier 1807. Rapport 20 9bre 1807.
109. SHDDT Xb 607 24ᵉ *Légère*. Dossier An 13. Rapport 10 Thermidor An 13.
110. SHDDT Xb 609 24ᵉ *régiment d'infanterie légère* 1811 a 1814. Dossier 1812. Rapport 10 Janvier 1812.
111. SHDDT Xb 609 24ᵉ *régiment d'infanterie légère* 1811 a 1814. Dossier 1813. Rapport 23 Juillet 113.
112. SHDDT Xb 609 24ᵉ *régiment d'infanterie légère* 1811 a 1814. Dossier 1814. Rapport 24 Mai 1821.
113. SHDDT Xb 610 25ᵉ *Légère*. Dossier An 13. Rapport 8 Thermidor An 13.
114. SHDDT Xb 611 25ᵉ *régiment d'infanterie légère* 1811 a 1814. Dossier 1812. Rapport 24 Mai 1812.
115. SHDDT Xb 585 10ᵉ *régiment d'infanterie légère* 1811 a 1815. Dossier 1814. Rapport 1 Aout 1814.
116. SHDDT Xb 612 26ᵉ *Légère*. Dossier An 13. Rapport 4 Vend An 13.

117. SHDDT Xb 612 26ᵉ *Légère*. Dossier An 13. Rapport 5 Thermidor An 13.
118. SHDDT Xb 613 26ᵉ *régiment d'infanterie légère* 1811 a 1814. Dossier 1813. Rapport 3 Mai 1813.
119. SHDDT Xb 614 27ᵉ *Légère*. Dossier An 13. Rapport 22 Vend An 13.
120. SHDDT Xb 615 27ᵉ *régiment d'infanterie légère* 1811 a 1815. Dossier 1814. Rapport 3 Avril 1821.
121. SHDDT Xb 614 27ᵉ *régiment d'infanterie légère*. Dossier 1808 Rapport 28 9bre 1807.
122. SHDDT Xb 590 13ᵉ *régiment d'infanterie Légère*. Dossier 1814. Rapport 1 7bre 1814.
123. SHDDT Xb 590 13ᵉ *régiment d'infanterie Légère*. Dossier 1814. Rapport 1 7bre 1814.
124. SHDDT Xb 618 29ᵉ *régiment d'infanterie Légère* 1811 a 1814. Dossier 1812. Rapport 14 Mars 1812.
125. SHDDT Xb 618 29ᵉ *régiment d'infanterie légère* 1811 a 1814. Dossier 1812. Rapport 25 Fevrier 1812.
126. SHDDT Xb 618 29ᵉ *regiment d'infanterie légère* 1811 a 1814. Dossier 1812. Rapport 25 Fevrier 1812.
127. AN AF/IV/1179.
128. SHDDT Xb 586 11ᵉ *régiment d'infanterie légère* 1811 a 1815. Dossier 1814. Rapport 4 Aout 1814.
129. SHDDT Xb 619 31ᵉ *Légère*. Dossier An 13. Rapport 16 Vend An 13.
130. SHDDT Xb 619 31ᵉ *Légère*. Dossier An 13. Rapport 1 Thermidor An 13.
131. SHDDT Xb 619 31ᵉ *Légère*. Dossier 1808. Rapport 24 Fevrier 1808.
132. SHDDT Xb 620 31ᵉ *Légère*. Dossier 1815. Rapport 19 Avril 1819.
133. SHDDT Xb 620 31ᵉ *Légère*. Dossier 1815. Rapport 21 Avril 1819.
134. SHDDT Xb 620 31ᵉ *Légère*. Dossier 1815. Rapport 26 Juillet 1815.
135. SHDDT Xb 621 32ᵉ *Légère*. Dossier 1807. Rapport 26 9bre 1807.
136. SHDDT Xb 592 14ᵉ *Légère*. Dossier 1814. Rapport 4 Aout 1814.
137. SHDDT Xb 622 33ᵉ *régiment d'infanterie légère* 1811 a 1814. Dossier 1814. Proces Verbal 15 Aout 1814.
138. SHDDT Xb 622 33ᵉ *régiment d'infanterie légère* 1811 a 1814 Dossier 1814. Proces Verbal 15 Aout 1814.
139. SHDDT Xb 622 33ᵉ *régiment d'infanterie légère* 1811 a 1814 Dossier 1814. Proces Verbal 19 Aout 1814.
140. SHDDT Xb 348 3ᵉ *de Ligne*. Dossier 1814. Rapport 16 Juillet 1814.
141. SHDDT Xb 492 76ᵉ *de Ligne* 1811 a 1815. Dossier 1814. Rapport 26 7bre 1814.
142. SHDDT Xb 419 35ᵉ *de Ligne* 1812 a 1815. Dossier 1812. Rapport 7 Mai 1812.
143. SHDDT Xb 391 9ᵉ *de Ligne* 1812 a 1815. Dossier 1814. Rapport 20 7bre 1814.
144. SHDDT Xb 490 75ᵉ *de Ligne* 1811 a 1815. Dossier 1814. Rapport 26 7bre 1814.
145. SHDDT Xb 583 9ᵉ *Légère* 1812 a 1815. Dossier 1814. Rapport 1 Aout 1814.
146. SHDDT Xb 440 47ᵉ *de Ligne* 1812 a 1815. Dossier 1814. Rapport 1 Octobre 1814.
147. SHDDT Xb 567 2ᵉ *régiment d'infanterie Légère*. Dossier 1815. Rapport 21 Juin 1821.
148. SHDDT Xb 570 3ᵉ *Légère*. Dossier 1815. Rapport 25 7bre 1815.
149. SHDDT Xb 577 7ᵉ *Légère* 1812 a 1815. Dossier 1815. Rapport 5 décembre 1821.
150. SHDDT Xb 581 9ᵉ *Légère*. Dossier 1808. Rapport 1 Janvier 1808.
151. SHDDT Xb 589 13ᵉ *Légère*. Dossier An 13. Rapport 9 Thermidor An 13.
152. SHDDT GR 2C 518 Résume d'revue 1 Mai 1811.
153. SHDDTGR 2C 518 Résume d'revue 1 Mai 1811.
154. SHDDT Xb 595 16ᵉ *Légère* An XII a 1811. Dossier 1808. Rapport 1 8bre 1808.
155. SHDDT Xb 597 17ᵉ *Légère*. Dossier An 13. Rapport 28 Thermidor An 13.
156. SHDDT Xb 605 23ᵉ *Légère*. Dossier 1808. Rapport 23 Mars 1808.
157. SHDDT Xb 607 24ᵉ *Légère*. Dossier An 13. Rapport 10 Thermidor An 13.
158. SHDDT Xb 610 25ᵉ *Légère*. Dossier An 13. Rapport 8 Thermidor An 13.
159. SHDDT Xb 619 31ᵉ *Légère*. Dossier 1808. Rapport 24 Fevrier 1808.
160. SHDDT Xb 583 9ᵉ *Légère* 1812 a 1815. Dossier 1814. Rapport 1 Aout 1814.
161. SHDDT Xb 586 11ᵉ *régiment d'infanterie Légère* 1811 a 1815. Dossier 1814. Rapport 4 Aout 1814.

162. SHDDT Xb 590 13ᵉ *régiment d'infanterie Légère*. Dossier 1814. Rapport 1 7bre 1814.
163. SHDDT Xb 594 15ᵉ *régiment d'infanterie Légère* 1811 a 1815. Dossier 1814. Rapport 1814.
164. SHDDT Xb 588 12ᵉ *régiment d'infanterie Légère* 1811 a 1815. Dossier 1814. Rapport 2 7bre 1814.
165. SHDDT Xb 592 14ᵉ *Légère*. Dossier 1814. Rapport 4 Aout 1814.
166. SHDDT Xb 590 13ᵉ *régiment d'infanterie Légère*. Dossier 1814. Rapport 1 7bre 1814.
167. SHDDT Xb 586 11e *régiment d'infanterie légère* 1811 a 1815. Dossier 1814. Rapport 4 Aout 1814.
168. SHDDT Xb 592 14ᵉ *Légère*. Dossier 1814. Rapport 4 Aout 1814.
169. SHDDT Xb 622 33ᵉ *régiment d'infanterie légère* 1811 a 1814. Dossier 1814. Proces Verbal 15 Aout 1814.
170. SHDDT Xb 391 9ᵉ *de Ligne* 1812 a 1815. Dossier 1814. Rapport 20 7bre 1814.
171. SHDDT Xb 567 2ᵉ *régiment d'infanterie Légère*. Dossier 1815. Rapport 26 7bre 1815.
172. SHDDT Xb 572 4ᵉ *Légère* 1814 a 1815. Dossier 1815. Rapport 16 juillet 1815.
173. SHDDT Xb 575 6ᵉ *Légère* 1812 a 1815. Dossier 1815. Rapport 22 Septembre 1815.
174. SHDDT Xb 590 13ᵉ *régiment d'infanterie Légère*. Dossier 1815.
175. SHDDT Xb 460 57ᵉ *de Ligne* 1812 a 1815. Dossier 1814. Rapport 16 Juillet 1814.
176. SHDDT Xb 606 23ᵉ *Légère*. Dossier 1814. Procès-Verbal de la vérification de la compatibilité.

Chapter 6

1. SHDDT, C2 130. Rapport 5 8bre 1812.
2. SHDDT, C2 135. Rapport 5 Janvier 1813.
3. SHDDT Xs 525 décret 18 Brumaire An XII.
4. Fondation Napoléon (2016), *Napoléon Bonaparte, Correspondance générale, Le commencement de la fin*, Tome 13, Fayard.
5. SHDDT, C2 135. Rapport 10 Fevrier 1813.
6. AN AF/IV/1119. Mouton to Napoleon, 21 February 1813.
7. SHDDT, C2 136 Rapport 1 Avril 1813.
8. *Mémoires du maréchal Marmont, duc de Raguse, de 1792 à 1814*, Perrotin, Paris, 1857. Tome 5.
9. Taken from '*Mémoires de Jean-Louis Rieu*, first trustee of Geneva', H. Georg, in 12, 1870.
10. Ibid.
11. SHDDT C2 138 Rapport 15 Avril 1813.
12. *Mémoires du maréchal Marmont, duc de Raguse, de 1792 à 1814*, Perrotin, Paris, 1857. Tome 5.
13. AN AF/IV/1119. Napoleon to Clarke, 23 Janvier 1813.
14. SHDDT GR 21 YC 914 Régiment d'infanterie de la garde de Paris, 1er avril 1812–17 avril 1813.
15. SHDDT Xb 624 37ᵉ *Légère*.
16. SHDDT Xs 528 décret 30 Thermidor An 13.
17. SHDDT Xs 528 décret 30 Thermidor An 13.
18. SHDDT Xs 528 décret 27 9bre 1807.
19. SHDDT Xs 528 décret 12 Juillet 1808.
20. SHDDT Xs 528 décret 1 8bre 1812.
21. SHDDT Xb 546 121ᵉ *de Ligne*. Dossier 1809. Rapport 25 Avril 1809.
22. Luis Sorando Muzas pers comm citing AHN, Estado 8612, exp. 350, rapport 27 Janvier 1809.
23. SHDDT Xb 546 121ᵉ *de Ligne*. Dossier 1809. Rapport 28 Avril 1809.
24. SHDDT Xb 546 121ᵉ *de Ligne*. Dossier 1809. Rapport 26 Octobre 1809.
25. SHDDT Xb 546 121ᵉ *de Ligne*. Dossier 1815. Rapport 21 Octobre 1816.
26. SHDDT Xb 548 122ᵉ *de Ligne* 1809 a 1814. Rapport 1 Juin 1809.
27. SHDDT Xb 548 122ᵉ de *Ligne*. 1809 à 1814.
28. AN AF/IV/1119.
29. SHDDT Xb 634 37ᵉ *Légère*.

Chapter 7

1. SHDDT Xs 528 État de la dépense de premier mise d'un Garde National, suivant le nouvel uniforme règle par le Décret impérial du 19 Janvier 1812.

Notes 267

2. *Journal Militaire*, 13 Mars 1812.
3. SHDDT Xs 525 décret 27 Novembre 1812.
4. SHDDT Xm 1 Documents Généraux, Lois décrets, règlements, rapports, comptes rendus 1790–1840.
5. SHDDT C2 137. Clarke au Napoléon 5 Janvier 1813.
6. SHDDT C2 137. Napoleon a Berthier 9 Janvier 1813.
7. SHDDT Xs 269.
8. SHDDT Xm 1 Documents Généraux, Lois décrets, règlements, rapports, comptes rendus 1790–1840.
9. AN AF/IV/1179. Lettre 25 Février 1813.
10. SHDDT Xs 526 circulaire 23 février 1813.
11. The expenditures associated with the 20,000fr grant covers, for each regiment: 2,500 buttons of which 56 are for the drummers, 89,55m of golden lace, 201,6m of woollen lace, 12,8m of silver lace, 2,500 *schako* plates and chinscales, 400 grenadiers' epaulettes, 400 grenadier *aigrette*s, 400 *voltigeurs' aigrette*s, 400 sabre belts, 2,500 numbers or other cartridge box ornaments, 400 red lace for grenadiers' *schako*s; 16 *sapeurs'* axes, 16 axe cases, 16 *sapeurs'* aprons, 16 pairs of *sapeurs'* gauntlets, 8 *voltigeur cornet*s and some musical instruments. SHDDT X^s 525-526.
12. SHDDT Xm 1 Documents Généraux, Lois décrets, règlements, rapports, comptes rendus 1790–1840.
13. The companies of the 135e, 136e, 139e, 144e, 146^3, 147^3, 148e and 150e to 155e line infantry regiments.
14. SHDDT Xm 3 Documents Généraux. See also SHDDT Xm 1 Documents Généraux, Lois décrets, règlements, rapports, comptes rendus 1790–1840.
15. Bibliothèque Musée de l'Armée. Fonds Rousselot. Infanterie de la *Ligne*. Extraits *Journal Militaire* 1812. Vol. 1 p.107.
16. SHDDT Xb 343 1e *de Ligne* 1814 a 1815. Dossier 1814. Rapport 22 Aout 1814.
17. SHDDT GR 21 YC 918 136e *régiment d'infanterie de Ligne*. 1813–1814.
18. SHDDT Xb 465 59e *régiment de Ligne*. Dossier 1814. Rapport 16 Aout 1814.
19. SHDDT Xb 465 59e *régiment de Ligne*. Dossier 1814. Rapport 16 Aout 1814.
20. SHDDT Xb 398 24e *de Ligne* 1809 a 1815. Dossier 1815. Rapport 3 Aout 1815.
21. SHDDT Xb 398 24e *de Ligne* 1809 a 1815. Dossier 1814. Rapport 1 Juillet 1814.
22. SHDDT GR 21 YC 923 138e *régiment d'infanterie de Ligne*. 1813–1814.
23. SHDDT Xb 404 27e *de Ligne* 1813 a 1815. Dossier 1814. Rapport 1 Aout 1814
24. SHDDT Xb 404 27e *de Ligne* 1813 a 1815. Dossier 1814. Rapport 1 Aout 1814.
25. SHDDT GR 21 YC 926 139e *régiment d'infanterie de Ligne*. 1813–1814.
26. SHDDT Xb 457 51e *de Ligne*. 1809 a 1815. Dossier 1814. Rapport 15 Septembre 1814.
27. SHDDT Xb 457 51e *de Ligne*. 1809 a 1815. Dossier 1814. Rapport 15 Septembre 1814.
28. SHDDT GR 21 YC 929 140e *régiment d'infanterie de Ligne*. 1813–1814.
29. SHDDT Xb 376 15 *de Ligne* 1812 a 1815. Dossier 1814. Rapport 16 septembre 1814
30. SHDDT Xb 486 70e *de Ligne* 1811 a 1815. Dossier 1814. Rapport 16 7bre 1814.
31. SHDDT GR 21 YC 932 à 933bis 141e *régiment d'infanterie de Ligne*. 1813–1814.
32. SHDDT C2 136.
33. SHDDT Xb 342 43e *de Ligne*, 1812 a 1815. Dossier 1814. Rapport 16 Juillet 1814.
34. SHDDT GR 21 YC 934 142e *régiment d'infanterie de Ligne*. 1813–1814.
35. SHDDT, C2 136.
36. SHDDT Xb 421 36e *de Ligne* 1812 a 1815. Dossier 1814. Rapport 1 7bre 1814.
37. SHDDT GR 21 YC 936 143e *régiment d'infanterie de Ligne*. 1813–1814.
38. SHDDT Xb 492 76e *de Ligne* 1811 a 1815. Dossier 1814. Rapport 26 7bre 1814.
39. SHDDT Xb 496 81e *de Ligne* 1812 a 1815. Dossier 1814. Rapport 18 7bre 1814.
40. SHDDT GR 21 YC 940 144e régiment d'infanterie de *Ligne*.
41. SHDDT Xb 444 50e *de Ligne*. 1811 a 1815. Dossier 1814. Rapport 28 Septembre 1814.
42. SHDDT Xb 444 50e *de Ligne*. 1811 a 1815. Dossier 1814. Rapport 28 Septembre 1814.

43. SHDDT Xb 444 50ᵉ *de Ligne*. 1811 a 1815. Dossier 1814. Rapport 28 Septembre 1814.
44. SHDDT C2 138, rapport 8 Mars 1813.
45. SHDDT GR 21 YC 942 145ᵉ *régiment d'infanterie de Ligne*. 1813–1814.
46. SHDDT Xb 510 93ᵉ *de Ligne* 1812 a 1815. Dossier 1814. Rapport 13 7bre 1814.
47. SHDDT Xb 378 16ᵉ *de Ligne* 1812 a 1815. Dossier 1814. Rapport 26 7bre 1814.
48. SHDDT GR 21 YC 146ᵉ *régiment d'infanterie de Ligne*.
49. SHDDT GR 21 YC 147ᵉ *régiment d'infanterie de Ligne*.
50. SHDDT Xb 561 147ᵉ *de* Ligne.
51. SHDDT GR 21 YC 944 148ᵉ *régiment d'infanterie de Ligne*. 1813.
52. SHDDT Xb 400 25ᵉ *de Ligne* 1812 a 1815.
53. SHDDTGR 21 YC 945 149ᵉ *régiment d'infanterie de Ligne*. 1813–1814.
54. SHDDT Xb 531 107ᵉ *de Ligne*. Dossier 1814. Rapport 21 Juillet 1814.
55. SHDDT Xb 531 107ᵉ *de Ligne*. Dossier 1814.
56. SHDDT GR 21 YC 947 150ᵉ *régiment d'infanterie de Ligne*. 1813–1814.
57. SHDDT Xb 408 29ᵉ *de Ligne*. Dossier 1814. Rapport 1 Aout 1814. See also SHDDT Xb 408 29ᵉ *de Ligne*. Dossier 1815. Rapport 21 Janvier 1816.
58. SHDDT GR 21 YC 949 151ᵉ *régiment d'infanterie de Ligne*. 1813–1814.
59. SHDDT Xb 492 76ᵉ *de Ligne* 1811 a 1815. Dossier 1814. Rapport 26 7bre 1814.
60. SHDDT Xb 385 18ᵉ *de Ligne* 1812 a 1815. Dossier 1814. Rapport 16 Juillet 1814.
61. SHDDT Xb 385 18ᵉ *de Ligne* 1812 a 1815. Dossier 1814. Rapport 16 Juillet 1814.
62. SHDDT GR 21 YC 954 153ᵉ *régiment d'infanterie de Ligne*. 1813–1814.
63. SHDDT Xb 455 55ᵉ *de Ligne* 1812 a 1815. Dossier 1814. Rapport 1 Aout 1814.
64. SHDDT GR 21 YC 957 154ᵉ *régiment d'infanterie de Ligne*. 1813–1814.
65. SHDDT Xb 424 37ᵉ *de Ligne* 1812 a 1815. Dossier 1814. Rapport 4 Aout 1814.
66. SHDDT Xb 444 50ᵉ *de Ligne*. 1811 a 1815. Dossier 1814. Rapport 21 Juillet 1814. NB the 54ᵉ *de Ligne* became the 50ᵉ *de Ligne* in May 1814, hence why this report is misfiled.
67. SHDDT Xb 410 30ᵉ *de Ligne* 1812 a 1815. Dossier 1814. Rapport 15 Juillet 1814
68. SHDDT Xb 369 12ᵉ *de Ligne*. Dossier 1814. Rapport 30 Juillet 1814.
69. SHDDT Xb 390 20ᵉ *regiment d'infanterie de la Ligne* 1812 a 1815. Dossier 1814. Rapport 6 8bre 1814.
70. SHDDT Xb 390 20ᵉ *regiment d'infanterie de la Ligne* 1812 a 1815. Dossier 1814. Rapport 6 8bre 1814.
71. SHDDT Xs 526 Décret 8 Avril 1813. See also Ibid, décret 24 Mai 1813.
72. SHDDT Xm 1 Documents Généraux, Lois décrets, règlements, rapports, comptes rendus 1790–1840.
73. SHDDT Xs 526 decret 17 Xbre 1813.
74. SHDDT Xm 3 Documents Généraux.

Chapter 8

1. Les Goupil (1812) *Administration des Masses*, Paris, Chez Magimel No. 36 *Devis de l'Artillerie à Pied*.
2. AN, AF/IV/1179. Bourcier to Berthier 30 Avril 1811.
3. Bibliothèque Musée de l'Armée, Manuscripts and printed books, Volume 1 du projet de règlement sur l'habillement du major Bardin. pp.116–122.
4. SHDDT Xd 6 1ᵉ *Artillerie à Pied*. Dossier 1814. Rapport 1 Septembre 1814.
5. SHDDT Xd 10 2ᵉ *Artillerie à Pied*. Dossier 1815. Rapport 25 7bre 1815.
6. SHDDT Xd 10 2ᵉ *Artillerie à Pied*. Dossier 1815.
7. SHDDT Xd 14 3ᵉ *Artillerie à Pied*. Dossier 1814. Rapport 7 7bre 1814.
8. Ibid.
9. SHDDT Xd 14 3ᵉ *Artillerie à Pied*. Dossier 1815. Rapport 21 7bre 1815.
10. SHDDT Xd 19 4ᵉ *Artillerie à Pied*. Dossier 1814. Rapport 3 7bre 1814.

11. SHDDT Xd 23 5ᵉ *Artillerie à Pied*. Dossier 1814. Rapport 1 7bre 1814.
12. SHDDT Xd 35 8ᵉ *Artillerie à Pied*. Dossier 1814. Rapport 12 7bre 1814.
13. SHDDT Xd 35 8ᵉ *Artillerie à Pied*. Dossier 1814. Rapport 12 7bre 1814.
14. SHDDT Xd 35 8ᵉ *Artillerie à Pied*. Dossier 1815. Rapport 8 Aout 1815.
15. SHDDT Xd 35 8ᵉ *Artillerie à Pied*. Dossier 1814. Rapport 12 7bre 1814.
16. Les Goupil Devis 39 Sapeur et Mineurs.
17. Fonds Rousselot. Dossier Sapeurs, Mineurs, Pontonniers.
18. Bibliothèque Musée de l'Armée, Manuscripts and printed books, Volume 1 du projet de règlement sur l'habillement du major Bardin, pp.130–132.
19. SHDDT Xs 525 to Comte de Cessac 17 Juin 1812.

Chapter 9

1. Les Goupil (1812) No. 37 Devis de l'Artillerie à Cheval.
2. Bibliothèque Musée de l'Armée, Manuscripts and printed books, Volume 1 du projet de règlement sur l'habillement du major Bardin, pp.269–271.
3. Bibliothèque Musée de l'Armée, Manuscripts and printed books, Volume 1 du projet de règlement sur l'habillement du major Bardin, pp.289–294.
4. SHDDT Xd 41 1ᵉ *Artillerie à Cheval*. Dossier 1814. Rapport 16 7bre 1814.
5. SHDDT Xd 41 1ᵉ *Artillerie à Cheval*. Dossier 1815. Rapport 26 8bre 1815.
6. SHDDT Xd 41 1ᵉ *Artillerie à Cheval*. Dossier 1815. Rapport 26 8bre 1815.
7. SHDDT Xd 42 2ᵉ *régiment Artillerie à Cheval*. Dossier 1814. Rapport 1 7bre 1814.
8. SHDDT Xd 43 3ᵉ *régiment Artillerie à Cheval*. Dossier 1814. Rapport 6 7bre 1814.
9. Ibid.
10. Ibid.
11. Ibid.
12. SHDDT Xd 43 3ᵉ *régiment Artillerie à Cheval*. Dossier 1815.
13. SHDDT Xd 43 3ᵉ *régiment Artillerie à Cheval*. Dossier 1815.
14. SHDDT Xd 44 4ᵉ *régiment Artillerie à Cheval*. Dossier 1812. Rapport 1 June 1812.
15. SHDDT Xd 44 4ᵉ *régiment Artillerie à Cheval*. Dossier 1814. Rapport 1 7bre 1814.
16. SHDDT Xd 41 1ᵉ *Artillerie à Cheval*. Dossier 1814. Rapport 16 7bre 1815.
17. SHDDT Xd 41 1ᵉ *Artillerie à Cheval*. Dossier 1814. Rapport 156 7bre 1815.
18. SHDDT Xd 43 3ᵉ *régiment Artillerie à Cheval*. Dossier 1814. Rapport 6 7bre 1814.
19. Ibid.
20. Ibid.

Chapter 10

1. SHDDT Xd 48 1ᵉ *train d'artillerie*. Dossier An 13. Rapport 13 Brum An 13.
2. SHDDT Xs 525 tarif 1 Vend An 14 pour train d'artillerie.
3. SHDDT Xs 525 tarif 31 Mars 1810 pour train d'artillerie.
4. SHDDT GR 2C 518 Résume d'revue 1 Mai 1811.
5. SHDDT Xs 528 Décret 6 Avril 1807.
6. SHDDT Xs 528 Lettre 26 Mars 1808.
7. SHDDT Xs 528 Lettre 10 Avril 1808.
8. Fonds Rousselot. Dossier trains des équipages.
9. SHDDT Xs 528 décret 14 Mars 1809.
10. AN, AF/IV/1179. Bourcier to Berthier 30 Avril 1811.
11. Bibliothèque Musée de l'Armée, Manuscripts and printed books, Volume 1 du projet de règlement sur l'habillement du major Bardin, pp.231–238.
12. SHDDT Xs 525 Tarif 7 Fevrier 1812 troupes du train.

Chapter 11

1. SHDDT Xk 31 Troupes au Grande Quartier General. Rapport 4 Brumaire An 14.
2. SHDDT X3 31 Guides de Berthier. Dossier An 12. Lettre 15 Brumaire An 12. Jones was born in Hamburg 24 July 1769. The *Legion Nantaise* was formed in June 1793. One of Jones' fellow *sous-officiers* was Pierre Jacques Etienne Cambronne, best known for his acts at Waterloo. After serving in the National Guard of Nantes and then in the 1st battalion of volunteers of Maine et Loire, Cambronne enlisted in June 1793 in *Legion Nantais* as a *Sous-officier* in the grenadier company. He was promoted to captain in October 1794. The legion fought at Quiberon in 1795. Jones and Cambronne, it seems, fought side by side.
3. Ibid., Lettre 11 Brumaire An 12.
4. Born in Wexford 24 June 1768, son of Francis Thomas Moffatt and Elizabeth Stafford.
5. Born in Dublin 15 October 1780, son of Nicholas Morley and Angelica Bouilly.
6. Born in Edinburgh 25 December 1773, son of Joseph Murray and Mary Walker.
7. SHDDT X3 31 Guides de Berthier. Dossier An 12. Control Nominatif.
8. Ibid., Lettre 29 Vend An 12.
9. Ibid., Lettre 22 Vend An 12.
10. Ibid., lettre 30 Brumaire An 12.
11. Ibid., Dossier An 12 Rapport 19 Pluviose An 12.
12. Ibid., Dossier An 13. Dupont Derval au Ministre de Guerre 2 Jour Complémentaire An 13.
13. Ibid., Dossier 1806. Dupont Derval au Marechal Berthier 4 Fevrier 1806.
14. Ibid., Dupont Derval au Marechal Brune 12 Fevrier 1806.
15. Ibid., Brune au Ministre de Guerre 7 Juin 1806.
16. SHDDT GR 2C 275 habillement.
17. SHDDT Xk 31. Dossier 1807. Lettre 16 Mai 1807.
18. SHDDT Xk 31. Guides de la Grande Armée. Lettre 17 8bre 1808.
19. Ibid., Dossier 1807. Lettre 23 Avril 1807.
20. Ibid., Dossier 1807. Lettre 8 May 1807. See also Ibid., Lettre 24 Mai 1807.
21. SHDDT GR 17 Yc 326 Compagnie de guides interprètes de l'armée d'Angleterre puis du ministre de la Guerre Dates complètes: 9 germinal an 12 – 4 juin 1810.
22. SHDDT Xk 31 Guides de Berthier. Proces Verbal Louis Gabriel Grumet, 12 Aout 1808.
23. SHDDT Xk 31 Guides du General en Chef. Rapport 10 Pluviose An 12.
24. SHDDT Xk 31 Guides du Massena. Rapport 4 Brumaire An 14.
25. Rigo le Plumet Nouveau sur les Guides. In *Tradition Magazine* 1989, p.12.
26. SHDDT Xk 31 Guides du Grande Armée. Rapport Brumaire An 14.
27. SHDDT Xk 31 Guides de Berthier. Dossier 1808. Rapport 26 Mai 1809.
28. SHDDT Xk 31 Guides de Berthier. Dossier 1812 Rapport 30 9bre 1811.
29. Ibid., Dossier 1812 Rapport 4 Fevrier 1812.
30. Ibid., Dossier 1812 Rapport 8 Fevrier 1812.
31. Ibid., Dossier 1814. Rapport 1 Juin 1814.
32. Ibid., Dossier 1814. Rapport 1 Juin 1814.
33. Ibid., Rapport 14 Juillet 1814.
34. SHDDT Xs 526 Décret 22 Avril 1810.
35. SHDDT C8 364 Situations Armée d'Espagne.
36. SHDDT C7 25 Situations Armée du Portugal.
37. Les Goupil (1812) No. 43 Devis des Infirmiers.
38. SHDDT C15 35 Situations Armée du Nord.
39. *Deshabille* was an informal style of clothes in the eighteenth century. It's what people would wear when not dressed up, or when about to dress. It's somewhere between underwear/bathrobe and formal wear. People would not wear this outdoors, but it was not uncommon to receive friends at home in this. It also frequently appears in paintings.
40. Quilted petticoats.

Notes 271

41. I found it very difficult to translate this piece of text into something that makes sense: 'Deux coussins pour attacher des monture' translates as 'two cushions suspended off a belt'. I suggest therefore that these are hip pads/panniers, which were common in the eighteenth century.
42. The *gilets*, I would guess, were sleeveless waistcoats with peplums fastened in front with laces or ties, likely quilted, worn under the gown or jacket for warmth. They were sometimes known in English as 'jumps'.
43. SHDDT Xb 392 21ᵉ *de Ligne*. Dossier 1811. Succession de l veuue Hotte 20 Mai 1811 a Hamburg.

Bibliography

Printed Sources

Anon (1779) *Reglement Arête pour le Roi pour l'habillement et l'equipment des ses troupes*. Imprimerie Royale Paris

Etienne Alexandre Bardin (1813) *Mémorial de l'officier d'infanterie*. Chez Magimel Paris. 2 Volumes

Etienne Alexandre Bardin (1808) *Manuel d'infanterie, ou Résumé de tous les règlements, décrets, usages, renseignements concernant l'infanterie, dans lequel se trouve renfermé tout ce que doivent savoir les sergents et caporaux*. Chez Magimel Paris

Honoré Hugues Berriat (1812) *Législation militaire* Paris: A. Alexandrie

Terry Crowdy (2015) Napoléon's Infantry Hand Book Pen & Sword Barnsley

Paul Lindsay Dawson (2019) *Napoléon's Imperial Guard Uniforms and Equipment: The Infantry*. Barnsley, Frontline

Les Goupil (1812) *Administration des Masses*, Paris, Chez Magimel

Mémoires du maréchal Marmont, duc de Raguse, de 1792 à 1814, Perrotin, Paris, 1857. Tome 5

Fondation Napoléon (2016), *Napoléon Bonaparte, Correspondance générale, Le commencement de la fin*, Tome 13, Fayard.

Mémoires de Jean-Louis Rieu, first trustee of Geneva, H. Georg, 1870.

Rigo le Plumet Nouveau sur les Guides. In *Tradition Magazine* 1989.

Bibliotheque Musée de l'Armée

Manuscripts and printed books, Volume 1 du projet de règlement sur l'habillement du major Bardin

Archives Nationales

AN AF/IV/1941
AN AF/IV/1179

Service Historique de la Armée du Terre

GR 1K61 Correspondence General Gerard
GR 1M 1419 Renseignements sur l'Angleterre
GR 1M 1422 Renseignements sur l'Irlande
GR 2C 518 Armée d'Allemagne
GR 2C 275 Habillement
GR 17 Yc 326 Compagnie de guides interprètes de l'armée d'Angleterre puis du ministre de la Guerre Dates complètes: 9 germinal an 12 – 4 juin 1810
GR 21 YC 914 *Régiment d'infanterie de la garde de Paris*, 1er avril 1812–17 avril 1813
GR 21 YC 918 136e *régiment d'infanterie de Ligne*. 1813–1814
GR 21 YC 923 138e *régiment d'infanterie de Ligne*. 1813–1814
GR 21 YC 926 139e *régiment d'infanterie de Ligne*. 1813–1814
GR 21 YC 929 140e *régiment d'infanterie de Ligne*. 1813–1814
GR 21 YC 932 à 933bis 141e *régiment d'infanterie de Ligne*. 1813–1814
GR 21 YC 934 142e *régiment d'infanterie de Ligne*. 1813–1814
GR 21 YC 936 143e *régiment d'infanterie de Ligne*. 1813–1814
GR 21 YC 940 144e *régiment d'infanterie de Ligne*
GR 21 YC 942 145e *régiment d'infanterie de Ligne*. 1813–1814

GR 21 YC 146ᵉ *régiment d'infanterie de Ligne*
GR 21 YC 147ᵉ *régiment d'infanterie de Ligne*
GR 21 YC 944 148ᵉ *régiment d'infanterie de Ligne*. 1813
GR 21 YC 945 149ᵉ *régiment d'infanterie de Ligne*. 1813–1814
GR 21 YC 947 150ᵉ *régiment d'infanterie de Ligne*. 1813–1814
GR 21 YC 949 151ᵉ *régiment d'infanterie de Ligne*. 1813–1814
GR 21 YC 954 153ᵉ *régiment d'infanterie de Ligne*. 1813–1814
GR 21 YC 957 154ᵉ *régiment d'infanterie de Ligne*. 1813–1814
C2 130
C2 135
C2 137
C2 138
C7 25 Situations Armée du Portugal
C8 364 Situations Armée d'Espagne
C15 6 Correspondance Armée du Nord 11 Juin a 20 Juin 1815
C15 35 Situations Armée du Nord
C15 39 Decrets 1815
Xb 343 1ᵉ *de Ligne* 1814 a 1815
Xb 348 3ᵉ *de Ligne*
Xb 361 9ᵉ *de Ligne* 1812 a 1815
Xb 369 12ᵉ *de Ligne*
Xb 376 15ᵉ *de Ligne* 1812 a 1815
Xb 378 16ᵉ *de Ligne* 1812 a 1815
Xb 385 18ᵉ *de Ligne* 1812 a 1815
Xb 390 20ᵉ *régiment d'infanterie de la Ligne* 1812 a 1815
Xb 392 21ᵉ *de Ligne*
Xb 398 24ᵉ *de Ligne* 1809 a 1815
Xb 400 25ᵉ *de Ligne* 1812 a 1815
Xb 404 27ᵉ *de Ligne* 1813 a 1815
Xb 408 29ᵉ *de Ligne*
Xb 410 30ᵉ *de Ligne* 1812 a 1815
Xb 419 35ᵉ *de Ligne* 1812 a 1815
Xb 421 36ᵉ *de Ligne* 1812 a 1815
Xb 424 37ᵉ *de Ligne* 1812 a 1815
Xb 438 46ᵉ *de Ligne* 1812 a 1815
Xb 342 43ᵉ *de Ligne* 1812 a 1815
Xb 440 47ᵉ *de Ligne* 1812 a 1815
Xb 444 50ᵉ *de Ligne* 1811 a 1815
Xb 457 51ᵉ *de Ligne* 1809 a 1815
Xb 455 55ᵉ *de Ligne* 1812 a 1815
Xb 460 57ᵉ *de Ligne* 1812 a 1815
Xb 465 59ᵉ *régiment de Ligne*
Xb 486 70ᵉ *de Ligne* 1811 a 1815
Xb 490 75ᵉ *de Ligne* 1811 a 1815
Xb 492 76ᵉ de Ligne 1811 a 1815
Xb 496 81ᵉ *de Ligne* 1812 a 1815
Xb 510 93ᵉ *de Ligne* 1812 a 1815
Xb 531 107ᵉ *de Ligne*
Xb 546 121ᵉ *de Ligne*
Xb 561 147ᵉ *de Ligne*
Xb 565 1ᵉ *Légère*

Xb 567 2ᵉ *régiment d'infanterie Légère*
Xb 568 3ᵉ *Légère*
Xb 570 3ᵉ *Légère*
Xb 571 4ᵉ *Légère*
Xb 572 4ᵉ *Légère* 1814 a 1815
Xb 573 5ᵉ *Légère* 1803 a 1814
Xb 573 bis 5ᵉ *Légère* 1815
Xb 575 6ᵉ *Légère* 1812 a 1815
Xb 577 7ᵉ *Légère* 1812 a 1815
Xb 581 9ᵉ *Légère*
Xb 583 9ᵉ *Légère* 1812 a 1815
Xb 584 10ᵉ *Légère*
Xb 585 10ᵉ *régiment d'infanterie Légère* 1811 a 1815
Xb 586 11ᵉ *régiment d'infanterie Légère* 1811 a 1815
Xb 587 12ᵉ *Légère* An XII a 1811
Xb 588 12ᵉ *régiment d'infanterie Légère* 1811 a 1815
Xb 589 13ᵉ *Légère*
Xb 590 13ᵉ *régiment d'infanterie Légère*
Xb 592 14ᵉ *Légère*
Xb 593 15ᵉ *Légère*
Xb 594 15ᵉ *régiment d'infanterie Légère* 1811 a 1815
Xb 595 16ᵉ *Légère* An XII a 1811
Xb 597 17ᵉ *Légère*
Xb 601 21ᵉ *Légère*
Xb 603 22ᵉ *Légère*
Xb 605 23e *Légère*
Xb 606 23ᵉ *Légère*
Xb 607 24ᵉ *Légère*
Xb 609 24ᵉ *régiment d'infanterie Légère* 1811 a 1814
Xb 610 25ᵉ *Légère*
Xb 611 25ᵉ *régiment d'infanterie Légère* 1811 a 1814
Xb 612 26ᵉ *Légère*
Xb 613 26ᵉ *régiment d'infanterie Légère* 1811 a 1814
Xb 614 27ᵉ *Légère*
Xb 615 27ᵉ *régiment d'infanterie Légère* 1811 a 1815
Xb 618 29ᵉ régiment d'infanterie *Légère* 1811 a 1814
Xb 619 31ᵉ *Légère*
Xb 620 31ᵉ *Légère*
Xb 621 32ᵉ *Légère*
Xb 622 33ᵉ *régiment d'infanterie Légère* 1811 a 1814
Xb 624 37ᵉ *Légère*
Xd 6 1ᵉ *Artillerie à Pied*
Xd 10 2ᵉ *Artillerie à Pied*
Xd 14 3ᵉ *Artillerie à Pied*
Xd 23 5ᵉ *Artillerie à Pied*
Xd 35 8ᵉ *Artillerie à Pied*
Xd 41 1ᵉ *Artillerie à Cheval*
Xd 42 2ᵉ *régiment Artillerie à Cheval*
Xd 43 3ᵉ *régiment Artillerie à Cheval*
Xd 44 4ᵉ *régiment Artillerie à Cheval*
Xd 48 1ᵉ *train d'artillerie*

Xk 31 Troupes au Grande Quartier General
Xk 31 Compagnie des Guides Interprètes du Premier Consul
Xk 31 Guides de Berthier
Xk 31 Guides du General en Chef
Xk 31 Guides du Massena
Xk 31 Guides du Grande Armée
Xm 1 Documents Généraux, Lois décrets, règlements, rapports, comptes rendus 1790–1840
Xm 3 Documents Généraux
Xs 269
Xs 525
Xs 526
Xs 528

Dear Reader,

We hope you have enjoyed this book, but why not share your views on social media? You can also follow our pages to see more about our other products: facebook.com/penandswordbooks or follow us on X @penswordbooks

You can also view our products at www.pen-and-sword.co.uk (UK and ROW) or www.penandswordbooks.com (North America).

To keep up to date with our latest releases and online catalogues, please sign up to our newsletter at: www.pen-and-sword.co.uk/newsletter

If you would like a printed catalogue with our latest books, then please email: enquiries@pen-and-sword.co.uk or telephone: 01226 734555 (UK and ROW) or email: uspen-and-sword@casematepublishers.com or telephone: (610) 853-9131 (North America).

We respect your privacy and we will only use personal information to send you information about our products.

Thank you!